EXPLORER'S GUIDE

AUSTIN, SAN ANTONIO, & THE HILL COUNTRY

D0047811

EXPLORER'S GUIDE

AUSTIN, SAN ANTONIO, & THE HILL COUNTRY

THIRD EDITION

AMY K. BROWN

THE COUNTRYMAN PRESS
A division of W. W. Norton & Company
Independent Publishers Since 1923

This book is dedicated to my family.

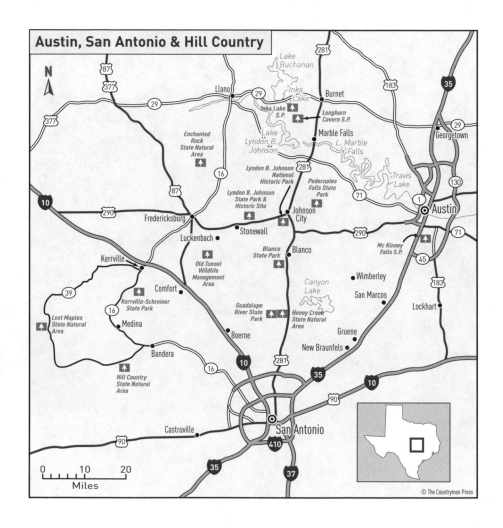

Austin, San Antonio & Hill Country

N

87
377
377
29
10
290
377

Llano
29
Inks Lake
Inks Lake S.P.
Lake Buchanan
281
183
35
Burnet
Longhorn Cavern S.P.
29
Georgetown
Enchanted Rock State Natural Area
Lake Lyndon B. Johnson
Marble Falls
L. Marble Falls
130
16
Lyndon B. Johnson National Historic Park
Pedernales Falls State Park
Travis Lake
1
Austin
87
281
71
Lyndon B. Johnson State Park & Historic Site
Fredericksburg
Johnson City
290
71
Stonewall
290
45
Luckenbach
Mc Kinney Falls S.P.
Kerrville
Blanco State Park
Blanco
183
39
Comfort
Old Tunnel Wildlife Management Area
Canyon Lake
Wimberley
Lockhart
Kerrville-Schreiner State Park
16
San Marcos
Lost Maples State Natural Area
Medina
Guadalupe River State Park
Honey Creek State Natural Area
Gruene
Boerne
New Braunfels
Bandera
16
10
281
Hill Country State Natural Area
35
10
90
Castroville
San Antonio
90
410
35
37

0   10   20
Miles

© The Countryman Press

CONTENTS

INTRODUCTION | 9

USING THIS BOOK | 10

WHAT'S WHERE IN AUSTIN, SAN ANTONIO, AND THE HILL COUNTRY | 11

AUSTIN | 29

SAN ANTONIO | 87

THE HILL COUNTRY | 137

BANDERA

BLANCO

BOERNE

COMFORT

FREDERICKSBURG

JOHNSON CITY

KERRVILLE

LUCKENBACH

MARBLE FALLS

WIMBERLY

NEARBY AND IN BETWEEN | 181

GEORGETOWN

NEW BRAUNFELS AND GRUENE

SAN MARCOS

SUGGESTED BIBLIOGRAPHY | 197

INDEX | 199

MAPS

AUSTIN, SAN ANTONIO & HILL COUNTRY | 6
AUSTIN AREA | 30
DOWNTOWN AUSTIN | 35
SAN ANTONIO AREA | 89
DOWNTOWN SAN ANTONIO | 93
HILL COUNTRY AREA | 139

INTRODUCTION

Everything really is bigger in Texas. The people in Central Texas have huge hearts, plenty of patience, and a friendliness that seems supersized.

As I traveled the region researching this book, Texans graciously answered numerous questions, refilled countless cups of coffee, and served up some of the biggest slices of pie I've ever seen. They shared generously the names of their favorites—from burgers to honky-tonks, enchiladas to swimming holes.

While the list was long, a guidebook can only be so big. This book is big enough to include all the basics and many of the extras, but as you make your way between the featured establishments, feel free to stray from the path I've laid out. Change your plans, pull into a farm stand, stop at a bakery, have a beer, and by all means ask a Texan for directions, suggestions, and recommendations. Let 'em lay some hospitality on you.

Extra-large thanks to all the good folks living in Austin, San Antonio, the surrounding communities, and the towns of the Hill Country. I gratefully appreciate your courtesy, knowledge, and kindness. Since most of you did not know I was writing a guidebook, the sincerity of your gestures was truly heartwarming.

Enormous thanks to the folks at Countryman and W. W. Norton for the opportunity to write about a region I love.

Deepest gratitude to my fantastic family.

Thank you.

Amy K. Brown
www.amykbrown.com

DINING ALONG THE RIVERWALK IN SAN ANTONIO

USING THIS BOOK

This book is divided into an introductory chapter followed by four main chapters—on Austin, San Antonio, the Hill Country, and Nearby and In Between—each with suggestions of lodging, dining, and things to see and do, arranged by neighborhood. The introductory chapter describes the region's shared landscape and common history. The unique histories of Austin and San Antonio and the towns of the Hill Country are addressed in the introductions to their respective chapters. Considering the scale of Texas, the cities, towns, and parks covered in this book are relatively close to one another, so as you read bear in mind that many destinations make easy stopovers or day trips.

All the information in this book was verified at the time of its writing. However, things change, and it is always prudent to call ahead or check online.

LODGING PRICE CODES

$	Up to $125 per couple
$$	$126–$175 per couple
$$$	$176–$250 per couple
$$$$	More than $250 per couple

WHAT'S WHERE IN AUSTIN, SAN ANTONIO, AND THE HILL COUNTRY

Deep in the Heart of Texas

The subject of legends and lore, Texas has a reputation that has always preceded it. And as an icon of strength and swagger, Texas plays an essential part in the story of America. Filled with opportunistic cattle rustlers and hunky cowboys thundering off into the endless crimson sunset, the Texas of myth and movies is larger than life, hotter than hell, and rougher than a ride at the rodeo.

Deep in the heart of Central Texas is a region that will challenge all your assumptions with its distinct mix of friendly casualness, edgy creativity, discerning taste, and a strong inclination toward celebration. Each city and town offers its own incomparable mix of culture, food, music, and heritage, and plenty of festivals—from cultural to culinary, kites to *kolaches*—which give visitors numerous opportunities to experience life in Central Texas as an honorary Texan-for-a-day.

With roots stretching back to the 17th century, San Antonio (see chapter 2) is now home to over a million people. Its pedestrian-friendly downtown, the celebrated Alamo, historic Mission Trail, and bustling Riverwalk cluster together to give the city an intimate feeling that belies its size. A strong sense of cultural history pervades all, with San Antonio's Native American origins, Spanish influences, and Mexican overtones zealously expressed in art, food, architecture, and festivals.

While San Antonio embodies something quintessentially Texan, people are fond of observing that Austin (see chapter 1) inhabits a category all its own. Austinites are an educated, energetic, and decidedly unconventional bunch, and while they tend to be less conservative than the rest of the state, their live-and-let-live attitude very much mirrors the overall spirit of Texas. Nightlife in Austin abounds, thanks to its internationally recognized live music scene, though acres of parks, bike trails, and gardens make recreational activities almost as popular.

The Hill Country (see chapter 3), easily accessible from either Austin or San Antonio, is the place to be if you really want to slow down and smell the bluebonnets. To drive the lazy, winding, rural roads past wineries and lavender fields, around limestone outcroppings, and through shady state parks is to experience carefree wanderlust at its most enjoyable. The region's rustic towns are brimming with gourmet restaurants, antique and knickknack shops, and bed and breakfasts, and make pleasant stopovers or destinations unto themselves. Nearby and In Between (see page 181), several towns along I-35 make wonderful day trips for the thrill of area amusement parks or tubing along cool spring-fed Texas rivers.

The folks in Central Texas are passionate about living here, and their infectious enthusiasm begins with the land that they love, a land rich in both resources and beauty that has been fought over for centuries.

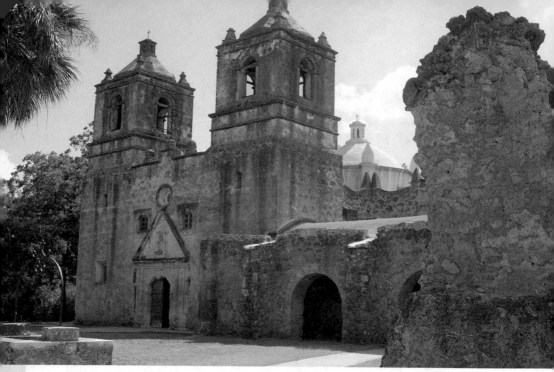

MISSION CONCEPCIÓN, SAN ANTONIO MISSIONS NATIONAL HISTORICAL PARK

Natural Wonders

Though now divided into two major cities, many towns, and numerous communities, Central Texas shares a common natural history that has been ages in the making.

Based on fossils of fish and aquatic plants, and other clues dating from the Cretaceous period (65–144 million years ago), we know that the Central Texas region was once submerged under a shallow lake. At some point, possibly 10–20 million years ago, movement along the Balcones Fault uplifted a massive hunk of limestone now known as the Edwards Plateau. The southeastern edge of this uplift was exposed to the elements, and its newer, softer rock eroded to form the dramatic cliffs and rocky outcroppings characterizing the present-day Balcones Escarpment, the ridge separating the undulating Hill Country to the west from the level Texas Coastal Plain to the southeast.

The movement in the earth's crust also created the Edwards Aquifer. A karst aquifer, the Edwards was formed over time as limestone-rich bedrock dissolved, creating an underground honeycomb network of pockets, caverns, and holes in which water collects and through which it percolates. The sinkholes, disappearing streams, and cave entrances of the Hill Country are all telltale signs of karst regions. When it rains, water rushes over the Cretaceous limestone streambeds of this "contributing zone" and into the aquifer, topping off its massive holdings. As the Edwards is also an artesian aquifer, the water within is held under hydrostatic pressure, producing the region's many springs, such as Barton Springs in Austin, Comal Springs in New Braunfels, and Aquarena Springs in San Marcos. While the aquifer contains enough water for use well into the future, if its levels drop, so too does the flow of its springs, threatening the vegetation and many endangered species that rely upon them. Central Texans are

LUCKY, TX

Always self-reliant, Texans have also been blessed with tremendous good luck. Rebounding from defeats suffered in the Civil War, Texans returned to find a population explosion of wild longhorn cattle. Rounded up by cowboys and taken to market along the Chisholm Trail in legendary cattle drives between 1867 and 1884, they provided a steady source of income for a state in dire need. Agriculture also flourished. Then, in 1901, one of the state's greatest natural resources was tapped at Spindletop, near Beaumont. After drilling for hours, amid much skepticism, exhausted workers struck "black gold," and a 150-foot geyser of the oil that would finance much of Texas's future came rocketing out of the ground.

aware of their own complete dependency on the Edwards Aquifer, a circumstance made increasingly complicated by rapid growth and growing demands for water.

For the nature enthusiast, the biodiversity of flora and fauna living in or migrating through Austin, San Antonio, and the Hill Country can be fascinating. For instance, millions upon millions of Mexican free-tailed bats roost in the nooks, crannies, and caves of Central Texas; the region is home to one of the largest maternity roosts for bats in the world. The bats give birth in the area's caves, take turns feeding and minding their young, and scour the countryside for insects, devouring tens of thousands of pounds' worth each night between May and October. While their presence has not always been met with much enthusiasm or tolerance, in time and with education folks around here grew to enjoy them, and public sentiment has morphed from fear to appreciation. With half a million bats, the Congress Avenue Bridge in Austin is home to the largest urban bat population in the world, and watching them take flight each night is a popular entertainment.

Sharing the great Texas sky with the bats is the state's huge variety of birds. An astonishing three-fourths of all American birds are represented throughout the diverse avian habitats of Texas. Some birds are residents and others migratory, passing through Central Texas on the 300-mile-wide "Central Flyway," one of the great routes for migration between Canada and Central and South America. Of the thousands of birds to make the trip, the golden-cheeked warbler is the only one to nest exclusively in Texas and, due to loss of habitat, is the most critically endangered of all warblers.

Also traveling the Central Flyway is the monarch butterfly, Texas's state insect. Monarchs are unusual among butterflies in that they migrate instead of hibernating; those that make the trip through Texas tend to originate in the upper Midwest, funneling through the Central Flyway on their way to Mexico. During this migration, in October, Central Texas enjoys the spectacle of millions of orange and black monarchs gliding along on favorable winds or resting and refueling at area gardens.

Central Texas has a wealth of parks and trails, making the region a natural spot for ecotourism. One of the best ways to commune with nature is to visit a state park, and there are many to choose from. From the bald pink dome of Enchanted Rock to the limestone canyons of Lost Maples, the state parks showcase the diversity of the regional landscape and the variety of wildlife it supports. Gray fox, armadillo, coyote, opossum, raccoon, bobcat, rock squirrel, roadrunner, white-tailed deer, and javelina are all common, and the patient observer can sometimes catch a glimpse of rarer species, such as the Cagle's map turtle, the San Marcos salamander, or the Guadalupe bass.

TEXAS HISTORY ONLINE

The history of Texas is fascinating in its depth and breadth. A cultural crossroads for centuries, the state is crisscrossed by the footprints of many. Some have just passed through, while others hung their hat for a while. Texas's roots are deep and spread wide. In addition to the recommended readings at the end of this book ("Suggested References" in the Information chapter), a wealth of information exists online for anyone wanting to learn more.

Briscoe Center for American History at the University of Texas at Austin (www.cah.utexas.edu): a useful site for locating sources of information regarding the various ethnic groups in Texas

Texas Almanac (www.texasalmanac.com): timelines, photos, and historical essays clearly presented

Texas Archeological Research Lab at the University of Texas at Austin (www.texasbeyondhistory .net): interactive website offering archaeological facts and information

The Texas State Historical Association (www.tshaonline.org): exhaustive online handbook of Texas history

Texas Historical Commission (www.thc.state.tx.us): comprehensive site including information on historic courthouses, cemeteries, and archaeological sites

Texas Parks and Wildlife (www.tpwd.texas.gov): information and photographs regarding the natural and cultural history of Texas

The Peoples of Texas

The unique terrain of Central Texas, with its clear springs, sheltering caves, and abundant wildlife, has made the region naturally attractive to humans for well over 11,000 years. Looking to the relatively recent past, Tonkawa and Lipan Apache Indians are thought to have lived here from the 14th century, with the Comanche and Kiowa arriving in the 18th century. While many of the other peoples living concurrently in neighboring regions had already begun to live in villages, the groups living in this region were fairly nomadic, following food sources throughout the seasons and varying weather conditions. Although there is still much to learn, the archaeological record of the region is extraordinary, certainly one of the longest continuous records of hunters and gatherers in North America. Prior to the arrival of Europeans, approximately 45,000 Native Americans lived in the region, organized in groups, each with its own language, identity, and customs.

However, the elements that attracted the first peoples would, of course, attract others, and people kept coming.

TEJANOS From the 1600s through the 1800s, pioneers from Mexico journeyed north and began settling the Texas frontier, creating towns, building roads and ranches, and governing themselves. Throughout the 1700s they put down

MIGRATING MONARCH BUTTERFLY

TEXAN HOSPITALITY

roots, establishing the settlements that would become El Paso, Galveston, Laredo, San Antonio, Victoria, and the large ranches of Central and South Texas. Those industrious pioneer ranchers were so successful that they were able to contribute 2,000 head of longhorn cattle to the Revolutionary War effort, driving a herd from Texas to New Orleans in 1776.

As the land under them shifted from Spanish, French, Mexican, Texan, then American governance (see sidebar, "Six Flags over Texas"), these people of Mexican, Spanish, or indigenous descent continued to live independently. Generations passed, citizenship changed, and cultural influences came and went; these early settlers created their own unique culture, calling themselves *Tejanos* as early as the 1830s. Distinguished Tejanos Gregorio Esparza and Toribio Losoya both died in 1836 defending the Alamo, the mission that had been their birthplace, and José Antonio Navarro and José Francisco Ruiz were the only native Texans to sign the Texas Declaration of Independence that same year.

SPANISH Though the Spanish explorer Alonso Álvarez de Pineda mapped the Texas coastline in 1519, the first Europeans to really get their boots dirty with Texas soil were Álvar Núñez Cabeza de Vaca and several companions, who found themselves shipwrecked on the Gulf Coast in 1528. Once ashore, Cabeza de Vaca and his men spent years living with Native Americans before heading to Mexico City and, eventually, back to Spain. The journey of these men, while extraordinary, might have been entirely forgotten had Cabeza de Vaca not prepared a report of his adventures and delivered it to the Spanish court in the late 1530s, thus providing the first written record of the land and peoples of Texas.

After colonizing Mexico the Spanish made inroads north, bringing with them the horse, which the Apache quickly mastered and rode to regional domination. The Comanche followed suit, and together the mounted Native Americans proved such a threat that the Spanish were hard pressed to set foot in the region for another 200 years. In the 1700s Franciscans passed through on their way to East Texas to convert Native Americans into Roman Catholics and Spanish citizens. There the threat of the

SIX FLAGS OVER TEXAS

The flags of six countries have flown over Texas, making it one of the most sought-after and fought-over pieces of land in North America. Spain was the first, claiming Texas as its own from 1519 to 1685 as an extension of its holdings in Mexico, but it never created much of an actual presence in its far-flung acquisition.

In 1685 the French, emboldened by their success in Louisiana, planted their flag on Texas soil just across the eastern border, but mishaps and misfortune caused them to abandon their claim in 1690, at which time the Spanish regained control, which they kept until 1821.

During their rule the Spanish focused on expanding their empire and establishing a solid foothold in North America. In Texas, *presidios* (forts) were built to protect and defend, and *misiones* (missions) were established in the hopes that self-sustaining communities of Spanish Catholic citizens might arise.

When Mexico won independence from Spain in 1821, Texas became the land of opportunity for both Hispanic pioneers from the south and Anglos from the north, all considering themselves citizens of Mexico. Out on the frontier people were used to being their own masters, however, and when General Santa Anna dismissed the Mexican Constitution, effectively declaring himself king, they revolted.

Battles at Gonzales and the Alamo in San Antonio tested the resolve of the revolutionaries, but the definitive battle at San Jacinto, on April 21, 1836, secured their independence, giving rise to the fourth flag, that of the Republic of Texas.

The republic had its ups and downs during its almost 10 years of existence from 1836 to 1845, but its rugged individualism, gritty determination, and boundless energy—not to mention lots and lots of land—made it a very attractive addition to the United States, which it joined on December 29, 1845.

Sixteen years later, the Civil War tore the fledgling nation apart, and Texas, though advised by Governor Sam Houston to remain neutral or reestablish a republic, sided with the Southerners, and the flag of the Confederacy flew over Texas from 1861 to 1865. While Texans valiantly fought, and won, the last battle of the Civil War, it was, unfortunately, after the Confederacy had already surrendered, and Texas suffered the rebels' fate. The flag of the United States of America has hung over Texas, the 28th state, since 1865.

Still, for many Texans, the flag that suits Texas best is its state flag, that of the tumultuous but short-lived former republic—the simple, straightforward, iconic Lone Star Flag, a proud reminder that though Texas may have been ruled by many, it has been controlled by none.

French and French-allied Native Americans near the Louisiana border forced them to backtrack to Central Texas, where they established the mission San Antonio de Valero, later known as the Alamo.

NATIVE AMERICANS The arrival of Europeans was clearly the pivotal historic moment for Native Americans in Texas, as elsewhere. When the Franciscans arrived in the 1700s proposing mission life, the reaction of the Native Americans varied immensely. Some wanted nothing to do with the newcomers, while some smaller groups saw the missions as a refuge from harassment and hostilities at the hands of larger groups. In the 1800s settlers came to Texas by the wagonload, bringing with them the notion of land claiming. Native Americans asked for, and were promised, ownership of the land they considered theirs, yet years of fighting, alliances, treaties, surprise attacks, and broken promises failed to yield documentation. While land ownership remained elusive, tensions boiled.

President Sam Houston of the Republic of Texas brokered treaties with the Tonkawas, the Lipan Apaches, the Comanches, Kichais, Tawakonis,

Wacos, and Taovayas throughout 1837 and 1838, creating a tenuous peace. In the 1850s, after Texas joined the United States of America, these many treaties and agreements were broken, and many Native Americans were forced to leave Texas or relocate to reservations. The disastrous Red River War in 1874 was the final straw, and in June 1875 the mighty Comanche surrendered at Fort Sill. In short, the 1800s were catastrophic for Native Americans in Texas, leaving their populations decimated by disease, violence, starvation, or genocide. These days, their descendants host the Austin Powwow and American Indian Heritage Festival, the largest annual Native American gathering in Texas, a huge celebration of Native American heritage and a commemoration of their shared history.

ANGLOS Anglos, a convenient term for people of various European backgrounds arriving primarily from the United States, came to Texas following the promise of plentiful, inexpensive land at precisely the time that Spain was having difficulty convincing its own citizens that this isolated, unknown, and generally hostile environment was a good investment. As long as these incoming Anglos agreed to become both Catholic and Spanish, they were guaranteed large land grants, and many, sincere or not in their desire to convert, took the bait. When Mexico gained independence from Spain in 1821, it extended the deal, giving *empresarios,* those willing to help organize and oversee large groups of immigrants, land grants to begin their settlements. During this time, immigrants came for many reasons. Some, Stephen F. Austin for one, made the trip with the promise of land ownership, while others came on the lam, taking advantage of the fact that the US and Mexico had not yet established an extradition agreement. Slave owners brought

LONGHORN CATTLE

LONE STAR STATE

slaves, incensing the Mexican government, which not only had forbidden the African slave trade, but whose president, Vicente Ramón Guerrero, had emancipated all slaves on September 15, 1829, in commemoration of Mexican independence. Nevertheless, slaves were bought and sold in Texas until 1840, with Mexico turning a blind eye in the hopes that the cotton production so dependent on slave labor might prove profitable.

Being so far removed from the long reach of government, over time the new Texans started to organize, think, and act for themselves. In 1830, after much tension and fearing rebellion, the Mexican government passed the Law of April 6th, effectively making unorganized immigration from the US to Texas illegal. Europeans, however, kept coming, and in 1831 Johann Friedrich Ernst, his wife, and their children were the first German family to arrive in Texas, settling near present-day Austin. Ernst was so impressed with his new surroundings that he wrote glowing letters back to Germany detailing his new home. Word spread, and by 1850 people of German descent totaled 5 percent of the state's total population, settling mostly in New Braunfels or fanning out into the Hill Country.

Texans soon began to chafe under Mexican leadership, growing restless for self-determination. In 1833 Antonio López de Santa Anna Pérez de Lebrón, the legendary Santa Anna, was installed as the president of Mexico. A lifelong military man, Santa Anna—though elected as a liberal—established himself as a dictator as soon as he was in power. After crushing opponents in Mexico, he headed north to San Antonio to confront the growing rebellion in Texas, attacking the Alamo in the early morning hours of March 6, 1836. His victory there—a dramatic example of winning the battle but losing the war—only galvanized Texans' support for independence. Months later, Mexico was defeated at the battle of San Jacinto, and the Republic of Texas was born. When Texas passed from a republic to a state, tiny Austin was thrust into the limelight—a brand-new city for a brand-new Texas.

Transportation

TO AND FROM THE REGION Interstate 35 links Austin and San Antonio. Sometimes called the NAFTA Highway, I-35 originates at the Mexican border and bisects the United States on its way to Duluth, Minnesota, on Lake Superior. Consequently, the six-lane route is constantly jammed with 18-wheelers, livestock trailers, delivery trucks, and overloaded pickups headed north and south. When traffic is flowing, I-35 is perfectly functional, but when it's not, be prepared to sit and wait . . . and wait, and wait. In and around both Austin and San Antonio, it is always wise to budget some extra time into your itinerary for

HAUPTSTRASSE, OR MAIN STREET, IN BOERNE

GOT WHEELS?

Most visitors to the region rent a car, and most major rental companies have kiosks in each airport. While it is possible to get around most of Austin or San Antonio using public transportation, a car is essential for touring the Hill Country. The percentage of uninsured motorists in Texas is high, and while lawmakers are attempting to curb the problem, a fender bender, regardless of fault, may end up costing you a pretty penny. Be sure to check your insurance policy before you drive.

Reservations are strongly recommended.

Advantage (800-777-5500; www.advantage.com)

Alamo (800-462-5266; www.alamo.com)

Avis (800-331-1212; www.avis.com)

Budget (800-527-0700; www.budget.com)

Dollar (800-800-3665; www.dollar.com)

Enterprise (800-261-7331; www.enterprise.com)

Hertz (800-654-3131; www.hertz.com)

National (844-382-6875; www.nationalcar.com)

Thrifty (800-847-4389; www.thrifty.com)

inevitable congestion. Conversely, traffic in the Hill Country flows at a leisurely pace; generally speaking, you can breeze undeterred over the winding, rural roads between towns.

Inside Austin and San Antonio the paths of interstate highways, U.S. highways, and state highways often merge. In San Antonio, for example, I-10 is also US 87 or US 90 at various points; US 281 north of town suddenly becomes I-37 south of town. Some state highways have names in addition to their numbers. Loop 360 in Austin is known as Capital of Texas Highway. Loop 1, also in Austin, is commonly referred to by its nickname, "MoPac." The Hill Country is traversed by plenty of small highways known as farm-to-market (FM) or ranch-to-market (RM) roads, which were built to be reliable trade routes between agricultural Texas and nearby cities or market centers. Constructed in the 1940s, these secondary roads are well maintained by the Texas Department of Transportation. County roads (CR), maintained by individual counties, are also secondary roads, though their size and conditions vary.

GETTING TO CENTRAL TEXAS

By Air: Air travelers coming to the region might consider flying into either Austin or San Antonio. Depending on your destination and time of travel, prices can vary widely; being flexible in your travel plans can sometimes yield big savings.

Austin-Bergstrom International Airport (512-530-2242; www.austintexas .gov/department/airport) 3600 Presidential Blvd., Austin, TX 78719.

The airport is located in southeast Austin, just east of the intersection of TX 71 and US 183, approximately 8 miles from downtown.

Taxi: **American Yellow Checker Cab** (512-452-9999; www.yellowcabaustin .com) Price: approximately $25-$30.

Airport Shuttle: **Super Shuttle** (512-258-3826 or 800-258-3826; www .supershuttle.com) Price: $12.

Bus: **Capital Metro Bus** (512-474-1200; www.capmetro.org) The *Airport Flyer* travels between the airport and two centrally located downtown stops, Sixth Street & Brazos, and 18th Street & Congress Avenue. It connects downtown and UT to the airport. Price: $1.

San Antonio International Airport (210-207-3433; www.sanantonio.gov/SAT) 9800 Airport Blvd., San Antonio, TX 78216. The airport is located near the intersection of Loop 410 and US 281, approximately 8 miles from downtown San Antonio.

Taxi: **San Antonio Taxis** (210-444-2222; www.sataxis.com) or **Yellow Checker Cab** (210-222-2222; www.yellowcabsa.com) Price: approximately $25–$30.

Airport Shuttle: **Super Shuttle** (210-281-9900; www.supershuttlesa.com) Price: one-way $19, round-trip $34.

Bus: **VIA Metropolitan Transit** (210-362-2020; www.viainfo.net) Price: $1.30.

By Train or Bus: While` train or bus travel to the region and between its cities and towns is possible, it is not very efficient.

Train: **Amtrak** (800-872-7245; www.amtrak.com)

Austin: 512-476-5684; 250 N. Lamar Blvd., Austin, TX 78703

San Antonio: 210-223-3226; 350 Hoefgen St., San Antonio, TX 78205

Bus: **Greyhound** (800-231-2222; www.greyhound.com)

Austin: 512-458-4463; 916 E. Koenig Lane, Austin, TX 78751

San Antonio: 210-270-5824; 500 N. St. Mary's St., San Antonio, TX 78205

Food and Drink

The secret to dining in Central Texas is to focus on the well done. Whether you're in an upscale restaurant or a neighborhood coffee shop, the charm of eating out in Central Texas is in the details, with an emphasis on quality and personality. At any price level, many menus feature creative seasonal fare accompanied by plenty of vegetables, meal-sized salads, and hearty soups, frequently made with organic ingredients. Vegetarians and the health-conscious will find themselves in unusually good company in this area, where restaurant menus tend to be diverse. Regional chefs love using locally grown or produced items, and regional wines, cheeses, game, fruits, and vegetables are often highlighted. The many, many individually owned and operated restaurants in Austin and San Antonio are very much rooted in their neighborhoods and their city, with a large number of them supporting local causes, participating in community events, and providing venues for local musicians and visual artists.

Now for the details. As you will undoubtedly notice, casual attire—some people wear shorts and flip-flops throughout the better part of the year—is commonplace. Wearing "business casual" is appropriate for most of the pricier establishments, though you won't feel out of place should you decide to dress up for a fancy, formal meal. Families seem especially welcome in Austin's eating establishments, most of which offer booster seats, kids' menus, and a friendly atmosphere. Generally, credit cards are accepted, and I have noted the occasional place where they are not. Reservations should be considered essential at the more expensive and popular spots, and I have recommended making them if necessary. You are not allowed to smoke in any public building or within 15 feet of the entrance to one. As with everything, details change, so please call ahead to ensure your visit goes smoothly.

In San Antonio, people like to eat out in style. For pricier establishments, "business casual" is generally appropriate. Families are welcome, particularly at the city's many casual restaurants, which are often family run themselves and quite kid friendly. If you are on a schedule or dining with a large group, consider making reservations or calling ahead.

Emergency Numbers

In an emergency, dial 911 and tell the operator your location and the nature of your emergency, and your call will be directed to the appropriate responder.

Poison Control is 800-222-1222; www.poison.org.

For further assistance, see "Hospitals" on page 23.

Area Codes

Austin	512

SAN ANTONIO

Bexar County	210
Comal County	830

THE HILL COUNTRY

Bandera	830
Blanco	830
Boerne	830, 210
Comfort	830
Fredericksburg	830
Johnson City	830
Kerrville	830
Marble Falls	830
Stonewall	830
Wimberley	512

NEARBY AND IN BETWEEN

Georgetown	512
New Braunfels/Gruene	830
San Marcos	512

Banks and Money

A good many national banks, or banks that participate in national networks, are represented in Austin and San Antonio. However, depending on the bank, you could incur several dollars in fees per ATM withdrawal. Alternatively, many national stores, such as Target or Walmart, grocery stores, and the post office will allow you to get "cash back" if you use your debit card to make a purchase. Though there is frequently a maximum withdrawal of $100, there is generally no additional fee. In the Hill Country, ATM machines are fewer and farther between, so plan accordingly, and be sure to check in advance that a shop or restaurant accepts credit cards.

Climate and Weather Reports

The weather in Austin, San Antonio, and the Hill Country is generally favorable, with about 300 sunny days a year, warm nights, and gentle breezes. Mid-July to mid-September is the hottest time of year, with temperatures easily reaching the high 90s. Austin and San Antonio can become stiflingly humid, the Hill Country somewhat less so; the farther west you travel, the more arid it becomes. Winters tend to be cool but not often freezing, with snow an aberration. The region gets most of its rainfall in the spring, when steady showers soak the ground and fill lakes and streams.

THE HEAT   When it gets hot in Texas, it gets really, really hot. When it gets humid in Texas, it gets really, really humid. In fact, the best way to describe the summertime in San Antonio, in particular, is tropical. Since dehydration and heatstroke are not uncommon conditions, it's important to be aware and prepared. Sunglasses, sunscreen, a light cotton long-sleeved shirt, a wide-brimmed hat, an umbrella, or even a small spray bottle filled with water for misting can help provide protection and relief. Staying hydrated is essential; steering clear of sodas and alcoholic beverages in favor of water, sports drinks, and juice is considered wise.

STORMS   Arriving sometimes without warning, summertime thunderstorms can bring torrential rain and flash floods. When flash-flood warnings are issued, it is best to exercise caution and avoid creeks, drainage ditches, and low-water road crossings, as signs in these areas will indicate. Tornadoes frequently accompany thunderstorms, so it is best to listen to or watch the news for any words of caution. A tornado or severe thunderstorm watch serves as an alert that conditions are favorable for either event, while a tornado or severe thunderstorm warning means that either event has been detected on radar and danger may be imminent. In this case, it is best to seek cover in a substantial building, away from windows. In cooler weather ice storms can occur, and since Central Texas does not maintain a large fleet of sand or salt trucks, the roads can become treacherously slick and hazardous. Texas drivers are inexperienced with slick or icy roads, and during storms accidents tend to be frequent.

Grocery Stores/ Drugstores

HEB is a grocery-store chain based in San Antonio with many locations throughout Austin, San Antonio, and the Hill Country. HEB also owns Central Market.

AUSTIN

HEB (512-459-6513; www.heb.com) There are many HEBs in Austin, but this one is open 24 hours a day with a 24-hour pharmacy (512-459-8308).

SAN ANTONIO

HEB (210-829-7373; www.heb.com) The store is open until 1 AM and the pharmacy is open Monday through Friday 9–9, Saturday 9–8, and Sunday 10–5. Pharmacy phone is 210-829-1705.

Accessible Services

In Austin and San Antonio, Wheelchair Getaways (800-723-6028; www .wheelchairgetaways.com) rents

accessible vans. In San Antonio, the Riverwalk will present some challenges for anyone with restricted mobility. Visit www.thesanantonioriverwalk.com for maps detailing access points, ramps, and walkways.

Hospitals

AUSTIN

University Medical Center Brackenridge Hospital (512-324-7000; www .seton.net)

Dell Children's Medical Center (512-324-000; www.dellchildrens.net)

Seton Medical Center Austin (512-324-1000; www.seton.net)

Seton Shoal Creek (512-324-2000; www .seton.net) Emergency psychiatric care

St. David's Medical Center (512-476-7111; www.stdavidsmedicalcenter.com)

BANDERO

Closest facility is in Kerrville.

BLANCO

Closest facility is in Fredericksburg.

BOERNE

Closest facility is in San Antonio.

BURNET

Seton Highland Lakes Hospital (512-715-3000; www.seton.net)

COMFORT

Closest facility is in Kerrville.

FREDERICKSBURG

Hill Country Memorial Hospital (830-997-4353; www.hillcountrymemorial .org)

GEORGETOWN

St. David's Georgetown Hospital (512-943-3000; www.georgetownhealthcare.org)

JOHNSON CITY

Closest facilities are in Fredericksburg or Marble Falls.

KERRVILLE

Peterson Regional Medical Center (830-896-4200; www.petersonrmc.com)

MARBLE FALLS

Marble Falls Minor Emergency Center (830-798-1122; www.mfmec.org)

Seton Highland Lakes Hospital (512-715-3000; www.seton.net)

NEW BRAUNFELS/GRUENE

McKenna Memorial Hospital (830-606-2180; www.mckenna.org)

SAN ANTONIO

Baptist Medical Center (210-297-7000; www.baptisthealthsystem.com)

Nix Medical Center (210-271-1800; www.nixhealth.com)

Christus Santa Rosa Health Care (210-704-2361; www.christussantarosa.org)

SAN MARCOS

Central Texas Medical Center (512-353-8979; www.ctmc.org)

STONEWALL

Closest facility is in Fredericksburg.

WIMBERLEY

Central Texas Medical Center (512-353-8979; www.ctmc.org)

Late-Night Food, Fuel, and Groceries

AUSTIN

Catering to students' insomnia and club-goers' late-night tendencies, there are a few spots to eat all day and night in Austin. Try **24 Diner, Kerbey Lane Cafe,** or **Magnolia Cafe**.

SAN ANTONIO

Mi Tierra serves Mexican food and **Lulu's** has breakfast treats 24/7.

Licenses

Hunting and fishing, popular recreational activities in Texas, require state-issued licenses, which are available at numerous locations, including some grocery and sports stores, online through the Texas Parks and Wildlife Department's website, www.tpwd.state.tx.us, or by phone at 800-895-4248. However, fishing from shore or pier within a Texas state park does not require a license; check at the park's headquarters for details. For a full overview of state hunting and fishing regulations, go to www.tpwd.state.tx.us/regulations. Texas game wardens are especially strict, and any violation of state hunting and fishing regulations will be taken very seriously.

Media

MAGAZINES AND NEWSPAPERS Both Austin and San Antonio have dailies as well as free weekly papers, all of which are likely to include information regarding events in the towns nearby and in between and in the Hill Country.

AUSTIN

Austin American-Statesman (www
.statesman.com) The Austin daily. The
Statesman's Entertainment, Calendar,
and Life sections and archived reviews
can also be viewed online at www
.austin360.com.

Austin Chronicle (www
.austinchronicle.com) Excellent free
weekly guide to entertainment, with politics and news thrown in. Published on
Thursdays.

SAN ANTONIO

San Antonio Express-News (www
.mysanantonio.com) The San Antonio
daily news; in print or online.

San Antonio Current (www.sacurrent
.com) News, culture, free. Published on
Thursdays.

HILL COUNTRY

Many of these tiny papers are regional,
serving the city mentioned and, often-
times, the entire county.

Bandera Bulletin (www.bandera
bulletin.com)

Blanco County News (www.blanco
countynews.com)

Boerne Star (www.boernestar.com)

Burnet Bulletin (www.burnetbulletin
.com)

Comfort News (www.comfortnews
.com)

Fredericksburg Standard (www
.fredericksburgstandard.com)

Herald-Zeitung (New Braunfels/
Gruene, www.heraldzeitung.com)

Johnson City Record Courier (www
.jcrecordcourier.com)

Junction Eagle (www.junctioneagle
.com)

Kerrville Times (www.dailytimes.com)

San Marcos Daily Record (www
.sanmarcosrecord.com)

Williamson County Sun (Georgetown,
www.wilcosun.com)

Wimberley View/Hill Country Sun
(www.hillcountrysun.com)

RADIO STATIONS

AUSTIN

KBPA 103.5 "BOB" FM. Their tagline,
"Bob plays anything," says it all.
KMFA 89.5 FM. Outstanding classical
music since 1967.
KUT 90.5 AM. National Public Radio and
outstanding music.
KVET 98.1 FM. Country music and Long-
horn sports.

SAN ANTONIO

KLEY 94.1 FM. Tejano music.
KPAC 88.3 FM. National Public Radio and
classical music.
KROM 92.2 FM. Mexican pop.
KRTU 91.7 FM. Trinity University station.
KSTX 89.1 FM. National Public Radio.

HILL COUNTRY

KTXI 90.1 FM. National Public Radio.

Pests

For whatever reason, pests love Texas
and tend to thrive in its temperate climate despite efforts to control them. The
truth is that many serve an important
ecological function and most are harm-
less, but there are a few pests that should
have you watching where you sit, step, or
stand.

FIRE ANTS The biggest pests in Central
Texas are the fire ants, for which you will
frequently see warning signs posted. Fire
ants tend to make mounds in sunny,
open fields and parks, by the side of the
road, and at the base of trees and other
objects, such as picnic tables. When their
nest is disturbed, they swarm and deliver
many simulta- neous stings, which are
similar to bee stings in look and feel.

Usually no medical intervention is required, but as with bees, a small percentage of the population may have a severe allergic reaction, in which case emergency medical care is essential. The only prevention is avoidance, so watch where you sit and stand, and be especially aware of small children.

SNAKES Snakes are common in Texas, but of the 72 native species and subspecies, only 15 pose any threat to humans. In Central Texas, snakes keep to themselves and do not tend to initiate interactions. Since both poisonous and nonpoisonous snakes bite, if you have the unfortunate experience of being bitten, a precautionary trip to the emergency room would be wise.

SPIDERS Of the 900 species of spiders present in Texas, only two groups pose any threat to humans: the recluse and widow spiders. In many cases, if you are bitten by one of these, you may not notice until the appearance of a suspicious wound coupled with fever, chills, nausea, pain, vomiting, or weakness, among other symptoms. In all cases, swab the wound with alcohol, relieve swelling and pain with ice, and call your doctor or, depending on the severity, visit the emergency room.

Religious Services

Texas is known for its religious enthusiasm, and there are plenty of places of worship in Central Texas. The *Austin American-Statesman,* the *San Antonio Express-News,* and the newspapers in the larger towns of the Hill Country list upcoming services in their Saturday editions. While many religious organizations in the region identify themselves as Christian, they are widely varied in focus, practice, and beliefs. You will find the most religious diversity in Austin and San Antonio, where Jewish, Islamic, and other religious communities are active.

Tourist Information

Local visitor centers and convention bureaus are great sources of information, maps, advice, and even coupons for discounts on tours and admission fees.

AUSTIN

Austin Convention & Visitor Bureau (800-926-ACVB; www.austintexas.org; 301 Congress Ave., Suite 200, Austin, TX 78701)

Austin Visitor Center (866-GO- AUS-TIN; www.austintexas.org; 209 E. Sixth St., Austin, TX 78701) Open Mon.–Fri. 9–5, Sat.–Sun. 9–6.

SAN ANTONIO

San Antonio Convention and Visitor Bureau (210-207-6700 or 800-447-3372; www.sanantoniocvb.com; 203 S. St. Mary's St., 2nd floor, San Antonio, TX 78205)

San Antonio Chamber of Commerce (210-229-2100; www.sanantonio.com; 602 E. Commerce St., San Antonio, TX 78205)

HILL COUNTRY

Bandera

Bandera County Convention and Visitor Bureau (830-796-3045 or 800-364-3833; www.banderacowboycapital.com; P.O. Box 171, Bandera, TX 78003)

Blanco

Blanco Chamber of Commerce (830-833-5101; www.blancochamber.com; 312 Pecan St., Blanco, TX 78606)

Boerne

Boerne Convention and Visitor Bureau (830-249-7277 or 888-842-8080; www.visitboerne.org; 1407 S. Main St., Boerne, TX 78006)

Greater Boerne Chamber of Commerce (830-249-8000 or 888-842-8080; www.boerne.org; 126 Rosewood Ave., Boerne, TX 78006)

Burnet

Burnet Chamber of Commerce (512-756-4297; www.burnetchamber.org; 229 S. Pierce St., Burnet, TX 78611)

Comfort

www.shopcomfort.com. Information available in Fredericksburg and Kerrville.

Fredericksburg

Fredericksburg Chamber of Commerce (830-997-6523 or 1-888-997-3600; www.fredericksburg-texas.com; 302 E. Austin St., Fredericksburg, TX 78624)

Johnson City

Johnson City Texas Chamber of Commerce (830-868-7684; www.lbjcountry.com) Located inside the **Hill Country Visitor Center** (830-367-2151; www.hillcountryvisitorscenter.com; 803 US 281 South, Johnson City, TX 78636)

DECORATIVE IRON FENCING ON THE CAPITOL GROUNDS IN AUSTIN

Kerrville

Kerrville Convention and Visitor Bureau (830-792-3535 or 800-221-7958; www.kerrvilletexascvb.com; 2108 Sidney Baker St., Kerrville, TX 78028) Open Mon.–Fri. 8:30–5, Sat. 9–3, Sun. 10–3.

Kerrville Chamber of Commerce (830-896-1155; www.kerrvilletx.com; 1700 Sidney Baker St., Suite 100, Kerrville, TX 78028)

Marble Falls

Marble Falls/Lake LBJ Visitor Center (830-693-4449 or 800-759-8178; www.marblefalls.org; 801 US 281, Marble Falls, TX 78654) Open Mon.–Fri. 8–5.

Stonewall

Stonewall Chamber of Commerce (830-644-2735; www.stonewalltexas.com; 115 St. Francis St., Stonewall, TX 78671)

Wimberley

Wimberley Chamber of Commerce and Visitor Center (www.visitwimberley.org; P.O. Box 12, Wimberley, TX 78676)

NEARBY AND IN BETWEEN

Georgetown

Georgetown Visitor Information Center (512-436-8696; www.visit.georgetown.org; 101 W. Seventh St., Georgetown, TX 78626)

New Braunfels

New Braunfels Chamber of Commerce (800-572-2626; www.nbjumpin.com; P.O. Box 311417, New Braunfels, TX 78131). **Gruene Historic District** (830-629-5077; www.gruenetexas.com)

San Marcos

San Marcos Convention and Visitor Bureau (512-393-5900 or 888-200-5620; www.toursanmarcos.com; 202 N. C. M. Allen Pkwy., San Marcos, TX 78667)

Tourist Information Center (512-393-5930; 617 I-35 North, San Marcos, TX 78666)

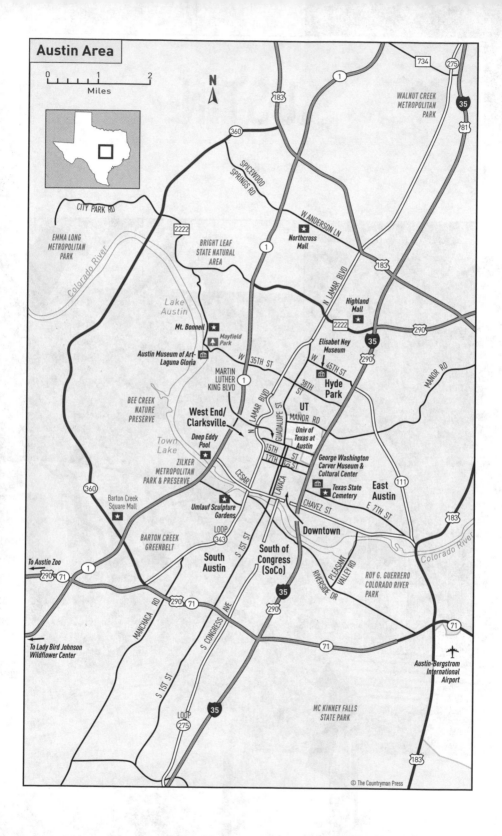

AUSTIN

The seat and center of Travis County, Austin is smaller than San Antonio and just a fraction of the size of Dallas or Houston, but is nevertheless the capital of Texas. The city is, and always has been, quick with opinions, purposeful in action, and unlikely to follow anyone else's lead. An intellectual powerhouse, Austin has a nationwide reputation for brains and creativity, encouraged and supported by the University of Texas, whose campus occupies a large swath of the city. Sunshine, hike-and-bike trails, parks, and rooftop bars satisfy the city's penchant for all things outdoors. At open-air concerts or just lounging under the shady oaks, Austin is a city that likes to hang out, having perfected the art of doing so. And here in the "Live Music Capital of the World," you can see performances every day and dozens of music festivals throughout the year.

EARLY DAYS Situated at the eastern edge of the Edwards Plateau, where the land of prairies and lakes is thrust suddenly into the dips and curves of the Hill Country, Austin is blessed with natural resources and beauty. In 1839 the then thinly settled area anchored by the tiny village of Waterloo was chosen for the capital of the Republic of Texas and was promptly named after its most famous Anglo-American, Stephen F. Austin, who was revered long before being immortalized along with the other fallen heroes of the Alamo. Standing on the edge of the western frontier, in full view of Mexicans and Native Americans, both of whom had their eye on the property, Austin seemed unsafe, its future uncertain. Some, including Sam Houston, were skeptical of the choice. But the republic's president, Mirabeau B. Lamar, who had become smitten with the location on a buffalo hunt, gave the go-ahead for the purchase of 7,735 acres along the Colorado River. Surveyors, planners, and workers immediately set about building a city, with the hope of having it finished by the next scheduled meeting of the Texas Congress, just months away in November 1839. A grid of 14 blocks was laid out on a 640-acre plot starting at the river, bounded on two sides by Shoal and Waller Creeks; Congress Avenue bisected the grid on its way northward to the hill on which a temporary one-story wooden capitol was built. Austin was incorporated on December 27, 1839, Congress successfully convened as planned, and the city welcomed diplomats from England, France, and its neighbor to the north, the United States.

Austin's status as capital didn't sit well with everyone. In 1842 Sam Houston, who had succeeded President Lamar, demanded that the national archives and state-related records be brought to Houston. Folks in Austin took the news personally, feeling that moving the papers would mean moving the fledgling capital, and staunchly refused. Houston acquiesced, allowing Austin to keep the documents, but moved the government all the same, first to Houston and later to Washington-on-the-Brazos. Houston quickly grew to regret his hasty compromise; he wanted the papers, and he sent armed men to Austin to get them. In what would become known as the Archive War, the men were met by enraged citizens, and in the end the papers remained in Austin while the government remained in Houston. It wasn't until the 1845 annexation of Texas by the United States that Austin was established, officially, as capital of Texas—with one caveat. The designation was temporary; a vote would be held in 20 years to let the people decide once and for all.

MURAL IN SOUTH AUSTIN

Taking its role as capital to heart, by 1853 Austin had completed a permanent capitol building and, by 1856, a Governor's Mansion. The city was growing, but it was still essentially an outpost on the edge of the frontier, with only unreliable roads for trading. Austin lobbied hard for railroads, but the Civil War halted all new construction as resources were diverted to the war effort. While the city was initially against secession, skyrocketing food shortages, inflation, and casualties shifted its sentiments. At the end of the war, in 1865, Union troops occupied a bedraggled Austin.

On December 25, 1871, Austin, still suffering the effects of the war and Reconstruction, was gratefully connected to the greater and newly unified country as the Houston and Texas Central Railway passed through the city. The city's economy took this shot in the arm, and Austin almost immediately became a bustling hub of materials, products, and, most importantly, immigrants. By 1870, five years after the end of the Civil War and the Emancipation Proclamation, 36 percent of Austin's population was African American. These newcomers quickly went to work settling various Austin neighborhoods, opening churches and businesses, and sending their children to local schools. By 1875 there were 757 residents from Germany, 215 from Ireland, 138 from Sweden, and 297 from Mexico—the first from that nation—with each group contributing to the economy of the young and growing city. Public life was getting crowded and chaotic; gas street lamps were installed in 1874, a streetcar line was established in 1875, and a bridge spanned the Colorado River the following year.

In 1872 Austin triumphed at the polls and was declared, once and for all, the Texas capital. In 1881 Austin prevailed again in a statewide ballot, this time for the site of the University of Texas, which started educating students two years later. Also in 1881, the city organized a public school system, and the Tillotson Collegiate and Normal Institute began offering instruction to African American students. Four years later

St. Edward's Academy was chartered as St. Edward's College. In 1888 the city finished construction of the huge granite Capitol, still so prevalent in its skyline, anchoring Austin at the symbolic center of Texas.

In 1905, despite its statewide importance, Austin had only one paved street, deplorable sanitary conditions, and very few public services. All this changed with the 1928 city plan, the first plan drawn up since the town's beginnings in 1839, and the passage of a $4.25 million bond issue. The money was used to finance a library, a hospital, an airport, roads, and sewers and to further the city's primary goal of boosting its image as the go-to city for education and culture in Texas. A recreation department was put into place; soon after, the city had made huge strides in beautification, giving itself parks, pools, and recreation programs. These public improvements asserted the ideals that define Austin today, a city with progressive ideas and proactive planning.

THE 20TH CENTURY The Great Depression of the 1930s did not spare Austin, but by all accounts it was the skills of Mayor Robert Thomas Miller and Congressman Lyndon Baines Johnson that kept the city afloat. The population exploded, increasing 66 percent in the 1930s, and with this growth came increasing demands on services. The University of Texas saw enrollment practically double and quickly began construction to expand the campus. The devastating flood of 1935 prompted plans to dam the Colorado River; the Tom Miller Dam, finished in 1940, gave the city Lake Austin, while the Mansfield Dam, completed the following year, created Lake Travis. Dams farther north created the Highland Lakes, used for recreation, water supply, and power. The dawn of World War II brought Del Valle Air Base, later called Bergstrom Air Force Base, and later still retrofitted to become the Austin-Bergstrom Airport.

The 20th century brought radical social changes to Austin. Mirroring other cities throughout the country, Austin was mired in the politics and interpersonal dynamics of segregation. While African Americans had previously lived throughout the city, the city plan of 1928 recommended a "Negro district" be established in the city's East Side. By the 1940s this ghettoizing allowed the city to systematically restrict African Americans' access to schools, parks, transportation, and other municipal services, despite the fact that blacks had established numerous businesses, dozens of churches, and two colleges in the city and had participated in civic life since the city's inception. As the city grew, the African American population remained relatively stable in numbers but dropped dramatically in percentage.

At the same time, the number of Hispanic residents jumped from 1.5 percent of the population to 11 percent. Though laws permitted discrimination against African Americans, the discrimination experienced by Mexican Americans, while pervasive, was not as systematic or organized. Over the years, local African American leaders and their supporters worked tirelessly to desegregate schools and other institutions, and in 1956 the University of Texas admitted black students, the first large southern university to do so. The nationwide demonstrations and sit-ins of the 1960s brought about the Civil Rights Act of 1964, which provided some measure of legal protection from discrimination. Ironically, while two African Americans sat on Austin's city council in 1880, African Americans did not serve again until 1968, an advance soon repeated by Hispanic citizens.

Austin is still a young city. Coming of age in the mid-20th century, it has seen its growth hastened by wars, railroads, and social movements. In the 1950s Austin began positioning itself for a future in technology, as several research laboratories and think tanks sprang up and prospered, benefiting from their proximity to the university. By the 1970s rapid growth in the city was met by a politically active population who formed civic groups to preserve the city's history, neighborhoods, and environment and to protect the rights of its citizens. Austin remains the state's undisputed educational and cultural center, with enough parks, lakes, recreation, and cultural events to keep everyone happy. As the popularity of the loosely organized movement "Keep Austin Weird" (www.keepaustinweird.com) demonstrates, the city loves its free-thinkers, artists, and musicians. If, as John Steinbeck wrote, "Texas is a state of mind," then Austin, an unencumbered free spirit of a city, is surely its perfect capital.

GETTING AROUND Austin is not a large city, so driving into, out of, or around it is not a particularly difficult task. However, the major routes that approximate the boundaries of the city are known by several names, making navigation a challenge.

I-35 runs along the eastern part of Austin, dividing East Austin from the rest of the city. Following the western border is Loop 1, also known as the MoPac Expressway, or MoPac, for the Missouri-Pacific Railroad, which runs parallel to it in many places. Farther west is Loop 360, often referred to as Capital of Texas Highway.

US 183 originates in East Austin as Ed Bluestein Boulevard, becoming Anderson Lane, Research Boulevard, and finally Bell Boulevard as it snakes it way along the northern edge of the city. At the southern reaches of the city, TX 71 is also known as US 290 and Ben White Boulevard.

Downtown Austin is more straightforward for both drivers and pedestrians. Spread out in a grid, with generously sized blocks, downtown is easily taken in on foot, but to get to sights in South Austin and beyond, consider riding one of the city's buses.

See Austin's Capital Metro's website for details; www.capmetro.org.

NEIGHBORHOODS

DOWNTOWN

Overseen by the Capitol, downtown is organized around Congress Avenue, which divides cross streets into east and west. Much of the city's nightlife is located either on Sixth Street, bounded by Congress to the west and Red River Street to the east, or the Warehouse District on Fourth and Fifth Streets between Congress and Guadalupe.

SOUTH AUSTIN AND SOUTH OF CONGRESS (SOCO)

While crossing over the Congress Avenue Bridge used to feel like crossing into a different world, a recent rejuvenation of the area has tempered its edge. Large-scale commercial and residential developments are now springing up in this artsy enclave. Filled with creative

THE FROST BANK BUILDING IN DOWNTOWN AUSTIN

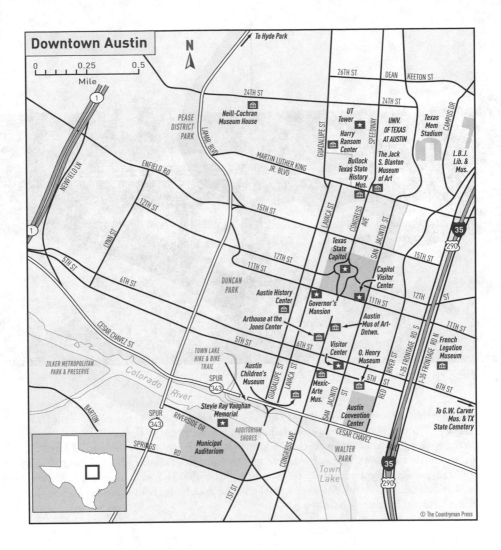

eateries, music venues, and funky art and resale shops, South Austin embodies some of the best of Austin.

WEST END/CLARKSVILLE

The area west of Lamar Boulevard between Enfield Road to the north and West Fifth Street to the south, West End and Clarksville is a deceptively modest-looking neighborhood conveniently located beside downtown. The area is atmospheric, with large trees, art galleries, several upscale restaurants, and sidewalks for strolling.

UT AND HYDE PARK

To the north of the Capitol, the sprawling 350-acre University of Texas campus is bounded by Guadalupe Street (also known as "The Drag") to the west, I-35 to the east,

BRIDGE OVER LADY BIRD LAKE AT DUSK

and Martin Luther King Jr. Boulevard to the south. Located just a mile north of the University of Texas, Hyde Park is bounded by Guadalupe Street to the west, Duval Street to the east, 45th Street to the north, and 38th Street to the south. Developed as Austin's first suburb, the neighborhood features homes from the 1930s and '40s interspersed with commercial centers, folksy restaurants, and coffee shops. Students, professors, and young families call Hyde Park home, and the area feels lived in, with bikes in the yards and swings on the porches.

EAST AUSTIN

Comprising the neighborhoods east of I-35, East Austin retains its historic roots. A diverse neighborhood, it is also home to significant cultural institutions such as the George Washington Carver Museum and Cultural Center and the Texas State Cemetery. Recent economic development has changed the face of East Austin, but its infectious community spirit is still thriving.

✳ To See

HISTORIC PLACES The Austin History Center is a good place to research the history of the city, and a visit to the Bob Bullock Museum will help you put the facts in the larger context of Texas history.

The Texas Capitol (512-463-4630; www.tspb.texas.gov) sits on a high point in the city, with the University of Texas to the north and Congress Avenue descending gently southward to the Colorado River. The massive Renaissance revival–style building, built to replace its predecessor, which had been destroyed by fire, was completed in 1888 at a cost of over $3.5 million—not paid for in cash, but with the enormous parcel of land in the Texas Panhandle that became the legendary XIT Ranch. The largest capitol building in the nation, save for the National Capitol in Washington, D.C, the Texas State Capitol is big, bold, and—right down to the engraving of "Texas Capitol" on the *inside* of the 7-pound bronze hinges of the massive entrance doors—very Texas.

The Capitol's exterior walls are made of distinctive pink-hued granite known as "sunset red," quarried at Granite Mountain in nearby Marble Falls. The building is topped with a gleaming aluminum Goddess of Liberty, clutching a Lone Star in her hand. The original zinc figure was removed in 1985, painted white, and put on permanent display at the Bob Bullock Museum (see "Museums" on page 38); her star rests at the Capitol Visitor Center. In 1995 the building underwent an extraordinarily expensive $98 million renovation and now sparkles inside and out, with original details restored. In the lobby Elisabet Ney's sculptures of Texas leaders Stephen Austin, Sam Houston, and Miriam "Ma" Ferguson, Texas's first woman governor and the country's second, are all on display, as are portraits of other notables and folk heroes such as Davy Crockett. Inside, centered in the impressive rotunda, a Lone Star of the Texas Republic looks down on a terrazzo floor mosaic of the seals of the six countries whose flags have flown over the state. The serene, parklike grounds, surrounded by the bustling city, are perfect for strolling, and the large shade trees and benches provide relief in the heat. The many monuments dotting the 22-acre grounds tell the stories of Texas and include statues of an armed Alamo defender, Texas Rangers and cowboys, pioneer women, children, and a volunteer firefighter, war memorials, and even a replica of the Statue of Liberty; they are all detailed in a brochure available at the visitor center. Admission is free.

THE CAPITOL

The **Capitol Visitor Center** (512-305-8400; www.tspb.texas.gov) and gift shop is located in the faux-medieval General Land Office Building on the southeast corner of the Capitol grounds and is chock-full of information, booklets, pamphlets, videos, art exhibits, and Texas-themed merchandise. Whether your questions regard history, camping, bus tours, or public restrooms, the folks here have the answer, not just for the Capitol, but for Austin and Central Texas as well. Interesting exhibits include the O. Henry Room, where you can listen to information about the writer's life and works on old-fashioned telephones, a 1:16 scale model of the Capitol dome, and a fascinating video that details the creative deal brokered between Texas and a group of

STATUE WITH A LONE STAR ATOP THE TEXAS CAPITOL

Chicago businessmen that financed the construction of the Capitol in exchange for the land that became the XIT Ranch.

The gleaming-white, beautifully proportioned Greek-revival **Governor's Mansion** (512-463-5516; www.governor.state.tx.us /mansion or www.txfgm.org) was built by self-taught master builder Abner Cook and completed in 1856. The house proved so big that governors at first had a difficult time furnishing and maintaining it, until Sam Houston, a man who liked to think big, moved in and had it properly appointed. Home to every Texas governor since 1856, in the fall of 2007 the Governor's Mansion was closed for maintenance and its contents placed in storage, a fortuitous fact since an arsonist set fire to the building in the summer of 2008. While the mansion sustained considerable damage, a four-year-long reconstruction has since restored its grandeur and dignity. Free guided tours are available Wednesday, Thursday, and Friday afternoons; reservations are required and must be made a week in advance. To reserve a spot, email Mansion.Tours@tspb.texas .gov or call 512-305-8524.

A division of the Austin Public Library, the **Austin History Center** (512-974-7480; www.library.austintexas.gov/ahc) is centrally located on Guadalupe, a few blocks southwest of the Capitol, and certainly worth popping into. Well-presented collections of photos, news clippings, maps, and records trace the history of Austin through exhibits on African American history, the women's suffrage movement, Austinites at work, and Victorian architecture.

MUSEUMS While music has deep roots in Central Texas, the formal establishment of museums for the visual arts is still relatively recent. The city's two big museums, the Austin Museum of Art and the Jack S. Blanton Museum of Art, are less than 50 years old, so their collections are still growing and their exhibition space is wonderfully intimate. Cultural museums, such as the Bob Bullock Museum, offer a dynamic introduction to the history and personality of the region, while interactive museums, such as the Thinkery, are just plain fun.

Brush up on your Texas history at the **Bullock Texas State History Museum** (512-936-8746; www.thestoryoftexas.com). The 35-foot-tall bronze star sculpture out front is your first indication that this museum thinks big. Spearheaded by former Lieutenant Governor Bob Bullock and opened in 2001, the Texas State History Museum has quickly become a must-see destination. Known for its elaborate and educational interactive exhibits, many of which challenge myths and misconceptions, the permanent collection of the museum is organized around the themes of Land, Identity, and Opportunity. Special exhibits have included *It Ain't Braggin' if It's True* which explores, among other things, the gray area between pride and swagger, and *The Faces of Texas*,

REMEMBER EAST AUSTIN

With so many of Austin's sights concentrated on the west side of I-35, the city's east side doesn't get as many visitors, but that doesn't mean there aren't interesting spots to check out, notably the Carver Museum and Cultural Center. Be sure to leave time to stop in at one of the neighborhood's eateries (see "Where to Eat" on pages 68–70) for a great taste of everyday Austin.

Originally built to house the French representative to the Republic of Texas, the French Legation Museum (512-472-8180; www.frenchlegationmuseum.org) comprises two buildings: the mansion and the kitchen. The mansion is the oldest building in Austin, having survived thanks to the good care of the Robertson family—who owned it from 1848 to 1940 and whose Victorian furnishings still grace the interior—and the Daughters of the Republic of Texas, who restored it in the 1950s. An example of French neoclassical architecture, the house feels very Continental, right down to the French wine cellar. The original kitchen burned down in 1880; the current building is a replica based on evidence from the archaeological record, and antique kitchenware adds authenticity. Docent-led tours bring the property to life. Each July, Bastille Day festivities add an air of celebration.

The George Washington Carver Museum and Cultural Center (512-974-4926; www.austintexas.gov) began in 1926 as a tiny library—no bigger than a house—serving the neighborhood's mostly African American population and has grown into a museum and cultural center celebrating African American heritage, the first of its kind in Texas. The centerpiece of the museum is its exhibit on Juneteenth (see "Festivals" on page 84), which celebrates the announcement of the Emancipation Proclamation of 1862. A thoughtful exhibit featuring the history of 10 African Americans in Central Texas whose lives illustrate perseverance is also interesting. There is also a small interactive area for children, an art gallery, and the Boyd Vance Theater, which hosts music and film events throughout the year. Just a block farther east is the Henry Madison Log Cabin (512-472-6838; www.austintexas.gov), built in the 1860s by the man who would become the first African American city councilman in Austin.

The parklike Texas State Cemetery (512-463-0605; www.cemetery.state.tx.us), in the heart of East Austin, is the final resting place of many of Texas's leaders and personalities. Governors, authors, Texas Rangers, Confederate generals, and signers of the Texas Declaration of Independence are all buried here. Originally planned in 1851, the cemetery underwent a much-needed restoration, spearheaded by former Lieutenant Governor Bob Bullock, who has since been buried there, in the 1990s. The results include a gallery and sleek visitor center with displays and information designed to make the cemetery as educational as it is reverential. Genealogists will appreciate the very thorough online master list of burials.

a lovely portrait series taken by Austin photographer Michael O'Brien. The vast sunsets, galloping herds of horses, and NASA space shuttles featured in *Texas: The Big Picture* are well suited to the enormous screen at the museum's IMAX theater. The Story of Texas Café on the second floor is a convenient spot to enjoy lunch or a snack, either inside or out on the balcony.

Directly across the street, on the edge of the University of Texas campus, the **Jack S. Blanton Museum** (512-471-5482; www.blantonmuseum.org) earns praise for both the focus and depth of its collection. The museum has a problem that every museum would like to have—collectors keep bequeathing it their collections. Consequently, what was a fledgling operation in the 1960s and '70s has grown to over 17,000 works of art and counting. The Blanton's 20th-century Latin American collection, for example, is almost unparalleled in the U.S. and one of a handful worldwide. Spacious, spare, and well lit, the environment at the Blanton showcases the artwork wonderfully and is both peaceful and provocative.

THE BULLOCK TEXAS STATE HISTORY MUSEUM

The Lyndon Baines Johnson Museum and Library (512-721-0200; www.lbjlibrary .org), on the eastern edge of the University of Texas campus near the Texas Memorial Stadium, provides a fascinating look at post-Depression era America. With the benefit of hindsight and a few intervening decades, it is easy to appreciate Lyndon Johnson's life, times, and presidency, as they were some of the most tumultuous and formative years for the country. LBJ's terms as vice president and president encompassed the Cuban Missile Crisis, the civil rights movement, the assassinations of John F. Kennedy, Robert F. Kennedy, and Martin Luther King Jr., and the Vietnam War. A Texan through and through, LBJ never forgot his childhood in the rural Hill Country, which fueled his passion for the enormous social reforms designed to bring about the "Great Society." A must for history buffs, who might also consider a trip to the LBJ National Historic Park (see Hill Country chapter).

A block away and also part of the university, the **Texas Memorial Museum** (512-471-1604; www.utexas.edu/tmm), located in the Texas Natural Science Center, is dedicated to geology, paleontology, zoology, and anthropology, which translates into an eclectic mix of meteorites and dinosaur skeletons, Texas wildlife taxidermy, and Native American artifacts. The knowledgeable and personable staff enlivens what is otherwise a fairly straightforward presentation. This is a good museum for the super-curious. The small gift shop stocks some real gems for gift giving.

Several blocks away, west of campus, you'll come across the **Neill-Cochran House Museum** (512-478-2335; www.nchmuseum.org). Built by the same architect responsible for the Governor's Mansion (see above), this Greek Revival–style mansion, dating to 1855, shares the neighborhood with others of its vintage, including the nearby Hotel Ella. Managed and maintained by the the National Society of the Colonial Dames of America in The State of Texas, the home, which has been restored to sparkling and filled with Victorian furnishings, offers a glimpse back in time to a historic Austin opulence. In addition to its permanent collection and special exhibits, the Neill-Cochran hosts interactive events, intriguing lectures, and educational presentations throughout the year.

The Contemporary Austin (512-453-5312; www.thecontemporaryaustin.org) is the result of a very complex relationship between the former Austin Museum of Art and the Arthouse at the Jones Center. To make a long story short, the two have been together, separated, and reunited, hyphenating their names to the **AMOA-Arthouse**, and moving in together on Congress Avenue in 2011. At that time, the Arthouse had finished an expensive renovation, leaving it with posh digs but little cash. At the same time, the Austin Museum of Art sold the real estate it had hoped to build on but never did, leaving it flush yet homeless. Suddenly it made good financial sense for these two modern and contemporary art lovers to join forces, so they did. Renamed The Contemporary Austin in 2013, the museum finally has a name which breaks from its past and is descriptive of an optimistic future. The city's modern art museum, The Contemporary exemplifies Austin's eclectic, forward-thinking creative spirit.

Lovely **Laguna Gloria** (512-458-8191; www.thecontemporaryaustin.org), part of the original AMOA-Arthouse, is still part of the Contemporary Austin arrangement. The very talented Clara Driscoll and her husband, Hal Sevier, onetime owner of the *Austin American* newspaper, built Laguna Gloria in 1916 and in 1943 donated it to the city of Austin, which established it as a museum in 1961. Situated on a bluff overlooking the Colorado River and the hills opposite, the Driscoll villa is surrounded by terraced gardens created by Clara herself and filled with native foliage. Tropical plants, statues and sculptures, and found objects such as a mission bell, an Italian wishing well, and other bits of whimsy dot the grounds. Contemporary works, such as the sculptures of Nancy

Holt, Clyde Connell, and Jesus Morales, have been added more recently. The focus of Laguna Gloria is its historic building and grounds.

Nestled near Zilker Park (see page 51), **The Umlauf Sculpture Garden and Museum** (512-445-5582; www.umlaufsculpture.org) is the home of the works of artist Charles Umlauf. A native of Michigan, Umlauf moved to Texas with his wife Angeline in 1941, when he took a teaching position with the fledgling University of Texas art department. Forty years and dozens of awards and accolades later, he retired, and in 1985 he and his wife donated their home, studio, and 168 pieces of art to the city of Austin. In 1991 a new museum was built on neighboring land, and today visitors are invited to tour both its interior and grounds. Themes of children, mothers, and docile animals dominate Umlauf's works, and the resulting sculptures tend to be sweet, tender, and lyrical—an especially nice fit for the lush gardens in which they are displayed.

Downtown, what began in 1983 as a 300-square-foot gallery/studio has grown into one of a very few museums in the U.S. dedicated to traditional and contemporary Mexican and Latino art. The **Mexic-Arte Museum** (512-480-9373; www.mexic-artemuseum .org) has two exhibition spaces; the main gallery is reserved for major exhibits, while the annex highlights new talent and is home to events such as the reverent display of commemorative altars for the celebration of Día de los Muertos (Day of the Dead). Exhibits can be political or personal, transcultural or transcendent, but they are always thought-provoking and timely. Recent shows have included such wide-ranging topics as *Los Hilos de Oaxaca*, an exhibition of textiles and costumes vividly embroidered by different indigenous groups living in the Mexican state of Oaxaca, and a retrospective of the legendary Mexican political cartoonist, muralist, and printer José Clemente Orozco. The **Emma Barrientos Mexican American Cultural Center** (512-974-3772; www.austintexas.gov) on the shores of Lady Bird Lake has a busy schedule of exhibits, performances, theater, music, and films illuminating not only Mexican American but also Chicano and other Latino cultures.

William Sidney Porter was many things in his life. Although to officials in Austin he was a convicted embezzler, to the rest of us he is simply O. Henry, or "master of the short story." The **O. Henry Museum** (512-472-1903; www.austintexas.gov/department/ o-henry-museum) is housed in the charming 1886 Queen Anne–style cottage he lived in for two years at the end of the 1800s and contains a sparse collection of memorabilia from his life. A National Literary Landmark of the City of Austin, the O. Henry Museum offers writing programs and workshops and promotes all manner of wisecracking and witticism at the annual O. Henry Pun-Off (www.punpunpun.com) held in May. The museum is located on Fifth Street, between Trinity and Neches.

Moving to the Hyde Park neighborhood, the **Elisabet Ney Museum** (512-458-2255; www.austintexas.gov/Elisabetney) was the home of Elisabet Ney, a 19th-century German-born sculptor. After moving to Texas in 1872, Ney relocated to Austin in 1892, building herself a neoclassical studio in what was then rural Hyde Park. Ney's studio was a salon of sorts, with those who would become leaders of Texas frequently gathering to discuss ideas, politics, and of course art. In 1893 she was asked to sculpt life-size likenesses of Texans Stephen Austin and Sam Houston for the Chicago World's Fair; these sculptures are on display at the state Capitol in Austin and the national Capitol in Washington, D.C. Today, Ney's studio is a museum, owned by the city of Austin, containing a collection of her sculptures and portraits of notable European royalty and American leaders. A plaster model of her favorite sculpture, one of Lady Macbeth, is prominently displayed; its marble counterpart is at the Smithsonian American Art Museum in Washington, D.C.

Located on the grounds of Camp Mabry, headquarters of the Texas National Guard, the **Texas Military Forces Museum** (512-782-5659; www.texasmilitaryforcesmuseum.org)

THE UNIVERSITY OF TEXAS AT AUSTIN

Founded in 1883 with only eight teachers and 220 students, the University of Texas at Austin (UT) has grown into one of the largest universities in the country, with close to 50,000 students, numerous departments, and an enviable reputation that reaches far beyond its 350-acre campus.

UT is located just north of the Capitol, roughly bounded by Martin Luther King Jr. Boulevard to the south, I-35 to the east, and Guadalupe Street ("The Drag") to the west. The campus, a nice place to stroll, is home to the Blanton Museum of Art, the Harry Ransom Humanities Research Center, the LBJ Library and Museum, and the Texas Memorial Museum. The UT Tower overlooks the plaza at Guadalupe and 22nd Streets and offers a bird's-eye view of the city from its observation deck (accessible only by tour). In the fall, Texas Memorial Stadium fills up with football fans every time the university's Longhorns are in town, while the Cactus Café in the Texas Union Building hosts music concerts year-round. (See separate listings below for more information on all of the above.)

THE MUSTANGS, SCULPTED BY ALEXANDER PHIMISTER PROCTOR

FOLK ART FROM OAXACA, MEXICO

keeps a low profile but has a much wider appeal than its name may suggest. Tanks, airplanes, artillery hardware, uniforms, posters, ephemera, and dioramas are all well displayed with details and descriptions for context. While the collection hails from Texas, the history, which includes both world wars and more recent events, is of national historical significance and interest.

Finally, the former Austin Children's Museum has been relocated and renamed **The Thinkery** (512-469-6200; www.thinkeryaustin.org), and the legacy of interactive, educational fun lives on in its current incarnation. Arts, crafts, STEM (science, technology, engineering, and math) activities, simple machines, water play, a kitchen lab, and a big backyard playscape all appeal to what kids love most—hands-on making, doing, and playing. The Thinkery is located in the Mueller Development, a collaborative, sustainable, mixed-used redevelopment of the former Mueller Municipal Airport, a few miles northeast of downtown.

THE PERFORMING ARTS Austin just loves to express itself. From classic, contemporary, and country music to dramatic theatrical productions and dance, the city hosts performances practically every day of the year, and the newly renovated, centrally located, state-of-the-art Long Center for the Performing Arts is one hub of activity. The city's performance arts organizations are listed alphabetically below.

Austin loves live music, including opera. The **Austin Opera** (512-472-5992; www.austinopera.org), founded in 1986 and formerly known as the Austin Lyric Opera, has weathered economic ups and downs but come up singing every time. With a packed performance calendar, acclaimed artistry, and an impressive ensemble of voices,

Austin Opera continues to charm audiences with spellbinding productions at the Long Center for the Performing Arts.

The **Austin Symphony Orchestra** (512-476-6064; www.austinsymphony.org) typically plays a classical concert series from September through May, but they aren't shy about mixing it up with local talent. Crossover concerts—western swing, boogie, and roots-music band Asleep at the Wheel on one occasion and the Grammy-winning choral ensemble Conspirare on another—were huge hits. The ASO offers a Fourth of July extravaganza of patriotic music and fireworks, a Halloween concert for families, Handel's "Messiah" at the holidays, and a popular Pops concert. All performances are at the Long Center for the Performing Arts.

Under the direction of Stephen Mills, **Ballet Austin** (512-476-2163; www.balletaustin .org) dances works such as Twyla Tharp's *The Golden Section,* a blithe rendition of *The Taming of the Shrew,* and the expected holiday tradition, *The Nutcracker.* This top-notch troupe impresses with stunning choreography, superb sets, gorgeous costuming, and plenty of passion. Ballet Austin Academy offers all manner of classes in its dramatic studio space, where floor-to-ceiling glass walls make for good views—of the city from inside and the dancers from the street.

Esther's Follies (512-320-0553; www.esthersfollies.com) serves up satirical comedy performed in campy costumes, outrageous makeup, and wacky hairdos. From magic to impersonations, juggling to political parody, Esther's Follies is hysterical. The fact that there is a window onto Sixth Street on the back wall of the stage, through which pedestrians see performers and vice versa, only helps to blur the line between reality and ridiculousness.

Located in the little theater district along Congress Avenue, the **Hideout Coffee House and Theatre** (512-443-3688; www.hideouttheatre.com) hosts entertaining improv classes by day and hysterical improv performances by night. This little gem is located in a historic building. It's no secret that shows sell out quickly, so buy tickets at least a day or so in advance to be on the safe side.

Home to the Austin Symphony, the Austin Lyric Opera, and Ballet Austin, the **Long Center for the Performing Arts** (512-474-5664; www.thelongcenter.org) rests center stage on the banks of Lady Bird Lake. A dazzling adaptive reuse of the distinctive, oval-shaped Palmer Auditorium, the Long Center is now spacious and modern, with roomy seating, fantastic acoustics, and expansive views of the city.

The **Paramount Theatre** (512-472-5470; www.austintheatre.org), on Congress Avenue, has been in the entertainment business since 1915, starting with vaudeville, then talkies, and now Broadway shows, classic films, and concerts. The regional hit *Greater Tuna,* a live comedy performance depicting small-town life in fictional Tuna, Texas, opened here in 1982 to rave reviews, and Lyle Lovett loves playing the Paramount when he's in town. The theater's enduring charm is in its detailed architecture, painted ceilings, twinkling chandeliers, balconies, and ushers—all hallmarks of a bygone era.

The **Salvage Vanguard Theater** (512-474-7886; www.salvagevanguard.org), in East Austin, has cut a path all its own, "defying theatrical tradition" without leaving audiences in the dust. Check its calendar for wacky improv, off-the-wall puppetry, contemporary dance, and vibrant multimedia presentations, with a few straight (-ish) plays mixed in. Located in dynamic East Austin, the theater is a good choice for an affordable, neighborhoody night out for dinner and a show.

The **University of Texas Performing Arts Center** (UTPAC) (512-471-1444; www .texasperformingarts.org) is made up of several venues: Bass Concert Hall, McCullough Theatre, and Bates Recital Hall on East Campus across from the LBJ Library, just north of the Memorial Stadium; and, on West Campus, Hogg Auditorium near the intersection of 24th and Guadalupe Streets. UTPAC hosts an impressive lineup of touring talent, performing everything from dance, opera, and comedy, to rock, classical, and world music.

Originally opened in 1932 as the Austin Civic Theatre, the **ZACH Theatre** (512-476-0591; www.zachtheatre.org) was renamed in 1968 to honor Zachary Scott, native Austinite and film star who relished playing scoundrels to the delight of audiences and who died of a brain tumor at 51, cutting short a flourishing career. A creative center of Austin, the ZACH hosts over 500 joyous, bittersweet, touching, and wonderfully exuberant performances a year—many on the main stage of the 420-seat Topfer Theatre—and is attended by over 100,000 yearly patrons.

Zilker Theatre Productions (512-479-9491; www.zilker.org) performs fun Broadway musicals under the stars in the summertime at the Zilker Hillside Theater. The theater is essentially a grassy knoll, so bring your own blanket to sit on.

CINEMA When writer/director Richard Linklater and cinematographer Lee Daniel joined forces to make *Slacker* (1991), they endeared themselves to a generation of 20-somethings trying to figure out what to do with their lives. Following up with *Dazed and Confused* (1993), Linklater garnered a national following and put Austin on the map as a city of slow and creative hipsters. Daniel's collaboration with director Margaret Brown, *Be Here to Love Me: A Film about Townes Van Zandt,* was a gem of a tribute to the beloved Texas singer-songwriter. The Austin Film Festival (see "Festivals" on page 85) offers yet more films to a city in which going to the movies is still about art.

The beauty of the **Alamo Drafthouse Cinema** (512-476-1320; www.drafthouse.com) is that it strives to fulfill the ultimate movie fantasy of great food delivered to your seat with permission to munch as much as you'd like throughout the movie. The menu here is extensive—from bottomless hot, buttered popcorn and fried dill pickles to a soba noodle salad and Hatch green chile macaroni and cheese—and limited only by what you think you can comfortably consume in the dark. The Alamo shows first-run movies all the time but also hosts special events like Anime Monday, Baby Day Tuesdays, and, on the last Thursday of the month, that essential flick shown by all great movie houses, *The Rocky Horror Picture Show.* Frequent theme nights pair food with film. Additional locations are scattered throughout the city.

What started as a bunch of friends watching movies together in 1985 has grown into the **Austin Film Society** (512-322-0145; www.austinfilm.org), a nonprofit organization dedicated to the promotion of films and support of creative filmmaking. This translates into a huge range of films, from foreign to independent to documentaries, and some a combination of all, flickering across the screens of the various Alamo Drafthouse Cinemas in the city. A must for film buffs.

✳ To Do

A tremendous online resource for all outdoor recreation in Texas is www.texasoutside .com.

BASEBALL **Round Rock Express** (512-255-2255; www.roundrockexpress.com). The thrill of minor league baseball. The Express play at the Dell Diamond, located on US 79 in Round Rock, just north of Austin.

BICYCLING Bicycling, both road and mountain biking, is big in Central Texas, especially in Austin and the Hill Country. Rentals are available through Bicycle Sport Shop

(512-477-3472; www.bicyclesportshop.com) and University Cyclery (512-474-6696; www.universitycyclery.com).

Austin Ridge Riders (www.austinridgeriders.org)
Bike Texas (www.biketexas.org)
Cycle Texas (www.cycletexas.com)

BIRD-WATCHING Austin is a great spot to catch a glimpse of rare, migratory, and native birds. Online, Texas Parks and Wildlife (www.tpwd.texas.gov) and the Travis County Audubon Society (www.travisaudubon.org) offer a wealth of information. See "Suggested References" in the Information chapter for a selection of bird-watching guides.

BOATING, CANOEING, AND KAYAKING Canoe, kayak, and paddleboat rentals are available on Barton Creek or Lady Bird Lake. Fees range from $15–$25 an hour and many accept only cash.

Capital Cruises (512-480-9264; www.capitalcruises.com)
The Rowing Dock (512-459-0999; www.rowingdock.com)
Zilker Park Boat Rentals (512-478-3852; www.zilkerboats.com)

CAMPING Emma Long Metropolitan Park (512-974-1831; www.austintexas.gov) is a favorite, as is **McKinney Falls State Park** (512-243-1643; www.tpwd.texas.gov), just

CYCLIST IN AUSTIN

south of the city. **Camp Ben McCulloch** (512-858-2084; www.campbenmcculloch.com) in Driftwood, southwest of the city, was once a reunion camp for Confederate veterans and is now a historic site, campground, and host of numerous gatherings, including the annual Old Settler's Music Festival (see "Festivals" on page 84). The various state parks in the Hill Country, Krause Springs, and the public and private parks surrounding the Highland Lakes offer a variety of camping options (see individual entries in Hill Country chapter).

CLIMBING **Texas Climbing Adventures** (512-590-2988; www.texasclimbingadventures .com) Weekend classes are held at Enchanted Rock State Natural Area near Fredericksburg.

DISC GOLF Disc golf is based on the rules of golf. Players throw a Frisbee-like disc toward a basket hanging approximately 2 feet from the ground in an effort to "sink" the disc. Points are added for extra throws over par, and the courses tend to have 18 holes, though some have 9 and others 27. Disc golf is extraordinarily popular in Austin, which has free courses scattered throughout the city. Find out all you need to know about disc golf at Disc Nation (512-280-1115; www.discnation.com).

FISHING Fishing in Central Texas is excellent, though developed or privately owned shoreline can make it difficult to find a spot to sink your lure in Austin. Emma Long Metropolitan Park on Lake Austin is a popular fishing spot, as are the Highland Lakes. Check www.tpwd.texas.gov; www.texasoutside.com, or www.txfishing.com. You don't need a license to fish from the shore in a Texas state park.

FOOTBALL **University of Texas Longhorns** (512-471-3333; www.texassports.com) Austin doesn't have a pro team, but it does have the UT Longhorns, who play at the Texas Memorial Stadium. Hook 'em Horns!

GOLF **Avery Ranch Golf** (512-248-2442; www.averyranchgolf.com) An excellent public golf course in northwest Austin.

SWIMMING People have been dipping their toes in the water around Austin for centuries. If you're looking to cool off in the city, try Barton Springs or Deep Eddy Pool (see page 54). Outside the city, Hamilton Pool (see "Take a Dip" on page 51), a natural grotto and waterfall, is about a 45-minute drive, as is Hippie Hollow (see "Highland Lakes" in the Hill Country chapter), everyone's favorite nudist hangout on Lake Travis. Krause Springs (see "Take a Dip" on page 51) in Spicewood also has camping.

TOURS Whether by foot, boat, amphibious vehicle, or Segway, touring Austin outside a car can give you a whole new perspective. The Austin Visitor Center (512-474-5171; www.austintexas.org) runs many worthwhile tours, all of which are listed on its website.

The Austin City Limits Tour (512-457-5550; www.acl-live.com) Studio tours available on weekdays at 11 AM.

The Austin Eats Tours (512-963-4545; www.austineatsfoodtours.com) The perfect mix of walking, talking, and noshing, with historic facts, quirky stories, and lots of local flavor thrown in.

Austin Overtures (512-659-9478; www.austinovertures.com) Guides guests through Austin and the Hill Country in its bright pink van; check its website for details.

LAKE AUSTIN

Austin Duck Adventures (512-477-5274; www.austinducks.com) Drive around Austin in an amphibious British Alvis Stalwart before splashing into Lake Austin.

Austin Steam Train (512-477-8468; www.austinsteamtrain.org) Restored vintage trains run from Austin south to Manor and from Cedar Park to Burnet in the Hill Country. The trips seem best suited to die-hard train aficionados.

Capital Cruises (512-480-9264; www.capitalcruises.com) Sight-seeing cruises leave Saturday and Sunday at 1 PM. Bat-watching cruises leave nightly 30 minutes before sunset. Check their website for dinner cruise details. Reservations are recommended.

Gliding Revolution's (512-495-9250; www.glidingrevolution.com) These tours are via Segway, the self-balancing, motorized two-wheel contraption, and are rumored to be great fun; just be prepared for plenty of stares.

Haunted Texas Tours (512-853-9826; www.austinghosttours.com) Tour paranormal Austin.

Lake Austin Riverboats (512-345-5220; www.austinriverboats.com) Relaxing riverboat tours.

Lone Star Riverboat (512-327-1388; www.lonestarriverboat.com) This old-fashioned, paddle-wheel riverboat cruises around Lady Bird Lake for a relaxing 90 minutes. There are also weekend bat-watching/sunset cruises; call for departure times. Reservations are recommended.

SegCity (512-499-0331; www.segcity.com) More tours on that funky self-balancing machine, the Segway.

Texas State Capitol (512-463-0063; www.tspb.state.tx.us) See "Historic Places" on page 36.

University of Texas Tower Tours (512-475-6633; www.ut.edu) for the best view of the UT campus and surrounding Austin, take a tour of the tower. Reservations are recommended; hours vary with the seasons.

TUBING Without a doubt, tubing is one of the more popular outdoor activities in Central Texas, and New Braunfels is the best place to experience it (see pages 188–189).

ZIP LINING **Cypress Valley Canopy Tours** (512-264-8880; www.cypressvalleycanopy tours.com) Tour participants use steel zip lines to travel between treetop platforms among old-growth cypresses. Get back to nature with an overnight stay in one of their custom-designed tree houses. Cypress Valley is located in the Hill Country 30 minutes west of Austin.

✳ Outdoor Activities

Austinites just like being outdoors, in the year-round fantastic weather, on the miles of trails, and in the swimming holes. There are many opportunities for recreation in the city, and when you factor in the proximity of the Highland Lakes and the state parks of the Hill Country (see the Hill Country chapter), the list of options grows exponentially.

CENTRAL AUSTIN

Zilker Metropolitan Park and Preserve (512-867-3080; www.austintexas.gov) is Austin's playground. In 1932, A. J. Zilker proposed a donation of his ranch land to the city of Austin in exchange for extra city funding for local schools. City Council agreed to the trade, investing an additional $200,000 in public education and gaining gorgeous land for the enjoyment of future generations. Today, the 351-acre urban park just south

TAKE A DIP: QUICK GETAWAYS

When it's hot in Texas, it's get-in-a-swimsuit-and-get-in-the-water hot. Some folks make a beeline for Barton Springs (see below) or Deep Eddy Pool (see page 54), and others make a day trip to the Highland Lakes (see pages 172–174) or go tubing (see pages 188–189) near New Braunfels. Hamilton Pool (512-264-2740; www.parks.traviscountytx .gov), with its grotto and 45-foot waterfall, is another alternative. A well-marked trail leads from the parking lot to the pool. Bring your own food and water and arrive early, as the park closes when it reaches capacity. The park is approximately 30 miles west of Austin. From the intersection of TX 71 and US 290, take TX 71 to FM 3238/Hamilton Pool Road. Or try **Krause Springs** (830-693-4181; www.krausesprings.net), a privately owned park with a large spring-fed swimming hole on Little Cypress Creek. With one of the nicest swimming holes around, combined with tent camping, Krause Springs is a great place to spend a hot day or two. From Austin take TX 71 west to Spicewood and follow signs.

of Lady Bird Lake and the Colorado River encompasses the Zilker Botanical Gardens, Zilker Nature Preserve, and Barton Springs Pool. It is dotted with sports fields, picnic tables, children's playgrounds, and a miniature railroad, the Zilker Zephyr. The park hosts many of the city's music, arts, and cultural events, including the Austin City Limits Music Festival and the Zilker Park Kite Festival. Miles of hike-and-bike trails traverse the park and connect with those of its neighbor, Lady Bird Lake. Zilker Park is a stop on the free Tour the Town weekend bus service. Parking is free on weekdays; on Saturday, Sunday, and holidays from March through Labor Day there is a $3 fee per car, collected at any gate, and valid throughout the day at any parking lot within Zilker Park. **Zilker Nature Preserve,** an expansive 60-acre preserve with meadows, a trickling stream, and an outstanding view of Austin from the Overlook Trail, is located just west of Loop 360.

Zilker Botanical Garden (512-477-8672; www.zilkergarden.org), with its verdant terraced gardens, winding stone paths, and great views of the city and hills, is a pleasant place to stroll. Educational features prove there's more to the garden than just smelling the roses. The Green Garden features native and adapted plants and flowers best suited to the Central Texas climate, while the Hartman Prehistoric Garden conceals a life-size bronze sculpture of *Ornithomimus,* the dinosaur whose tracks were discovered here in 1992, nestled in among plants representing the Cretaceous period.

The hot Texas sun can be a great equalizer. **Barton Springs** (512-867-3080; www .austintexas.gov) attracts just about everyone in Austin with a swimsuit and a few dollars to pony up for a chance to cool off. It has always been a gathering place. Native Americans believed it held healing powers, and the Spanish, impressed and inspired by it, set up temporary missions here in the 1730s. The springs became a city park in 1917, and dams were added in 1929 and 1932, creating the swimming area. Today, Barton Springs is still a constant and bracing 68 degrees, a fact people approach with strategies ranging from dipping a toe in the cool dark water to belly flopping off the diving board. The expansive, grassy lawn rimmed with trees is a big draw. Unless you are a dog-lover, consider paying the fee for entrance to the gated portion of the springs, where the water is deep and the grassy knoll clean. The shallow free-and-open-to-the-public section below the dam tends to be overrun with canines fetching, splashing, and frolicking with their owners. And while the dog population runs high, the Barton Springs salamander has declined to the point of critical endangerment in this, its only known habitat. The little lungless salamander is now a protected endangered species,

ORNITHOMIMUS IN THE HARTMAN PREHISTORIC GARDEN OF THE ZILKER BOTANICAL GARDEN

which means that Zilker Park's managers, scientists, and various environmental agencies are doing all they can to support its survival.

Take a ride on the little green **Zilker Zephyr**. This miniature train makes a leisurely 25-minute loop through the park, past Barton Springs and Lady Bird Lake before heading back to the playground in front of the Barton Springs Pool entrance.

Adjacent, the peaceful **Umlauf Sculpture Garden and Museum** (see page 42) has lovely indoor/outdoor sculpture exhibits tucked within its lushly landscaped gardens. Also nearby, scoot underneath the highway overpass and you'll find the **Austin Nature and Science Center** (512-974-3888; www.austintexas.gov) just west of Zilker Park. School-age children enjoy this hands-on place, where you can dig up bones in the Dino Pit, be an "eco-detective" on the path around the nearby pond, use a science lab, and see some native Texas animals up close, courtesy of the center's program to care for animals who cannot be returned to the wild.

Right across the street the **SPLASH! Into the Edwards Aquifer** (512-481-1466; www.austintexas.gov) interactive exhibit at the Beverly S. Sheffield Education Center (located at the old Barton Springs Pool Bathhouse) does a nice job of explaining the fragility of the region's underground ecosystem.

When the city of Austin reconstructed the Congress Avenue Bridge in 1980, its architects unwittingly created a perfect **Mexican free-tailed bat** (www.batcon.org) habitat. Before long, close to a million migratory bats began using the nooks and crannies under the bridge decking as their summer home. From April to October, the bats live, give birth, and raise their young under the bridge, taking flight each night at dusk to scour the greater metro area for tens of thousands of pounds of insects *per night;* they head back to Mexico at the first nip of winter winds. Once Austin's biggest nuisance—early on there was talk of poisoning the colony—the bats are now its most innovative form of pest control, not to mention one of its most asked-about attractions.

The best time to see the bats is in August. Call the Bat Hotline at 512-327-9721 for information about observing the colony from either the *Austin American-Statesman*

TUMBLING WATER AT ZILKER BOTANICAL GARDEN

Bat Observation Center at 305 S. Congress Ave. or the *Bat Boat,* a nightly cruise run by either Capital Cruises Boat Tours (512-480-9264; www.capitalcruises.com) or Lone Star Riverboat (512-327-1388; www.lonestarriverboat.com).

WEST AUSTIN

Built in 1916, the concrete expanse of **Deep Eddy Pool** (512-472-8546; www.austintexas .gov) was the first outdoor pool in Texas and once part of a larger resort area that included rental cottages, bustling concession stands, and a Ferris wheel. While all those amusements are long gone, the main attraction remains—the water. The pool is spring-fed, with areas for laps, wading, and just splashing around. The fantastic combination of swimming and a movie make the family-friendly Splash Party Movie Night a big hit in the summertime. The Friends of Deep Eddy (www.deepeddy.org), a crew of dedicated volunteers, have recently undertaken a thorough restoration of the 1936 bathhouse aimed at bringing it back to its former glory. Amenities such as family restrooms, wheelchair and stroller-accessible ramps, and more landscaping will keep the pool and its environs as well used and well loved in the future as they are now.

SOUTH AUSTIN

The **Austin Zoo** (512-288-1490; www.austinzoo.org) is really more of an "educational sanctuary" dedicated to the rescue and rehabilitation of animals and the education of the public. The zoo was originally known as the Good Day Ranch, a fitting moniker since 90 percent of the animals at the zoo are rescued, in many cases from the unfortunate "roadside attraction" outfits that dot Texas's highways. There are lions, bears, monkeys, exotic birds, zebras, emus, Texas longhorns, a little petting zoo, and a sweet miniature train, which takes visitors on a 2-mile journey through the surrounding countryside. The zoo is neither large nor elaborate, but well intentioned; consider the price of admission a donation to a worthy cause.

The **Lady Bird Johnson Wildflower Center** (512-232-0100; www.wildflower.org) is a lovely swath of nature in the midst of the growing Austin suburbs. Proving that it is never too late to follow a dream, on her 70th birthday, December 22, 1982, Lady Bird Johnson and her friend, the actress Helen Hayes, started the center to protect and preserve North America's native plants and diverse natural landscapes. Lady Bird is quoted as once saying, "Ugliness is so grim, a little beauty can help create harmony." Always one to follow words with action, Lady Bird was a tireless environmentalist, promoting the simple idea that we are all custodians of beauty as nature intended it. While its lovely gardens are populated by plants and flowers native to Texas, diligently tended by the center's staff and volunteers, the center, through its website and hotline, is a clearinghouse of invaluable information to gardeners throughout the U.S. and Canada. Beyond flowers, the center also models both new and recycled ideas, such as its rainwater harvesting system, which diverts water from the roofs of its structures into several cisterns, supplying 10 to 15 percent of the center's annual water demand. The Wildflower Café serves drinks, sandwiches, and treats, and the gift shop, Wild Ideas, has nifty nature-themed items.

NORTH AUSTIN

Pioneer Farms (512-837-1215; www.pioneerfarms.org) is a collection of pre–Civil War structures, plus some new ones made to look old, arranged on a parcel of land to re-create some of the look and feel of pioneer life. Within each barn, home, and shop,

LADY BIRD JOHNSON WILDFLOWER CENTER

HIKING, BIKING, RUNNING, STROLLING

While Zilker Park provides plenty of opportunities for recreation, outdoor enthusiasts will also enjoy the other gems of Austin's extensive system of parks, hike-and-bike trails, and greenbelts. The city's Parks Department website has excellent maps of the greenbelts; see www.austintexas.gov for details. The following list is not exhaustive, but includes highlights. All these listings offer activities appropriate for any ability level.

Barton Creek Greenbelt This enormous greenbelt, spreading south from Zilker Park and then west of Loop 360, includes climbing walls, swimming areas, hike-and-bike trails, and abundant natural scenery.

Bright Leaf Park (www.brightleaf.org) A 200-acre natural area located in central northwest Austin, north of Camp Mabry, offering guided hikes only.

Hike and Bike Trail at Lady Bird Lake (www.austintexas.gov or www.thetrailfoundation.org) Officially named the Ann and Roy Butler Hike-and-Bike Trail and Boardwalk at Lady Bird Lake, this 10-plus-mile trail runs through the urban core of Austin and along the shores of Lady Bird Lake. Dotted with drinking fountains and rudimentary restrooms, the popular trail is a favorite for runners, dog walkers, families, and those out just to enjoy a stroll.

Mayfield Park Twenty-two peaceful acres with easy-to-navigate trails—and free-range peacocks—located beside Laguna Gloria.

McKinney Falls State Park (512-243-1643; www.tpwd.texas.gov) Straddling the banks of Onion Creek, McKinney Falls is 13 miles southeast of Austin off US 183 and offers swimming, hiking, fishing, camping, and picnicking. When the river is high, the falls are lovely, but drought can lessen them to a trickle.

Mount Bonnell (512-974-6700; www.austintexas.gov) The 785-foot-high mount is a popular place to watch the sun set over the hills. Climb the steep stairs and behold the wide views of Lady Bird Lake and the West Lake Hills.

Shoal Creek Greenbelt connects with the Hike and Bike Trail at Lady Bird Lake (see above) and continues for 4 miles, following Shoal Creek. The disc golf course in Pease Park is very popular with 20-something Austinites.

Veloway (www.veloway.com) A 3-mile paved loop designed specifically for bikers and inline skaters. The trail traverses parkland, and its entrance point is across from the Lady Bird Johnson Wildflower Center.

volunteer interpreters dressed in period costumes go about their work cooking, blacksmithing, spinning cotton into thread, making cheese, and woodworking. The General Store sells reproduction toys. Die-hard history buffs might enjoy taking a class at Pioneer School. Topics range from Dutch-oven cooking to the efficiency of the foot-powered lathe.

✳ Lodging

Hotel chains dominate the lodging choices in Austin, and many of them cater primarily to business travelers and politicians, charging additional hefty fees for parking, use of fitness facilities, and Internet service; be sure to inquire about such details when making your reservation, and keep in mind that parking on the streets in Austin is free on the weekends. Austin has several historic hotels, boutique hotels, and bed and breakfasts located throughout the city that offer character and individuality, not to mention free Wi-Fi and parking. They are also quick to hand out snacks, drinks, business discounts, flowers, and restaurant advice without batting an eyelash or charging you an extra penny. If you appreciate this sort of personal attention, consider patronizing one of these very worthy alternatives.

When choosing an area of town, keep in mind that the neighborhoods surrounding Sixth Street tend to stay up late for the nightlife on which the city has grown its reputation. If you are staying downtown, consider asking for a room as high up as possible. They don't call Austin the Live Music Capital of the World for nothing; if you are used to city sounds, the noise level may not bother you, but if you require silence to sleep, you might consider a hotel in a quieter neighborhood several blocks removed, or one of the B&Bs, which have strictly enforced quiet hours. Keep in mind that rates tend to rise during holidays, festivals, and special events. B&Bs often require a two-day minimum stay, possibly three days during holidays, festivals, and special events.

DOWNTOWN

The Driskill Hotel (512-439-1234; www.driskillhotel.com), 604 Brazos St. Constructed by cattle baron Jesse Lincoln Driskill in 1886, a time when the rest of the city was built low to the ground, the hotel was the largest, grandest, and most elaborate structure in Austin. Financial problems came to plague the hotel, and eventually the Heritage Society of Austin stepped in, drumming up support, investment, and interest in the building and making it what it is today—the elegant centerpiece of downtown. Dine at the Driskill Grill, have a drink at the bar, or eat a muffin at the 1886 Bakery while enjoying the stylish atmosphere of the hotel. Now owned by Hyatt, the vintage building has been treated to a recent refreshing facelift, but remember that it is old through and through, so modestly sized rooms and quirky layouts are the norm. All amenities have been modernized; the bathrooms have granite countertops, and the decor is refined, with soft linens, sumptuous drapes, and rich accents. While this sort of luxury isn't cheap, experiencing this grand piece of Austin history is worth it. $$$.

InterContinental Stephen F. Austin (512-457-8800; www.austin.intercontinental.com), 701 Congress Ave. This downtown charmer was built in 1924 and consequently does not have the cookie-cutter consistency associated with many of Austin's newer downtown hotels. In general, the standard rooms tend to be small, though tasteful decor keeps them from feeling cramped. The hotel's age also means different floor plans and different levels of service and amenities, so spending the extra to upgrade to deluxe rooms may very well be worth the money; be sure to inquire about specifics. While the Stephen F. Austin may not have the historic provenance of the Driskill, it is lighter, brighter, and just as well situated. $$$.

THE DRISKILL HOTEL IN DOWNTOWN AUSTIN

The Four Seasons (512-478-4500; www.fourseasons.com/austin), 98 San Jacinto Blvd. Perched on a bluff overlooking Lady Bird Lake just south of Cesar Chavez Street near the Congress Avenue Bridge, the Four Seasons is wonderfully located, within easy driving distance and, in many cases, walking distance of all major points of interest. Directly outside the hotel is a hike-and-bike path where you can join locals for a run. The lovely pool, with lake views, is a great spot for a dip. Inside, rooms are average size; though the ceilings are somewhat low, the generous windows help compensate. Rooms have either a city view or a lake view (extra charge), and each is enjoyable in its own way. Downstairs, the hotel's restaurant, **TRIO** (512-685-8300; www.trioaustin.com) is a favorite spot for locals to unwind over after-work drinks or Sunday brunch, especially on the terrace, with its gentle breezes and views of Lady Bird Lake. $$$$.

The Hotel Ella (800-311-1619; www.hotelella.com), 1900 Rio Grande St. The Goodall Wooten House was built in 1898–1900 by Goodall Wooten, a local doctor and son of a founder of the University of Texas, along with his wife, Ella. In 1910, extensive renovations and additions gave the structure its Classical Revival style, and Ella later commissioned the luxury department store Neiman Marcus to redecorate the entire interior. Listed on the National Register of Historic Places and now a boutique hotel, the building has been refreshed and reworked, and its elegance and style still shine through. The grand columns, the wide front porch, and the home's original artwork, including a sculpture garden showcasing pieces from the Umlauf family (see page 42), hark back to yesteryear, while the rooms are well appointed with modern amenities and soft linens. Over the years, a pool, restaurant, and annex with additional rooms have been added to the property; inquire before you book. $$$.

The Hotel Van Zandt (512-542-5300; www.hotelvanzandt.com), 605 Davis St. This Kimpton property has established a presence in the vibrant Rainey Street District, and it's just a hop from the hike and bike path along Lady Bird Lake or a 15-minute stroll from South Congress Avenue. The scale of the hotel is grand and dramatic. Artistic touches include shiny chandeliers made of what look like repurposed parts of a brass band hanging in the lobby, and a flock of painted birds taking flight from the horn of a Victrola. The rooms feel cozier and more tailored, with deep grays, browns, and blues accented by crisp white sheets, towels, and curtains. $$$$.

SOUTH AUSTIN

Austin Motel (512-441-1157; www.austinmotel.com), 1220 S Congress Ave. This eclectic boutique hotel is known for its telling tagline: "So close, yet so far out." The oldest part of this independently owned motel dates to 1938; the kidney-shaped pool was constructed in the 1950s, and the two-story addition in 1968. There are spacious suites, cozy singles, and poolside rooms, all with various bed configurations, making this a popular choice for small groups in town for festivals. Rooms are individually decorated, and the decor includes everything from wall-sized photo murals of sunsets to vintage kitsch and fluffy floral coverlets covered with pandas. The Austin Motel is an older establishment and very reasonably priced—just bear in mind that one person's worn-in might be another's worn-out. $$.

Hotel San José (512-852-2350; www.sanjosehotel.com), 1316 S Congress Ave. Opened in 1939, this hotel has since been remodeled in a style that harks back to its roots as an "ultramodern motor court," but which might now be best described as hacienda-meets-bento-box. It's compact and efficient, with an understated simplicity that is utterly serene. The European-style hotel has only 40 rooms, ranging from the small and spartan shared bathrooms to the generously sized Courtyard Suite with a balcony view. The minuscule pool, lovely gardens, laid-back bar, and adjacent coffee shop amplify the air of yesteryear and create a sophisticated oasis of calm on South Congress. $$$$.

Hotel St. Cecilia (512-852-2400; www.hotelsaintcecilia.com), 112 Academy Dr. Tucked into an old home located in a shady neighborhood just a few blocks off South Congress, the St. Cecilia embodies rock-meets-Texas-meets-beat-poet, with an overarching feeling of free-spirited romance. There are five quirky suites, six peaceful poolside bungalows, and three spacious studios on its expansive grounds. Each room is unique and the details make the difference—worn wood floors, tons of art, velvet couches, record players, pressed tin ceilings, and whimsical wallpapers. It's pricey but one of a kind. $$$$.

Kimber Modern Hotel (512-912-104; www.kimbermodern.com), 110 The Circle. This modern, cozy hotel has just a few rooms, two suites, a common area, and an enormous shared deck under the sprawling shade of a grove of live oak trees. Dramatic design shines—plenty of crisp white walls, linens, and furniture, with a pop of color here and there—but floor-to-ceiling windows and whimsical touches keep the hotel from feeling too cool. Though located in the heart of the SoCo bustle, the Kimber Modern feels private and intimate, with a folksiness you might expect of a hipster hostel for well-behaved grownups. $$$$.

South Congress Hotel (512-982-4815; www.southcongresshotel.com), 1603 S Congress Ave. Luxury here leans toward minimalistic boho-chic. From the serene lobby to the sparsely decorated rooms, the textures of Texas stand out: potted succulents, leather chairs, denim details, and tile and hardwood floors. The custom-crafted furniture is inspired by midcentury design, but still has a rough-hewn Texas sensibility. While the ambiance may be cool, the service is warm, friendly, and very Austin. Located in the heart of SoCo, the hotel's outdoor

THE HOTEL SAN JOSÉ ON SOUTH CONGRESS AVENUE

pool and balconies mean fresh air, views, and the sounds of the bustling street below. $$$$.

UT/HYDE PARK

The Adams House Inn (512-453-7696; www.theadamshouse.com), 4300 Avenue G. The inn's four rooms and freestanding bungalow are light, bright, and airy, with wood floors, plantation shutters on the windows, and a few well-chosen antiques. Spotlessly clean and refreshingly uncluttered, the inn has all the character you'd expect of an older home paired with a freshly updated modern feel. Sit down with a book in the sunroom of the Adams Suite, and you just might stay all afternoon. Warm and welcoming innkeepers Liz and Eric are the icing on the cake. $$.

WEST END/CLARKSVILLE

Brava House (512-478-5034; www .bravahouse.com), 1108 Blanco St. Lofty ceilings, hardwood floors, and dark wood moldings are all hallmarks of this Victorian beauty built in the 1880s. The two rooms and three suites in Brava House are well decorated with antiques that feel casual and comfortable, not formal or fussy. The small and sweet Van Gogh Room is wheelchair accessible, the generously sized and dapper Garbo Suite and art deco Fitzgerald Suite have foldout couches for extra guests, and the large Monroe Suite is really more of a mini apartment with a full kitchen. A buffet-style breakfast is served each morning, and the cozy backyard deck is a nice place to sit and enjoy it. Brava House is remarkably well located in a quiet West Austin neighborhood near the intersection of North Lamar Avenue and 12th Street, just four blocks north of the Whole Foods Market on Lamar. $$$.

NORTH AUSTIN

Lone Star Court (512-814-2625; www .lonestarcourt.com), 10901 Domain Dr.

Mixing modern and vintage, this hipster motor court feels like the best of summer camp. Fire pit, food trucks, rocking chairs by the front door, tacos, and cocktails are all arranged with hanging out in mind. Rooms are sparse, designed with a nod to midcentury style and the functionality and fun of an international hostel. Despite the look and feel, the Lone Star is not a renovation, but new construction, well-situated in the trendy and walkable Domain mixed-used complex in North Austin. Sister properties include Hotel San José and St. Cecilia, and Hotel Havana in San Antonio. $$$.

EAST AUSTIN

The Heywood Hotel (512- 271-5522; www.heywoodhotel.com), 1609 E Cesar Chavez St. The hotel is composed of a renovated bungalow and its attached addition, which together capture all the design of a modern hotel and the charm and warmth of a B&B. The rooms have clean lines, stylish decor, sumptuous sheets, and clean-as-a-whistle bathrooms. Other pluses include a lovely outdoor patio, proximity to funky East Austin eateries, and the owner, Kathy, who is as friendly and helpful as can be. The Heywood is the perfect boutique hotel for guests who prefer personal touches and a just-off-the-beaten-path location. $$$.

OUTER AUSTIN

The Lake Austin Spa and Resort (512-372-7300; www.lakeaustinspa.com), 1705 S Quinlan Park Rd. While *Travel + Leisure* and *Condé Nast Traveler* have given it high praise, Lake Austin Spa's biggest compliments have come from its guests, who leave relaxed and rejuvenated. With views of the lake at every turn and expansive use of native Austin limestone and huge cedar beams, this midsize resort with 40 guest cottages has that earthy, laid-back, rustic feel that typifies the area; the overall effect is both cozy and chic. A popular place for couples, the Lake Austin Spa has a more feminine, weekend-of-pampering vibe, easily enjoyed by some men, though the lack of testosterone may be noticeable to others. Prices include three gourmet meals a day and access to all fitness classes, including yoga, Pilates, hiking, and fun salsa aerobics. A bevy of activities and classes, from cooking to stargazing to watercolor, is also on offer. All spa services are à la carte. Of course, the price of this level of luxury is steep, but the Lake Austin Spa is a good value when compared to similar facilities nationwide. $$$$.

Travaasa (855-868-7282; www .travaasa.com), 13500 FM 2769. This is a full-service, campus-style spa resort with a twist. Challenge yourself to a ropes course, walk the Hill Country trails, horseback ride, or learn to play harmonica. You can take a yoga class, practice your mechanical bull-riding skills, and finish off with a wine tasting. Nature takes center stage at Travaasa. Each of the 70 rooms features rustic headboards, clean lines, big windows, and wide views of the surrounding countryside. There are leather couches, stone fireplaces, soaring ceilings, shady patios, and an infinity pool overlooking Lake Travis and the hills beyond. From sunrise to stunning sunset, Travaasa is well matched with its surroundings in both atmosphere and spirit. $$$$.

✳ Where to Eat

In general, Austinites are an adventurous and easygoing bunch, and the restaurants that serve them tend to reflect this sensibility. Austin is a relatively small city, and its roots as an overgrown college town are most apparent in its food scene, which is largely dominated by modestly priced menus served in a relaxed atmosphere. Not surprisingly, the most represented cuisines in Austin are American, barbecue, Continental, Mexican, southern, and Tex-Mex, and the variations and combinations of these themes seem endless. While those who live here would warmly welcome

HEYWOOD HOTEL IN EAST AUSTIN

more selection—new restaurants are quickly mobbed—visitors still have plenty to choose from.

The restaurants below are local favorites and include those that are frequently and enthusiastically voted onto citywide "best of" lists. Many have been around for years, changing with tastes or remaining exactly the same. Some are uniquely Austin, and others have a more universal appeal. Some are exquisitely appointed, with lovely stemware and thick napkins, while others are earthy, with sticky beer-stained barstools and self-serve plastic cutlery, but all are filled with the locals who love them. This list is by no means exhaustive, and if your taste buds have you salivating for something specific, check out www.austin360 .com, the *Austin American-Statesman's* online listing of food, entertainment, and events, for a full listing of their restaurant reviews, organized by cuisine. Pick up a free copy of the *Austin Chronicle* (www.austinchronicle.com) for weekly specifics, or check out *Edible Austin* (www.edibleaustin.com) for a more in-depth look at specific establishments, farms, markets, ingredients, or trends.

DOWNTOWN

In downtown Austin you are as likely to find a $100 meal as you are a $2 breakfast taco. This variety is what makes it a great place to eat for politicians, professionals, visitors, and students alike.

The **Driskill Grill** (512-391-7162; www .driskillhotel.com), 604 Brazos St. In the Driskill Hotel at the corner of Brazos and Sixth Streets, this restaurant marries lovely, old-time surroundings with a level of opulence not usually witnessed in Central Texas and innovative offerings. The menu is market driven, as in the farmers' market. Items such as heirloom tomatoes served with mozzarella and a black pepper brioche, hot smoked Bandera quail with a coriander orange curd, and the local Jameson Farms rack of lamb accompanied by a mushroom

risotto are the sorts of dishes that make the Driskill Grill so very representative of Austin and the surrounding region. The attached Driskill Bar is a good place for drinks.

1886 Café and Bakery (512-391-7066; www.1886cafeandbakery.com), 604 Brazos St. Also located in the Driskill Hotel, this café, or as the hotel likes to call it, "Austin's Original Socializing Parlor," serves wonderful soups, sandwiches, baked goods, and desserts amid lavish surroundings. The all-day menu is more modestly priced than the Driskill Grill and is served until 10 PM. The Hippie Hollow, a breakfast scramble of eggs, spinach, and goat cheese, the waffles with Texas pecans, bananas, and blackberry jam, and the eggs Benedict with grilled beef tenderloin, jack cheese, and salsa on a toasted muffin are several items that make this café a great place to stop in for a taste of Texas.

Second Bar and Kitchen (512-827-2750; www.secondbarkitchen.com), 200 Congress Ave. Chef David Bull's posh yet still casual spot is located in the Second Street District, just south of the Warehouse District, a block or so west of Congress Avenue. Try the small plates, including the avocado *fundido* with super fresh chunks of avocado and spicy chorizo, the black truffle pommes frites with aioli, the garlic and chive potato gnocchi, and the fried pickles with Gorgonzola. A good choice for evening drinks and noshes.

Frank (512-494-6916; www .hotdogscoldbeer.com), 407 Colorado St. Stop in at this gourmet hot dog spot on Colorado, just south of Fifth Street, for a taste of the popular "Jackalope"—an antelope, rabbit, and pork sausage hot dog served with huckleberry compote, sriracha aioli, and cheddar. Make any frank a veggie dog for 75 cents, or, for a buck sixty-five, they'll take the Daily Dog, stuff it with white American cheese, wrap it in bacon, and plunge it into the deep fryer for ya. Round out your meal with waffle fry nachos, and finish with a bacon

TEXAS FOR FOODIES

Central Texas makes some fantastic food, much of it easily found in the upscale food emporiums of Austin-based Whole Foods (512-476-1206; www.wholefoodsmarket .com) and San Antonio-based Central Market (512-206-1000; www.centralmarket .com).

With an emphasis on quality produce and products, both Whole Foods and Central Market have tapped into the market of conscious consumers. While doing all your grocery shopping at these stores can get pricey, the elaborate deli services, self-serve soup and salad bars, a variety of prepared foods, and wonderful coffees and baked goods make them the perfect spots to grab a bite. The wide range of regional produce, products, and specialties, including Texas wines, makes for fun browsing. Both establishments have become destinations in their own right, places locals love to bring out-of-towners.

chocolate chip cookie. Or go out on a limb and try one of Frank's super creative and intensely flavorful mixed drinks.

Moonshine Patio Bar & Grill (512-236-9599; www.moonshinegrill.com), 303 Red River St. Just the place for an early-morning brunch buffet that includes comfort food favorites like sweet potato casserole with mini marshmallows, ham smothered in pineapple chipotle glaze, and savory green chile cheese grits. Try the "corn dog" shrimp with honey mustard and blueberry sauce, the beer-battered fried asparagus, or the green chile macaroni with grilled chicken, corn relish, and a smooth green chile cheese sauce, and you'll know why there's a line out the door. Moonshine is in a sweet little two-story stone building with a patio on Red River, between Third and Fourth Streets.

Banger's Sausage House and Beer Garden (512-386-1656; www .bangersaustin.com), 79 Rainey St. A half mile south and a part of the Rainey Street scene, this place draws crowds with live music, dozens of picnic tables, a hundred types of beer, and 30 different kinds of housemade "bangers," meaning sausages. There are classics like jalapeño cheddar bratwurst, Cajun andouille, and spicy Italian with plenty of fennel and red pepper, as well as more exotic and even vegetarian options. Sides include cheddar cheese grits, German potato salad, and mashed potatoes with gravy.

Bangers are available fresh by the pound from the deli case, though it's hard to beat the taste of one that's just been grilled on the spot.

La Condesa (512-499-0300; www .lacondesaaustin.com), 400 W 2nd St. Vibrant, colorful, and energetic, La Condesa has made a name for itself with ambitious, upscale Mexican and Latin dishes. The must-order item here is the piping-hot, creamy, and slightly spicy Mexican-style street corn, known as *elote*. Folks also love the margaritas and guacamole sampler appetizer, which includes a mix of chipotle and almonds, watermelon with pomegranate molasses, and crab, apple, and coconut vinegar. The simple, citrus-rubbed half rotisserie chicken with three-day *mole* and grilled *cebollitas* (green onions) is fantastic, and *chile rellenos* stuffed with quinoa, butternut squash, and manchego cheese is a tasty twist on a classic. The desserts here are exceptional.

Lamberts Downtown Barbecue (512-494-1500; www.lambertsaustin.com), 401 W 2nd St. "Fancy BBQ" isn't an oxymoron here, where the food is served on plates, not butcher paper. The dining room blends cosmopolitan and country, as does the menu, where updated comfort foods such as daikon slaw, fried okra with rémoulade, and sautéed lemon spinach are served alongside classics such as baked mac and cheese and jalapeño cornbread muffins. The crispy wild boar ribs with honey, sambal, and blue cheese;

FOOD TRUCKS

Food trucks are a great fit for Austin, and the city has embraced the scene, spawning a mobile food vendor culture that's become a culinary incubator, social connector, and a creative way to bring new life into empty city lots. The combination of tasty take-away food and Austinites' love of eating outside at picnic tables has given many food trucks a devoted following of adventurous diners. In fact, the love between food trucks and their fans has been so intense that many mobile eateries have evolved to brick and mortar restaurants, where the hungry are happy to follow. Austin seems to have no shortage of new trucks popping up each year; some are seasonal, some are mobile, and hours vary. Since not all accept credit cards, it's wise to keep cash on hand just in case. Food Trailers Austin (www.foodtrailersaustin .com) does a great job keeping up with who exactly is parked where, open when, and serving what. You'll probably pass right by The Picnic (www.thepicnicaustin.com), a popular food truck trailer park on Barton Springs Road between South Lamar and Barton Creek that's home to some local favorites, including Hey! . . . You Gonna Eat or What? (see page 67). Torchy's Taco, (see page 68) and Holy Cacao (512-851-2253; www.theholycacao.com) have moved in together at the South Austin Trailer Park on South First Street, which means you can start with a fantastic Trailer Park Taco—fried chicken with green chiles, drizzled with a poblano sauce—and finish with a frozen Mexican Drinking Chocolate infused with ancho chile, cayenne, and cinnamon. You'll find additional food trucks up and down South First Street, dotting East Sixth and East Cesar Chavez Streets in East Austin, and along Rainey Street, a nightlife hot spot near downtown.

FOOD TRUCK

the black Angus brisket with a crusty, caramelized brown sugar and coffee rub; the pork ribs with maple and coriander; and the rib eye with brown sugar and mustard served with a whole roast garlic bulb are all standouts.

Hut's Hamburgers (512-472-0693; www.hutsfrankandangies.com), 807 W 6th St. This is one of those crowded, chock-full-of-memorabilia places that everybody loves. Diners happily overlook sticky soda spills and elbow-to-elbow seating because the great burgers always come out hot, smothered with creative toppings, and accompanied by mounds of fries or onion rings. Blue-plate specials change constantly, and the two-for-one deal offered Wednesdays from 6 to 10 PM is a hard bargain to resist. Vegetarians are surprisingly well served.

24 Diner (512-472-5400; www.24diner .com), 600 N Lamar Blvd. As delicious for midmorning brunch as it is for the midnight munchies. Some say the chicken and waffles, covered in maple syrup and brown sugar butter, are worth the trip alone. There are burgers, milkshakes, and fancy deviled eggs all week long and chicken and dumplings every Tuesday until midnight. Sure, it's a little pricey, but it's really more of a bistro than a diner, so it's hard to complain. After all, the doors are open 24/7.

Counter Café (512-708-8800; www .thecountercafe.com), 626 N Lamar Blvd. This tiny place grills up pimento cheese sandwiches, massive bacon-n-blackberry pancakes, and some of the best burgers in the city. Though the café is casual, it's not your average greasy spoon, and while the high-quality ingredients command slightly higher prices, one bite of a Counter Burger and you'll rest assured you got just what you paid for. They also have a second location on the East Side.

SOUTH CONGRESS, SOUTH FIRST STREET AND BARTON SPRINGS

Directly across Lady Bird Lake from downtown, South Austin is home to a disproportionate number of fun and funky local favorites, which are usually filled for breakfast, lunch, and dinner.

Perla's (512-291-7300; www .perlasaustin.com), 1400 S Congress Ave. The first thing you'll notice is the spacious front deck spread out under the oak trees and dotted with colorful umbrellas. The restaurant's casual upscale atmosphere is a great match for its menu, which features an oyster bar, scallops, and Texas Gulf snapper served with spicy garlic, tomato *sofrito,* and wood-grilled vegetable sides. The weekend brunch offerings are a mix of seafood—crab Florentine on an English muffin, for instance—and breakfast treats like brioche French toast served with coconut sorbet, maple syrup, and fresh berries.

Hopdoddy Burger Bar (512-243-7505; www.hopdoddy.com), 1400 S Congress Ave. Hopdoddy makes ultra-juicy, freshly ground Angus beef burgers served with a multitude of tasty toppings on warm homemade buns. Diners love the Texas goat cheese with pesto and roasted poblano chiles paired with apple-smoked bacon, and the Primetime justifies its high price ($12) with plenty of Brie and truffle aioli. Vegetarians will enjoy the La Bandita—a blackbean veggie patty with avocado, goat cheese, cilantro pesto, and a tab of chipotle mayo.

Güero's Taco Bar (512-447-7688; www .guerostacobar.com), 1412 S Congress Ave. In the 100-year-old Central Feed and Seed building, the cavernous dining rooms are always filled with the sound of diners munching chips and the clatter of its bustling wait staff. Güero's enormous menu is centered on classic favorites such as enchiladas, tacos, and fajitas, reshuffled into endless combinations; nightly specials keep things interesting. Handmade tortillas, a self-serve salsa bar, and a great number of margaritas made with fresh-squeezed limes add to the cantina-like appeal. The adjacent oak grove, festooned with tiny white lights, is Güero's music venue; check the website for the lineup.

Home Slice Pizza (512-444-7437; www .homeslicepizza.com), 1415 S Congress Ave. Stop in for NY-style pies made with zesty sauce, gooey cheese, and a crisp, yeasty crust. Eat in the bustling sit-down restaurant or order by the slice at the take-out outpost nearby. Huge, crisp salads, hot garlic twist rolls, and smooth, dense, and creamy cheesecakes make Home Slice a home run.

South Congress Café (512-447-3905; www.southcongresscafe.com), 1600 S Congress Ave. Folks come for the piping-hot *migas*, carrot cake French toast (that's right, carrot cake!), and the crab cakes eggs Benedict with chipotle hollandaise. The brunch menu is available every day until 4 PM, when dinner picks up the slack. The smoked duck breast finished with a port cherry chipotle glaze is outstanding. While the menu can feel fancy, the open, airy dining room—with its big windows, fresh flowers, and friendly servers—is chic yet casual.

Vespaio (512-441-6100; www .austinvespaio.com), 1610 S Congress Ave. Italian for "hornet's nest," Vespaio is constantly buzzing; diners swarm to this wonderful Italian trattoria and are willing to wait over an hour for the chance to sit at one of the 15 tables and dig in. While the standard menu of pasta, pizza, and antipasto is superb, regular diners enjoy ordering from the specials menu, featuring offerings like oak fire-grilled, prosciutto-wrapped Hill Country quail filled with carnaroli rice and served with caramelized brussels sprouts, shaved honey crisp apple, and arugula. A well-thought-out wine list provides the final touch. The wonderful food aside, the sophistication without pretension, fairly reasonable prices for such fare, and that feeling of enjoying a glass of wine surrounded by the casual and comforting din of other diners, make Vespaio a destination unto itself.

Enoteca (512-441-7672; www .austinvespaio.com), 1610 S Congress Ave. Run by the same folks as Vespaio, Enoteca has a much more casual look and feel, with small, informal, cloth-covered bistro tables dotting the room, as well as seating under umbrellas for alfresco dining. As befits a relaxed, European-style café, the simple all-day menu, served from 11 AM onward, features panini, pasta, pizza, salads, and daily specials. An extensive wine list leaves many opportunities for pairings. Dessert here is hard to resist after you've caught sight of the lovely *panna cotta* in the dessert case near the entrance. Enoteca is a wonderfully atmospheric place for a simple cup of morning coffee, pastry, or Sunday brunch.

Magnolia Café (512-445-0000; www .cafemagnolia.com), 1920 S Congress Ave. This is the place to go for gingerbread, whole wheat, buttermilk, or cornmeal pancakes 24 hours a day, seven days a week. Omelets, breakfast tacos, *huevos rancheros,* and a tantalizing version of *migas* made with what Magnolia calls "LOVE butter" (butter with fresh garlic and serrano peppers) are also available all day long. There are huge salads with homemade dressings and plenty of burgers, including the Jalapeño Cheese Burger and the Voodoo Bleu Cheese Burger with blackened spices. Vegetarians and the health conscious will enjoy ample choices.

Threadgill's World Headquarters (512-472-9304; www.threadgills.com), 301 W Riverside Dr. This Austin landmark is built on the former site of the Armadillo World Headquarters, the legendary dance hall whose 10-year run figures prominently in local lore. Loaded with memorabilia, Threadgill's pays tribute to the history of the Austin music scene. The menu is classic stick-to-your-ribs southern cooking, with items like fried green tomatoes, chicken-fried steak, and fried okra. While the food is fine, many come for the ambience, the live music lineup, and to experience a little bit of nostalgia. The Sunday Gospel Brunch is a great time to visit, especially for families.

Over on South Lamar, James Beard Award–winning Chef Tyson Cole has

DESSERTS AT ENOTECA ON SOUTH CONGRESS AVENUE

captivated Austin with **Uchi** (512-916-4808; www.uchiaustin.com), 801 S Lamar Blvd. The restaurant is completely at home in an old South Austin house painted a deep red, whose interior has been carved out to reveal vaulted ceilings, views into the kitchen, and a combination of tables and minimalist booths for diners. Appetizers are categorized as either Cool (for example, maguro sashimi and goat cheese with cracked pepper, apples, and pumpkin seed oil) or Hot (panko-fried green tomatoes). The sushi and sashimi menu includes delicate, melt-in-your-mouth tuna, baby yellowtail, snow crab, striped bass, octopus, salmon roe, and sea urchins, some raw and some cooked. If you like surprises, consider the *Omakase*, or tasting menu, which is designed for two and decided entirely by the chef. The desserts at Uchi are a must, and examples include the Valrhona chocolate and wasabi fondant with five-spice *tuile* and chocolate curry cookie, and the hydroponic basil-Prosecco sorbet. **Uchiko** (see page 73), Cole's second restaurant, is at 4200 N Lamar Blvd.

The restaurants on Barton Springs Road are a great place to stop before or after a trip to Zilker Park, the Umlauf Sculpture Garden, or Barton Springs itself. **Shady Grove** (512-474-9991; www.theshadygrove.com), 1624 Barton Springs Rd. Enjoy an archetypal burger with all the fixings here, where the style is best described as 1940s burger joint meets state park lodge. While some may consider it heresy, Shady Grove also makes a nice veggie burger. Take in live music or classic movies in the pecan grove under the stars. Check the website for the lineup. Owned by the same folks, **Chuy's** (512-474-4452; www.chuys.com), 1728 Barton Springs Rd., is a local chain of Tex-Mex restaurants known for its wacky decor, super-casual atmosphere, and huge portions of fresh, hot, homemade food. **Hey! . . . You Gonna Eat or What?** (512-296-3547; www.heyyougonnaeatorwhat.com), 1720 Barton Springs Rd. This bright red food truck in The Picnic food truck park along Barton Springs, is particularly famous for its "Shiner Monte Cristo," a pit-smoked ham, turkey, cheddar, and provolone sandwich dipped in a Shiner Bock beer batter, deep fried, dusted with confectioners' sugar, and served with a homemade cherry fig jam. Several other delicious sandwiches are in rotation, each served with homemade potato chips and a side of no-nonsense. **Austin Java Company** (512-482-9450; www.austinjava.com), 1608 Barton Springs Rd. An overgrown college town café that has imaginative coffee-based drinks and a substantial menu of healthy sandwiches, salads, pastas, and breakfast items all day.

South First Street offers a stretch of tasty informal dining. Started as a food truck, graduated to brick and mortar, and rapidly risen to a regional chain, **Torchy's Tacos** (512-366-0537; www .torchystacos.com), 2809 S 1st St., hasn't forgotten its Austin roots—the food trailer on First Street is still hot. You can't go wrong with any of the tacos here and you can mix and match until you find your favorite. Fillings include everything from green chile pork and fried avocado to grilled jalapeño sausage and Jamaican jerk chicken with mango. Don't expect classic Mexican street food—Torchy's is a delicious Austin-style take on tacos. Once just a First Street food truck churning out hot, delicious donut creations, **Gourdough's** (www.gourdoughs .com) has expanded its sweet and sticky empire, with several locations around Austin, including 1503 S 1st St. While the venues range from pub-style tables to picnic-tables-in-a-gravel-lot, the menu is essentially the same, with the classic donut a vehicle for any number of toppings of all imaginable types. There are donut burgers, donut sandwiches, and fried chicken on donuts, but, best of all, there are donut desserts. Something about "Granny's Pie," with cream cheese icing, caramel, pecans, bananas, and crushed graham crackers, or the "Blackout"—chocolate icing, brownie batter, and brownie bites with chocolate chips— lures diners every time.

Vegetarians, vegans, and gluten-free folks appreciate the menu at **Bouldin Creek Café** (512-416-1601; www .bouldincreekcafe.com), 1900 S 1st St., but they certainly aren't the only ones, as this place is routinely packed for brunch. In fact, breakfast is so popular here that it's served all day. Tofu scrambles, omelets, blueberry cornbread, sweet potato tamales, and anything with the spicy chipotle pecan pesto are all delicious, as is the ever-popular lavender mocha. Enormous salads, overstuffed sandwiches, stir-fries, and tacos round out the large and eclectic menu, all served on mismatched vintage plates and in wacky coffee cups, surrounded by kitschy decor.

Heading east to South Lamar, you'll find another Austin food-truck-to-full-restaurant success story. When brothers Bryce and Dylan Gilmore purchased an old trailer to house their dream of creating meals and menus from the bounty of Austin's area farms, **Odd Duck** (512-433-6514; www.oddduckrestaurant .com), 1201 S Lamar Blvd., took flight. The concept caught on, and soon the eatery outgrew its mobile kitchen and gravel lot, so Bryce opened the brick and mortar restaurant Barley Swine (see page 73). Ironically, after the land on which the trailer once stood was sold to developers, and through a few twists and turns of fate, the brothers opened a new version of Odd Duck in a restaurant built on the same exact location as the original. While the menu changes with the seasons, quality and creativity are constant. Examples include pork belly with pecan jerk glaze served with a sweet potato cake, or the kale salad with lamb heart and field pea hummus. The burger, topped with fried egg, pimento, tomato, bacon rillette, and tobacco onions is often on offer.

EAST AUSTIN

East Austin has a lot of homegrown favorites, each serving up comfort food and a warm welcome. Trendy coffeehouses, restaurants, and eateries have also been staking their claim. All give diners good reason to cross the I-35 divide to the east side.

Franklin Barbecue (512-653-1187; www.franklinbarbecue.com), 900 E 11th St. The fact that this place has sold out of meat every single day since it opened in 2009 should impress you. If that doesn't, the line outside the door and snaking around the block just might. Aaron Franklin started serving his piping-hot brisket from a food truck and quickly expanded it into a restaurant; demand hasn't slowed one bit. We're talking melt-in-your-mouth, fall-off-the-bone barbecue that's set a high bar for 'cue. Meats are served with purple cabbage slaw and mustard-based potato salad. There are even some wonderful pies and Dublin Dr Pepper, which retains the original Dr Pepper recipe, with cane sugar instead of high fructose corn syrup. The sign out front says they're open from "11 AM until out of food," and food this good goes fast!

No matter how much great barbecue there is in Austin, there always seems to be room for more. **La Barbecue** (512-605-9696; www.labarbecue.com), 1906

PULLED PORK SANDWICH AT FRANKLIN IN EAST AUSTIN

E Cesar Chavez St., slices and serves tender meats from its food truck in East Austin, each with the perfect balance of dark, burnt bits—or bark—on the outside and juicy goodness inside. Give El Sancho Loco a try: a trio of pulled pork, chopped brisket, and housemade sausage, piled high on a bun with a scoop of pickled red onions on top. The 'cue here rivals the best around, and eating it outside at the communal picnic tables seems to make it just that much tastier. Lines start early and grow long; free beer is often on offer.

Juan in a Million (512-472-3872; www.juaninamillion.com), 2300 E Cesar Chavez St., makes a breakfast burrito to be reckoned with. An enormous mound of eggs, onions, and potatoes, barely contained in a flour tortilla and priced to sell, the Don Juan is the sort of dining experience some walk away from and others run toward. Either way, it's hard not to appreciate the warm welcome and hearty handshake from the owner.

The **Blue Dahlia Bistro** (512-542-9542; www.bluedahliabistro.com), 1115 E 11th St., is a sweet French bistro that's both simple and special. The cozy backyard terrace is a big draw, and folks like to dine alfresco on fancy *tartines*. The Brie with walnuts and apricot preserves or the *chevre* with olive tapenade, roasted red pepper, and Parmesan are lovely appetizers. Diners also enjoy the fresh pastas, unfussy fish dishes, and refreshing soups.

Deeply rooted at 2305 E 7th St., **Joe's Bakery & Mexican Food** (512-472-0017; www.joesbakery.com) has no-frills, family-style Mexican food, including hot and spicy *migas* in the morning and all sorts of Mexican pastries. Open only for breakfast and lunch, Joe's has been feeding Austinites for over 50 years.

When the folks at the **Eastside Café** (512-476-5858; www.eastsidecafeaustin.com), 2113 Manor Rd., say "fresh," they mean, quite literally, "We are on our way out the back kitchen door to dig around in our on-site organic garden and

FRANKLIN BARBECUE IN AUSTIN

pick the ingredients just for you!" Now *that's* fresh. The menu leans toward the free-spirited and health-conscious, with the grilled ruby trout with a shiitake mushroom ginger cream sauce; wild mushroom crepes with walnuts, ricotta, and Jack cheese; and salmon dumplings with a spicy yellow coconut curry sauce being several examples. The chef's specials chalked on the blackboard change daily.

At 2002 Manor Rd., **Hoover's Cooking** (512-479-5006; www.hooverscooking.com) is honest-to-goodness cooking inspired by owner/chef Hoover Alexander's mother, Dorothy, and his Texas roots, which run five generations deep. For diners this translates into great chicken-fried steak, meat loaf, charbroiled catfish, and Elgin sausage from down the road a piece, served with mashed potatoes made from scratch and jalapeño creamed spinach, and washed down with homemade lemonade. Whether it's barbecue smothered with pickles, onions, and sauce, chicken-fried chicken breast smothered in a homemade cream gravy, or fresh fruit pie smothered in Blue Bell ice cream, Hoover's is just aching to smother you

with its comfort food the same way your grandmother might smother you with love—in a good way! Austin loves Hoover's for its fantastic, no-nonsense food served in a no-frills dining room and for its no-holds-barred use of the good stuff.

The **Salty Sow** (512-391-2337; www.saltysow.com), 1917 Manor Rd. A gastropub well known for its exceptional triple-fried duck fat fries topped with a fried egg, and its melt-in-your-mouth crispy brussels sprout leaves with golden raisins and pecorino. There are more substantial entrees on the menu—duck breast with turnips, oil-cured olives and cardamom orange sauce, for example—but simple ingredients and expert preparation make every dish a standout. Many save room for dessert since the bananas Foster beignets with honey nutmeg ice cream are well worth it. The Salty Sow is casual dining with a refined menu.

UT/HYDE PARK

Bright, light, funky, and friendly, the **Kerbey Lane Café** (512-451-1436; www.kerbeylanecafe.com), 2606 Guadalupe St., started in 1980 in the minds of two

UT grads looking for a healthy, affordable, and casual spot to eat in Austin. The idea proved to be so good that now, over 35 years later, there are seven area locations—each with its own distinct identity but all serving Kerbey Lane's exhaustive menu 24/7. The food here is healthy, creative, and affordable. The huge buttermilk, gingerbread, blueberry, or apple whole-wheat pancakes are very popular, as are the French toast and the signature sticky muffin, a gooey, sticky bun/muffin hybrid. Additionally, there are inventive sandwiches, hearty soups, meal-sized salads, and the usual Tex-Mex roster of enchiladas, quesadillas, and tacos, each with its own health-food spin. In an effort to serve super-fresh produce, Kerbey Lane has partnered with an independently owned area farm and now grows some produce of its own. The owners' energetic philanthropy has benefited many communities within their beloved Austin.

The closer you get to UT, the more likely you'll find sandwich shops. One local favorite is **Fricano's** (512-482-9980; www.fricanosdeli.com),2405 Nueces St. The Tenacious Deli Sandwich, a house specialty, involves a slice of "every meat available at Fricano's," provolone cheese, something called "rocket sauce," and a turn on the grill. The pesto and curry chicken salads are two specials to watch for, and the Reubens are probably the best in Austin (they have the trophy to back that up).

Foodheads (512-420-8400; www .foodheads.com), 616 W 34th St. In a cute little house-turned-café, this is a fantastic place to stop for lunch. Try the pork tenderloin ciabatta with smoked Gouda cheese and a sweet-n-spicy apple relish, or the vegetarian grilled squash and fresh mozzarella sandwich with cilantro pesto and a spritz of blackberry balsamic vinaigrette.

Dirty Martin's Place (512-477-3173; www.dirtymartins.com), 2808 Guadalupe St. Known simply as Dirty's, this is a venerable Austin institution. Close to campus, Dirty's has cooked up countless burgers to feed the scores of UT students who every day buzz by the white frame drive-in looking for that perfect lunch, dinner, or late-night snack. Counter seating gives you a great view of the griddle. Russet fries and thickly breaded onion rings round out an experience that some would say is a must. Speaking of burgers, head over to **Burger Tex II** (512-477-8433) 2912 Guadalupe St., for one of its outstanding bulgogi burgers—strips of thinly sliced beef marinated in a soy sauce, ginger, and garlic marinade that are served on a homemade bun. The saucy twang keeps diners coming back for more.

Built in 1868 by George Franklin, a freed slave, the Franzetti building has stood the test of time, serving as a residence, church, publishing house, grocery store, and gathering place of the neighborhood. Today **Freedmen's** (512-220-0953; www.freedmensbar.com), 2402 San Gabriel St., named to honor its history, specializes in slightly up-market barbecue, dozens of whiskeys, and a menu of specialty cocktails. The smoked beets with goat cheese and balsamic glaze appetizer is very popular, as is the Holy Trinity Plate with brisket, pork spare rib, and housemade sausage served with slaw and focaccia bread. If you prefer a stiff drink with your meat, try the Holy Mary, a quart of Forty Creek whiskey, smoked tomato, lemon, and worcestershire with a half pound brisket, sausage, and spare ribs balanced on top. The old-school ambiance and location close to the UT campus make Freedmen's a local favorite.

Meandering into Hyde Park, the **Hyde Park Bar & Grill** (512-458-3168; www .hpbng.com), 4206 Duval St., serves burgers, sandwiches, pastas, and any number of southern comfort foods in a slightly upscale business-casual atmosphere. But what sets this place apart are its french fries—strings of Idaho potatoes, dipped in buttermilk, dredged in seasoned flour, and fried in peanut oil just before arriving,

HYDE PARK BAR & GRILL

the mint green counter and spin in the salmon-colored swivel seats while you wait for your simple, juicy burger to do its time on the grill in this old-fashioned pharmacy. If the ambiance doesn't take you back to being a kid, the homemade Blue Bell shakes, malts, and crispy-on-the-outside, gooey-on-the-inside grilled cheese sandwiches just might. In addition to burgers, Nau's also serves breakfast.

Aptly named, **Wink** (512-482-8868; www.winkrestaurant.com), 1014 N Lamar Blvd., is personal, intimate, and flirty, with food so deceptively simple and earnestly pure you feel as if you are experiencing taste for the first time. Samples from a recent menu include roasted quail with ginger quinoa, shiitakes, baby leeks, and golden raisin sauce, and a sauté of monkfish with cauliflower, alba mushrooms, amaranth, and pistachio oil emulsion. Wink's menu is simple yet complex, unfussy yet anything but ordinary. The extensive and carefully chosen wine list only heightens the experience and, for dessert, Wink's lemon meringue pot is a revelation. The dining room, with crisp white tablecloths offset by a sweet-potato-colored wall and mobiles of semi-translucent "eyes" hanging from the ceiling, is both stylish and comfortable. Wink is simple done perfectly. Or, rather, perfection simply done.

Finding themselves in cattle country, many visitors to Austin set out in search of a steak. **Austin Land and Cattle** aims to please (512-472-1813; www.alcsteaks .com), 1205 N Lamar Blvd. Rib eye, filet mignon, top sirloin, New York strip, and the extraordinary 2-pound T-bone, served with the chef's choice of vegetables and your choice of potato or rice, are sure to satisfy any craving (though they will set you back close to $40). On the menu for non-red-meat eaters are chicken, seafood, and pasta dishes, and vegetarian diners will be relieved to discover that Austin Land and Cattle also serves a plump and juicy giant portobello mushroom steak. And for dessert,

hot and crisp, at your table. The Hyde Park Bar & Grill stays open late, making it both a neighborhood hangout and a citywide favorite for nocturnal noshing. The enormous fork marks the spot.

WEST END, CLARKSVILLE, AND NORTH LAMAR

Residential in feel and dotted with commercial centers that are home to restaurants, art galleries, and antiques shops, the West End, Clarksville, and North Lamar neighborhoods are wonderful, less urban options for diners who might like to eat and take a stroll through leafy, local neighborhoods.

Enjoy the simply things at **Nau's Enfield Drug** (512-476-1221; www .nausdrug.com), 1115 W Lynn St. Sit at the tart, fresh raspberry pie served with homemade whipped cream is a sweet ending.

Uchiko (512-916-4808; www .uchikoaustin.com), 4200 N Lamar Blvd. Chef Tyson Cole's second restaurant roughly translates as "offspring of Uchi" and is every bit as inspired as its namesake. The theme here is "Japanese farmhouse," and everything from the decor to the dishes embodies a down-to-earth simplicity. The cuisine is vibrant, honest, intense, absolutely delicious, and worth every penny. The menu is perfectly balanced. While every item is a taste revelation, be sure to wrangle at least a sample of the wagyu beef seared over Japanese river rock, the brussels sprouts with lemon chile, and the fried milk dessert.

WINK ON NORTH LAMAR

Don't be shy about asking for recommendations from the sushi menu. After all, you wouldn't come to a place like Uchiko to hold back.

BURNET ROAD AND BEYOND

Austin is a small enough city that "North Austin" really means only several miles north of center, a 10- to 15-minute drive, for which you will be richly rewarded with great local fare well off the beaten tourist path. The restaurants in this section stretch from 45th Street north to Burnet Road and beyond.

Burnet Road has become the road to eat your way up and down. On the south end, you'll find **Noble Sandwiches** (512-666-5124; www.noblesandwiches.com), 4805 Burnet Rd., serving up meaty gourmet sandwiches on squares of parchment paper. Diners cite the smoked duck pastrami, the spicy ham, pulled pork, and bacon sandwich known as the "Noble Pig," and meaty beef tongue on bacon bread as front-runner favorites. Casual counter service, outdoor patio, a nice list of beer and wine, and a selection of sweets for a bite of dessert round out the dining experience.

Entwined at the roots with Odd Duck (see page 68), Chef Bryce Gilmore's **Barley Swine** (512-394-8150; www .barleyswine.com), 6555 Burnet Rd., bends and flexes with the seasons, featuring multicourse, shared plate, and tasting menus of regionally farmed goodness. In Texas, this means plenty of meat and vegetables, and while the meats are outstanding the kitchen has converted skeptics with the creative heights it has reached with the vegetables. There is a sense of earthiness here: wooden tables, pottery, pickling jars, and cutting boards. The same earnest, handcrafted feel extends to the food, which is beautifully presented and always on point, mixing complex spicy, smoky, and tangy acidity to deliver delicious results. "Swine Time" happy hours (weekdays 5–6:30 PM) are the perfect opportunity to enjoy a taste alongside a cocktail. Reservations recommended.

Fortunately for the rest of us, some people have vision enough to create the things we all grow to love, and such is the case with **Fonda San Miguel** (512-459-4121; www.fondasanmiguel.com), 2330 W N Loop Blvd. Started in 1975 by Tom Gilliland and Miguel Ravago, who were undaunted by the scarcity of ingredients north of the border at the time or the public's skepticism, Fonda San Miguel won over diners one homemade tortilla and fresh lime margarita at a time. Starters include a hot corn soup with cheese and roasted poblano peppers, a nopal cactus salad with chopped tomatoes and onions with *queso fresco,* and a *chile con queso* that has never, ever been violated by the addition of Velveeta. Main courses offer a choice of rotisserie-broiled meats, filet of fish broiled with *achiote* (a bright and earthy spice), variations of the *chile relleno*—including one with spinach, goat cheese, raisins, and pine nuts—and *pollo pibil*: chicken baked in a banana leaf, a Yucatan specialty. Its popular Sunday brunches are terrific—the perfect chance to sample a huge array of dishes and delicacies to your heart's content.

✳ Entertainment

Austin is well known for the scene on Sixth Street, roughly bounded by Red River Street to the east and Congress Avenue to the west and taking in a several-block strip of bars, restaurants, and clubs on Fifth Street. The adjacent Warehouse District, on Fourth and Fifth Streets between Congress Avenue and Guadalupe Street, is also hopping at night, and together these areas have an irresistible nighttime allure for the students and 20-somethings that pack the streets with boisterous revelry. Radiating out from Sixth Street, things mellow out considerably. Slightly east, on Red River Street, a more local scene prevails, and farther south, the South Congress neighborhood offers individual music venues and late-night eateries. Heading east on Cesar Chavez, you can stop in the Rainey Street District to the south or continue under I-35 to East Austin, both of which host live music many evenings and weekends.

Practically speaking, clubs and bars card people religiously; so whether you consider it a hassle or a compliment, have your ID at the ready. Those under 21 will not be allowed to drink but are sometimes allowed in for the entertainment; call in advance for the official policy. While credit cards are accepted for sit-down drinks and meals, cash is generally used for tips, cover charges, and the $2 beer specials. Since ATM machines in these areas see a lot of use, they are frequently out of cash, so consider bringing with you what you plan to spend.

For up-to-the-minute information on Austin's very active nightlife, pick up one of the free copies of the *Austin Chronicle* available around town at bookstores, breakfast and lunch spots, and sidewalk kiosks, or visit its website at www.austinchronicle.com. Additionally, Austin 360 at www.austin360.com is a comprehensive online guide to nightlife, movies, entertainment, and dining, and the Calendar section of the *Austin American-Statesman,* Austin's local newspaper, accessible online at www.statesman.com, lists more of the same.

The line between music venues, bars, and restaurants is blurred in Austin, with many offering a variety of everything. Austinites love to debate the triumphs and shortcomings of the city's best-loved nightlife, but one thing is certain—the classics are classics, and the rest aspire to be.

MUSIC The "Live Music Capital of the World" doesn't disappoint. Venues are listed alphabetically below.

Antone's (512-814-0361; www.antonesnightclub.com) has been around the block a few times. Opened

OUTLAWS

Some of the best portraits of Texas are sung by its family of musicians, many of whom have earned national recognition for the genius of their technique, the depth of their songwriting, and the sheer amount of heart in their songs. "Outlaw" country music, which took roots in the bars and honky-tonks of Austin and bloomed prolifically throughout the 1970s, offers up some great examples.

In the 1960s a disillusioned Willie Nelson decided he'd had his fill of predictable drinking and cheating songs, shined to a high gloss in Nashville studios, and quit Tennessee for Texas. In Austin he met renegades Waylon Jennings, Billy Joe Shaver, Kris Kristofferson, and Townes Van Zandt, among others, and they put their guitars and songs together and invented the genre of outlaw country.

While the name came from Jennings's 1972 song, "Ladies Love Outlaws," the spirit came directly from the musicians themselves. Intent on bucking the system, they wrote raw country music influenced by the revolutionary rock and folk music of their era, and their intensely personal lyrics struck a chord with listeners. Powered by fierce individuality and abundant talent, this antiestablishment music broke into the mainstream, influencing countless musicians along the way.

Besides the pioneers listed above, Johnny Cash, Guy Clark, David Allan Coe, Jessi Colter, Joe Ely, Jimmy Dale Gilmore, Butch Hancock, Johnny Rodriguez, Kimmie Rhodes, and Jerry Jeff Walker, though they are not all from Texas, are classic outlaws. Have a listen.

STATUE OF WILLIE NELSON OUTSIDE THE MOODY THEATER

by Clifford Antone in 1975, the club has relocated several times before landing in its current home just blocks from where it started. Throughout the years, Antone's has earned a reputation for serving up the finest blues around, and the club, not to mention the music store (see "Shopping" on page 82) and recording label, is still a hands-down favorite among aficionados. Antone himself passed away back in 2006, breaking the city's heart, but the music he dedicated his life to nurturing stills envelopes the club he built.

AUSTIN CITY LIMITS

In 1975 the local PBS affiliate, KLRU—riding the wave of the city's burgeoning music scene—began taping live performances of singers, songwriters, and musicians to broadcast, calling its show *Austin City Limits*. Simple production and an intimate stage allowed the music to stand on its own, and the combination was an immediate hit. Since its inception, the show has hosted more than 500 artists, some well known and others less so, but all immensely talented. *Austin City Limits* has brought a tremendous range of music to its viewers, from country and bluegrass to blues, folk, and zydeco. Watching the show is both a pleasure and an education.

It is possible to watch a live taping of *Austin City Limits*, but only a precious few have the privilege each year. Visit www.acltv.com for details of the recording schedule and complicated ticket distribution process. For decades, the show was taped in a small studio on the sixth floor of the University of Texas College of Communications Building B; a site now designated by the Rock and Roll Hall of Fame and Museum as an official rock 'n' roll landmark and marked with a plaque. The music lives on at *Austin City Limits'* new digs inside the impressive, state-of-the-art Moody Theater. While chances of seeing a taping of the show might be slim, visitors are able to tour the studio and purchase tickets to see extraordinary musicians perform year-round at the Moody Theater; visit www.acl-live.com for a schedule of tours and performances. Don't miss the fantastic Austin City Limits Music Festival (see "Festivals" on page 85) in October.

A huge open-air venue nestled into the Hill Country, shaded by hundreds of live oak trees, **The Backyard** (512-651-5033; www.backyardaustin.com) hosts music events filled with pure magic. With multilevel decks, patios, and a grassy knoll, the Backyard is so relaxed that it feels like, well, your own backyard—except, of course, Willie Nelson, Norah Jones, the Neville Brothers, and Lyle Lovett probably wouldn't play at your house.

Pull up to the nondescript, low-slung building on South Lamar that houses the **Broken Spoke** (512-442-6189; www.brokenspokeaustintx.net) and you won't guess that you are sidling up to a venerable Austin legend. The Broken Spoke has been hosting honky-tonk a good long time, and they've booked everyone from Tex Ritter to Willie Nelson, George Strait to Jerry Jeff Walker, and they have the pictures on the wall to prove it. The Broken Spoke sells chicken-fried steaks, burgers, and the like, which you can wash down with a Lone Star longneck before hitting the dance floor.

Not many university campuses have a music venue with a national reputation for superb acoustics and a list of past performers that reads like a Who's Who of the country, folk, and singer-songwriter circuit. Then again, when that university is UT-Austin, it all makes sense. The **Cactus Café** (512-475-6515; www.cactuscafe.org) opened in 1979 in the Student Union and has since hosted such musicians as Lyle Lovett, Lucinda Williams, Alison Krauss, the Dixie Chicks, Nanci Griffith, and Loudon Wainwright III, to name a few. A café by day with pizza, baked goods, and light lunch fare, the Cactus transforms into an intimate coffeehouse by night, serving coffee and beer. Tickets are first come, first served unless otherwise noted on its website. Advance tickets are available for special attractions, booked at the larger Texas Union Theatre and the much larger Texas Union Ballroom. Call the Texas Box Office (512-477-6060) for more information.

The only place in Austin where you get to pick the music, the **Casino el Camino** (512-469-9330; www

.casinoelcamino.net) on Sixth Street has ruled the realm of self-serve sounds for years. Order up a table full of burgers, hot dogs, buffalo wings and french fries, pop quarter after quarter into the legendary jukebox, and sit back and enjoy your customized evening soundtrack. That is, until someone else's intervenes.

The **Cedar Street Courtyard** (512-495-9669; www.cedarstreetaustin.com) on Fourth Street mixes drinks and dancing with live music in its outdoor courtyard. Music from the '80s and '90s is popular, as best performed by the Spazmatics (www.thespazmatics.net), the well-loved Austin band with an awesome following.

The **Continental** (512-441-2444; www.continentalclub.com) has been a heavy hitter in the live-music scene since it opened in 1955, but its current owner is responsible for giving it the retro look and feel that have become such a part of its identity today. Known for booking fantastic music almost every night of the week, what makes this place really popular are its small size, simple bar, and that "if these walls could talk" feeling only a legendary landmark delivers. The Continental is smack in the middle of SoCo, so it's always a good time.

Even though it is in a basement, the **Elephant Room** (512-473-2279; www.elephantroom.com) is the high-water mark for jazz in Austin. Identifiable by the small neon sign that glows from a window at sidewalk level, the club is intimate, dim, and alluring in the way that these sorts of venues should be. Twenty different draft beers and plenty of high-quality acts make this Congress Avenue venue a great alternative to the Sixth Street scene.

THE SCENE COMES ALIVE AT NIGHT ON SIXTH STREET

ANTONE'S NIGHTCLUB, LEGENDARY LIVE MUSIC VENUE

While **Elysium** (512-474-2285; www
.elysiumonline.net) "encourages fabu-
lousness always," you can wear anything
you'd like to this good-natured industrial
Goth dance lair on Red River Street.
Weekends (Thursday through Saturday)
are reserved for live music, and Wednesday and Sunday are earmarked for popular throwback '80s theme nights.

Emo's (512-800-4628; www
.emosaustin.com) has had many incar-
nations over the years, but one constant
is that the bands here tend to be loud,
the energy high, and the patrons young.
Emo's is known for top-notch, almost-
nightly bookings, but the lack of seating
means an evening on your feet.

For 25 years, **Maggie Mae's** (512-478-
8541; www.maggiemaesaustin.com) has
been keeping Sixth Street rocking with
that archetypal college town combination of beer and cover bands. The maze
of rooms and outdoor areas, each with its
own music and scene, makes this bar an
endless party.

Free-flowing draft beer and nightly
music, mostly singer-songwriters and
Texas talent, make **The Saxon Pub** (512-
448-2552; www.thesaxonpub.com) on
South Lamar a terrific spot to kick back
with the locals. The free happy-hour concerts Tuesday through Friday start at 6.
Darts, pool, sports on the big screen, and
free Wi-Fi keep patrons busy in between
sets. Great music and down-to-earth affa-
bility put The Saxon Pub on the short list
of classic Austin hangouts.

Scholz Garten (512-474-1958; www
.scholzgarten.net) has been in business
since 1866, and this German *biergarten*
is the place to stop in, wet your whistle,
and listen to some oompah music courtesy of the house Wurst Band. Or maybe
you'll just want to join the pandemonium
of the crowds on game night. Located on
San Jacinto, just south of campus.

The story of **Stubb's Bar-B-Q's**
(512-480-8341; www.stubbsaustin
.com) beginning is a tale unto itself.
With personality, talent, and sheer
will, Christopher "Stubb" Stubblefield
managed to cook his way from Lubbock,
on through the Korean War with the
96th Field Artillery (the last all-black
army infantry), and into to the center
of the burgeoning music scene in 1970s
Austin. Combining two loves, barbecue
and music, Stubb's restaurant was soon
booking musicians like Muddy Waters,
John Lee Hooker, Willie Nelson, Johnny
Cash, and many others who loved playing the outdoor venue to the sweet smell
of slow-cookin' 'cue. These days, a more
commercial and streamlined Stubb's on
Red River Street is a major music venue
and sells sauce in a bottle, but the old
Austin favorite remains 100 percent
pure Texas.

While it doesn't look like much more
than a shack with peeling red paint,
the **Scoot Inn** (512-524-1932; www
.scootinnaustin.com) has weathered time
admirably. Opened in 1871 as a grocery
store—with a little bootlegging and gambling on the side—and later home to a
string of saloons and bars, it acquired its

STEVIE RAY VAUGHAN MEMORIAL

A tribute to the Austin bluesman whose life was cut tragically short when he died in a helicopter crash in 1990, the statue of Stevie Ray Vaughan was placed on the south shore of Lady Bird Lake by the city of Austin in 1993. At the time of his death, at age 35, Vaughan had released five albums and won three Grammy Awards, and an additional two were awarded posthumously. He was a revered musician, and tracks from the solo albums *Family Style* and *The Sky Is Crying*, along with those recorded with his band Double Trouble—*Couldn't Stand the Weather, Soul to Soul, Texas Flood, and Live at Carnegie Hall*—are radio mainstays. Vaughan left a legacy of heartfelt music to his fans; for Austin his statue is an expression of love and respect for all its musicians.

name along the way from a former owner, Aubrey "Scoot" Ivy. These days, the historic building comes alive each night with an eclectic lineup of music, basic drinks, plenty of people, and a vegan food truck out back. It's a small, intimate venue with a great backyard, and has been serving the East Side for decades.

DRINKS Sometimes the best way to get to know a town is just to sit down and have a casual drink with the locals. The following are a few suggestions of where to do so, scattered about town.

DOWNTOWN/WAREHOUSE DISTRICT

Bringing a little spice to downtown, gourmet hot dog joint **Frank** serves up some ultra-creative and super-tasty drinks on Colorado near Fifth. Like bacon? Try the Red Headed Stranger, a combination of housemade, bacon-infused Tito's Vodka and Bloody Mary mix that's garnished with bacon, cheddar cheese, jalapeño stuffed olive, and pepperoncini. Frank is open for happy hour and dinner, but not late night bar hours.

STREET MUSICIAN ON SOUTH CONGRESS AVENUE

crowd with everything from liqueurs to lattes, with plenty of long necks and a chocolate espresso martini thrown in. The make-your-own s'mores are a hit. Down the street, **Ginger Man** (512-473-8801; www.gingermanpub.com) offers a huge selection of bottled microbrews (with even more on tap rotation), a wide variety of local labels and national favorites, and a pleasant, low-key environment to drink them in. The mixologists at posh **Péché** (512-494-4011; www.pecheaustin .com) on West Fourth specialize in "pre-Prohibition style cocktails" with top-shelf gin, whisky, vodka, rum, tequila, and even absinthe. Try the mussels in a habanero and coconut broth or the macaroni and cheese with Gruyère and duck confit for an appetizer. One block up, **Gourdough's Public House** (512-645-0255; www.gourdoughspub .com) serves many of the same sweet, savory, gooey, and sticky donut creations featured in their food truck, but the brick-and-mortar locations allow them to offer indoor seating, craft beers, and mixed drinks. Their second location is on South Lamar.

For the taste of a classic German *bier-garten*, head over to **Easy Tiger** (512-614-4972; www.easytigeraustin.com), where you can sample a snappy garlic sausage, served on a pretzel bun with a generous dollop of their housemade bourbon-bacon relish and German mustard, then wash it down with craft beer.

Rainey Street, located in a little slice of downtown sandwiched between Lady Bird Lake and I-35 south of Cesar Chavez, offers a hopping bar scene. Stop by **Banger's Sausage House and Beer Garden** (see page 63) for a beer and a brat. **Icenhauer's** (512-473-0005; www .icenhauers.com) has mixed drinks, live music, and a fire pit, all in a fantastic backyard. The Emily—Tito's Handmade Vodka with muddled strawberries and basil, basil-infused syrup, and a splash of fresh lemon juice—is a popular choice.

Part bar, part café, part coffee shop, and part lounge, **Halcyon** (512-472-9637; www.halcyonaustin.com), on West Fourth at Lavaca, caters to a laid-back

SOUTH CONGRESS

South Austin has plenty of places to stop in for a drink. Step off busy South Congress Avenue and into the serene courtyard of the **Hotel San José**, where everyone is welcome for drinks. **Hop-doddy** (see page 65) has a nice selection of craft beers on tap, chosen to complement its fantastic gourmet burgers. Try a watermelon martini at the **South Congress Café** (see page 66) or a stiff, unsweetened, minty mojito at **Güero's Taco Bar** (see page 65). **The Continental** (see page 77) and the **Broken Spoke** (see page 76) top the list of dive bars that double as venerable music venues.

Head west to South First Street and pop in at **Freddie's** or **Shady Grove** on Barton Springs, both of which offer casual drinks and food with plenty of shade trees under which to enjoy them.

Climb the rustic stone steps to the relaxed rooftop patio of **El Alma** (512-609-8923; www.elalmacafe.com) and while away an afternoon. A popular choice for brunch, this Tex-Mex restaurant has also become a go-to spot for drinks, especially the sweet and spicy "chilanga." The signature frozen margarita is made with orange juice and a splash of Valentina hot sauce and served in a glass rimmed with a homemade chile powder.

UT/HYDE PARK

Predictably, the watering holes around the university cater to students; the offerings mature the deeper you press into Hyde Park and surrounding neighborhoods.

Spider House (512-480-9562; www.spiderhouse.com), a student hangout located just north of the University of Texas campus near the intersection of Guadalupe and 30th Streets, serves some food but also dozens of hot and cold caffeinated drinks, frozen fruit smoothies and shakes, bottled beer, draft beer, and a coffee martini known as the Brown Recluse. Grab a L'Orangina—Orangina plus a splash of gin or vodka—or a glass of its refreshing signature sangria, and relax on the backyard patio under the oaks.

Just north of campus, the **Crown & Anchor Pub** (512-322-9168; www.crownandanchorpub.com) has pool tables, video games, dartboards, and plenty of seating. You'll also find good grub and plenty of beer to wash it down with—30-plus taps and a hundred bottles and pitchers of local brew.

Tucked into a neighborhood a block west of Central Market on Lamar and 42nd Street, a short but well-removed drive from the downtown bar scene, the **Draught House** (512-452-6258; www.draughthouse.com) seems like a leap across the pond. The British feel of this pub and beer garden tends to be a good fit for folks who prefer a neighborhood watering hole. There are dozens of beers on tap—both local and guest brews—and plenty of bottles to choose from.

In nearby Hyde Park, the offerings at **Vino Vino** (512-465-9282; www.vinovinotx.com) include fantastic wines, artisanal cheeses, and plump mussels served with hot frites and a dollop of aioli. Try the orange olive oil cake with citrus tuile and avocado ice cream for dessert. Prices, but not quality, come down during happy hour, making it a great time to stop in. Epicureans will enjoy **Barley Swine** (512-394-8150; www.barleyswine.com), a cozy gastropub on Burnet Road featuring a fantastic drink menu, with a nice representation of local brew and ingenious "small plates" to match.

EAST AUSTIN

A selection of trendy dive bars has sprung up along East Sixth Street, part of East Austin's rapidly evolving nightlife scene. **The Liberty** (512-514-0502; www.thelibertyaustin.com), is a slightly divey bar, with the fantastic East Side King (www.eastsideking.com) food truck

featuring Japanese-inspired street food out back. The quirky **Shangri-La** (512-524-4291; www.shangrilaaustin.com) has cheap beer, pool tables, outdoor space, and a great Asian fusion food truck on-site. Breezy **Whisler's** (512-480-0781; www.whislersatx.com) feels like a saloon, with exposed limestone walls and soaring ceilings, but the creative cocktails, artsy outdoor area, and mezcal tasting room add a sophistication to an otherwise laid-back bar. **The Salty Sow** (see page 70) is a foodie favorite for drinks and nibbles.

✳ Selective Shopping

Austin has perfected the look of vintage urban chic. Shops are filled to the brim with coffee tables, clothing, housewares, signs, and any number of knickknacks from various eras. With other shops selling books, music, and folk art, as well as museum stores and galleries, Austin is great fun for folks who love the thrill of the hunt. Art Austin, a program of Art Alliance Austin (www.artallianceaustin.org), promotes the visual arts in the city and lists additional art galleries on its website, www.artaustin.org.

DOWNTOWN AND WEST AUSTIN

Antone's Record Store (512-322-0660; www.antonesrecordshop.com) offers jazz, folk, bluegrass, tons of Texas music, and lots of great blues. This is a great place to buy vinyl.

Book People (512-472-5050; www.bookpeople.com) is Austin's much-loved independent bookstore and "an outpost for the literate." Almost daily readings, author visits, and public events make it a great destination for bibliophiles young and old. In addition to all manner of books spread out on two floors, Book People carries quirky Texas-themed gifts, both in its store and online.

By George (877-472-5951; www.bygeorgeaustin.com), a smart clothing store with distinctive style, has been a part of Austin since 1977. Urban, sophisticated, and modern without being faddish, the designer clothing reflects the store owners' personalities, and the store itself is a work of art. They have locations on North Lamar and in SoCo.

Tesoros Trading Company (512-447-7500; www.tesoros.com) is a purveyor of colorful folk arts, crafts, furniture, clothing, and jewelry from more than 15 countries, and has a wonderful selection of items from Latin America.

Waterloo Records (512-474-2500; www.waterloorecords.com) is a perennial favorite and a die-hard music lover's music store run by die-hard music lovers, a love affair in which sparks still fly. Though the store itself has evolved from its humble beginnings into something big and modern, its philosophy has not. The staff at Waterloo has encyclopedic knowledge of Texas music and would be thrilled to send you home with some local music you'll just love.

The intriguing **Women and Their Work** (512-477-1064; www.womenandtheirwork.org) art gallery hosts dozens of events each year, featuring the visual art, dance, theater, music, literature, and film of female artists; check its website or call for current listings. The gift shop is packed with pieces from local artisans.

SOUTH AUSTIN

Stroll South Congress Avenue for antiques, resale, and vintage shops.

Allens Boots (512-447-1413; www.allensboots.com) on South Congress carries a huge selection of boots, hats, shirts, and belt buckles for cowboys and cowgirls of all ages. Boots range from the modestly priced utilitarian ropers to the always fashionable Lucchese Classics, expertly made of soft leather, with a 4-inch heel, square toe, and plenty of fantastic detailing, which can set you back upward of $1,200.

Mi Casa Gallery (512-707-9797; www .micasagallery.com) began as one family's love affair with Latin America and has grown into a large collection of international treasures ranging from a $4,000 antique hand-carved walnut chair upholstered with Argentine leather to one-of-a-kind devotional art pieces created by talented, self-taught folk artists.

Yard Dog (512-912-1613; www.yarddog .com) gallery, on South Congress, gravitates toward folk, outsider, and contemporary art, pieces created by self-taught artists, and anything else that seems to fit its ethos. The small gallery shows national artists, and its exhibits tend to be dynamic and varied.

EAST AUSTIN

The Flatbed Press (512-477-9328; www .flatbedpress.com) is both a publishing workshop specializing in etchings, lithographs, woodcuts, and monoprints, and an art gallery exhibiting the same, as well as paintings, drawings, and photographs.

✳ Special Events

FESTIVALS If you are lucky enough to be in town at the right time and get tickets, Austin's festivals are as impressive as they are fun. Maybe it's the first breezes of spring that make everyone so frisky, but **South by Southwest** (SXSW), held in March, is one big, weeklong party. Sure, it's technically more of a conference for those in the music, film, and multimedia industries where talent is "discovered" and deals are signed, but for the bar and club owners who have to clean up after the crowd leaves, it's just one long, beer-soaked bash. In October the **Austin City Limits Music Festival** (ACL) is tamer, but it's growing fast as word catches on. Festivals are what

Austin does best, and it hosts plenty of them. For specific information, check the calendars online at the Austin CVB (www.austintexas.org) or the *Austin American-Statesman* (www.austin360 .com).

Annual Festivals

The following organizations host a variety of events throughout the year.

Austin Food and Wine Alliance (512-348-6847; www.austinfoodwinealliance .org) A celebration of wine, food, and Central Texas, with events in Austin and the surrounding Hill Country. Admission charged.

Austin Shakespeare Festival (512-470-4505; www.austinshakespeare.org) Experience the timeless works of Shakespeare. Performances run throughout the year, with a season that kicks off in September. Admission charged.

Monthly Festivals

The Sustainable Food Center's Farmers' Market (www.sustainablefoodcenter .org) This Saturday-morning market in Republic Square Park, 422 Guadalupe St., is not exactly a festival. But with 100 vendors, a café under the Auction Oak, live music, and space for impromptu picnics, it makes for a festive atmosphere.

February: **The Mid-Winter Music Festival** (830-825-3108; www.aftm.us) A celebration of traditional, folk, and international music and dance organized by the Austin Friends of Traditional Music organization, which sponsors additional festivals throughout the year. Admission charged.

March: **The ABC Zilker Kite Festival** (www.zilkerkitefestival.com) A family-friendly festival with dozens of colorful kites dancing above Zilker Park. Flying high and admission free since 1929.

Rodeo Austin (512-919-3000; www .rodeoaustin.com) Livestock show, rodeos, a barbecue cook-off, and the popular kickoff event—the Cowboy Breakfast. Admission and free.

South by Southwest (SXSW) (512-467-7979; www.sxsw.com) An enormously popular conference for film, multimedia, and of course music, with performances and presentations. Admission charged.

Texas Rock Fest (512-913-8889; www.texasrockfest.com) Also known as the "The Heart of Texas Quadruple Bypass Music Festival," this event features plenty of indie talent. Admission charged.

April: **Art City Austin** (512-609-8587; www.artallianceaustin.org) Featuring art, local food, and plenty of music. Admission charged.

Eeyore's Birthday (www.eeyores.org) This groovy event benefits nonprofit groups in Austin and is more than 40 years old. Admission is free.

Old Settler's Music Festival (www.oldsettlersmusicfest.org) International, national, and regional artists performing Americana music. Held at Camp Ben McCulloch in Driftwood, just south of Austin. Admission charged.

May: **Austin Ice Cream Festival** (www.icecreamfestival.org) Extra sweet, since profits benefit local charities. Admission charged.

Cinco de Mayo (www.cincodemayoaustin.com) Commemoration and celebration of the Mexican army's victory over the French at the Battle of Puebla on May 5, 1862. This is a joyous cultural festival featuring events throughout the city, and its free.

Hot Luck Food Festival (www.hotluckfest.com) Aaron Franklin, of Franklin Barbecue (see page 69), the organizer of Fun, Fun, Fun Fest (see page 85), and partners from near and far have teamed to create a hot new weekend fetstival of live-fire cooking and sizzling concerts.

Pachanga Music Fest (www.pachangafest.com) High-energy Latin music, food, and culture fest has since evolved into a quarterly concert series

at Austin City Limits Live at The Moody Theater (ACL Live). Admission charged.

June: **Juneteenth** (512-974-4926; www.austintexas.gov) Commemorating June 19, 1865, the day that slaves in Texas first received word of the Emancipation Proclamation, this is a spirited citywide celebration of freedom. Visit the George Washington Carver Museum and Cultural Center (see "Museums" on page 39) in East Austin for more information. Admission charged.

Keep Austin Weird Fest & 5K (www.keepaustinweirdfest.com) "The ultimate toast to Austin." Cheers. Admission charged.

Republic of Texas Biker Rally (512-906-9954; www.rotrally.com) A massive three-day fest of music and biker culture. Hop on a Harley and come on down. Admission charged.

July: **Austin Chamber Music Festival** (512-454-0026; www.austinchambermusic.org) Enjoy chamber music in various venues throughout the city. Free.

Bastille Day (512-472-8180; www.frenchlegationmuseum.org) A Frenchfest hosted by the French Legation Museum (see "Museums" on page 39). Free.

Fourth of July Fireworks & Symphony (512-476-6064; www.austinsymphony.org) Patriotic music and fireworks over Lady Bird Lake.

Zilker Summer Musical (512-479-9491; www.zilker.org) Outstanding family-friendly musicals performed outdoors. Free.

August: **Austin Chronicle Hot Sauce Contest** (www.austinchronicle.com) Beer, music, and lots of spicy sauce. Take a taste and feel the burn. Admission charged.

Bat Fest (512-441-9015; www.roadstarproductions.com) Lots of arts, crafts, food, music, and fun on the Congress Avenue Bridge, with proceeds to benefit Bat Conservation International. Admission charged.

September: **Austin International Poetry Festival** (www.aipf.org) Annual celebration of poets and poetry. Free.

Diez y Seis Celebration (www.diezyseis.org) A celebration of Mexico's independence from Spain on September 16, 1821. Offers celebrations at Republic Square, Fifth and Guadalupe Streets. Free.

Pecan Street Festival (www.pecanstreetfestival.org) A juried arts festival, including food, live music, and family-friendly fun. Admission charged.

Out of Bounds Comedy Festival (www.outofboundscomedy.com) A seven-day extravaganza of improv, sketch, stand-up, and comedy performances

LIVE MUSIC ALL YEAR ROUND IN AUSTIN

straddling August and September. Admission charged.

October: **Austin City Limits Music Festival (ACL)** (www.aclfestival.com) More than a hundred bands play to the crowds for three days straight. An internationally regarded Austin original. Admission charged.

Austin Film Festival (512-478-4795; www.austinfilmfestival.com) A multiday film festival attracting big Hollywood names and independent upstarts. Film buffs will enjoy the quality and range of the offerings. Admission charged.

Austin Gay and Lesbian International Film Festival (512-257-6227; www.agliff.org) Edgy films tackling a wide range of topics. Admission charged.

Austin String Band Festival (830-825-3108; www.aftm.us) Fiddles, banjos and guitars galore, coupled with dancing, workshops, and a gospel jam. A laid-back gathering in a busy month of festivals. Admission charged.

November: **Austin Celtic Festival** (www.austincelticfestival.com) Celtic bands from Austin and around the world. Admission charged.

Austin Powwow and American Indian Heritage Festival (512-371-0628; www.austinpowwow.net) Spectacular celebration of Native American culture, the largest of its kind in the region, with food, music, and performances. Admission charged.

Día de los Muertos/Community Altars: A Celebration of Life (512-480-9373; www.mexic-artemuseum.org) "The Day of the Dead," the ancient cultural tradition in which families "welcome back" departed loved ones, commemorating them through special altars and cemetery visits. Poetry readings and *calavera* processions, in which participants dress as skeletons, are especially moving. Free.

East Austin Studio Tour (512-939-6665; www.eastaustinstudiotour.com) Enjoy a weekend visiting the open studios of East Austin artists. Free.

December: **Armadillo Christmas Bazaar** (512-447-1605; www.armadillo bazaar.com) An enormous yet casual art market with lots of gifts ideas. forty years old and counting. Admission charged.

Fun, Fun, Fun Fest (www .funfunfunfest.com) A weekend of indie rock, hip-hop, punk, electronica, and metal bands. Admission charged.

Trail of Lights and Zilker Christmas Tree (512-974-6700; www .austintrailoflights.org) Austin makes up for a lack of snow with a plethora of lights. Admission charged.

SAN ANTONIO

SAN ANTONIO

There is something special about San Antonio. You notice it when you are there, and it stays with you when you leave. Even Mark Twain felt it, naming San Antonio one of America's "unique cities," along with Boston, New Orleans, and San Francisco. Both a crossroads and a destination, San Antonio has attracted people for centuries, and its roots are deep and widespread. It is in many ways the birthplace of Texas; as Frank Tolbert, a noted Texas historian and journalist, once said, "Every Texan has two homes, his own and San Antonio."

ROOTS Native Americans were the first settlers of the area, drawn to the banks of the San Antonio River (or, as they called it, the Yanaguana, meaning "refreshing waters" or "clear waters"). Indeed, San Antonio's raison d'être is water, flowing from the San Antonio and San Pedro Springs into the San Antonio and San Pedro Rivers, supporting the lush ecosystem of the surrounding Olmos Creek basin. Tools and other artifacts found in this region attest to over 11,000 years of human habitation, and it is known that Native Americans used this area as a popular meeting and camping spot and a productive area for hunting and gathering. Though drilling, damming, and diverting have altered the location, flow, and personalities of the area's waterways, it is still easy to envision the practicality, charm, and charisma the water held for those who encountered it. Gurgling springs, the rushing river, and the surrounding vegetation are the center around which the city's history, most of its contested issues, and its civic pride have revolved.

While it is unclear exactly when the first explorers of European origin entered the region, what is known is that on June 13, 1691, a group of Spanish priests, en route to visit missions in East Texas, paused to camp at the clear-running river's edge, beside a group of welcoming Native Americans. The day happened to be the Feast of Saint Anthony of Padua, and the priests, so taken with the area's beauty, decided to name it San Antonio de Padua. In the late 1700s, the French were eyeing Texas, and the Spanish moved to put down deeper roots. Between 1709 and 1722, organized Spanish expeditions, called *entradas,* started to search the region for strategic spots to claim in advance of any French incursions. By 1718, the Spanish had staked a claim in San Antonio and founded the San Antonio de Béxar Presidio. In the same year, Franciscans, eager for citizens and converts, established the first of the five missions they would build in the area, including the Alamo. The inhabitants of the missions, in turn, built seven *acequias,* a series of interconnected irrigation ditches and aqueducts linking the missions and transporting water from the San Antonio River and the San Pedro Creek to the outlying farmlands, an outstanding feat of engineering for its day. In 1731 the village of San Fernando de Béxar was chartered by Canary Islanders, who went on to establish the San Fernando de Béxar Cathedral, and in 1772 the small town, by this time called San Antonio de Béxar, was made the capital of Spanish-ruled Texas.

When the Republic of Texas was formed in 1836, just months after the legendary battle of the Alamo, San Antonio was chartered as the seat of Bexar County. Located near a hotly contested border, San Antonio endured several Mexican invasions, and its population declined significantly until the Civil War in 1861. After the Civil War, San Antonio became a nexus of distribution, supplying the cattle-trail drives and serving

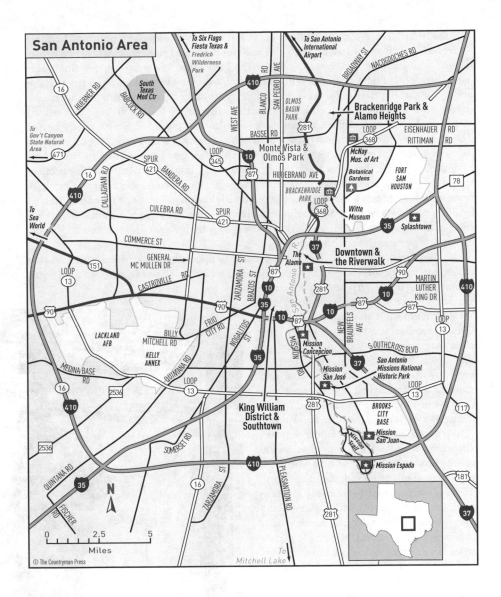

as a gateway to the Southwest. Five railroad routes passed through between 1877 and 1900, setting the city on track to participate in the economic growth and modernization of the nation and hastening immigration. By the 1920s just over 161,000 residents called San Antonio home, making it the largest city in the state. The city was already a diverse mix of Tejanos, Mexicans, German Americans, and Anglos from the American South when the Mexican Revolution of 1910 fueled substantial Mexican immigration, enhancing the city's already intimately intertwined history with Mexico.

THE RIVER Over time, each group in each era has left its mark on San Antonio. From the food and architecture, to historic sites and festivals, San Antonio is a fascinating interplay of cultures and history. One of the city's most recognizable landmarks—the lovely Riverwalk—is also one of its newest, though its story begins in the 19th century.

Back then, San Antonians relied on the river for drinking, swimming, bathing, hydropower, and irrigation. By 1890, the need for more and more fresh water had grown urgent, and many artesian wells were drilled into the Edwards Aquifer. Snatching water directly from its source meant an inevitable decline in water flow on the surface, and by 1896 the spring-fed river was in jeopardy, its current reduced to a gloomy trickle dotted with garbage. The social consequences were steep for the diverse community of residents who would flock to the river to swim and picnic along its shady banks. The final blow came, with a swift chop, in 1904, as city workers used axes to fell two beloved willow trees in the name of river "cleanup." After enraged citizens turned out in droves to berate their city and its misguided plan, officials responded with promises to beautify and protect the waterway. Civic associations formed and began to push for revitalization of both the river and the public life that had flourished along it. In 1912 local architect Harvey L. Page designed a plan for reinforcement of a 13-mile stretch of river using what are known as "Surkey seawalls," which were to be traversed by decorative bridges and lined with benches.

Mother Nature, it seems, had other plans. Six major floods between 1914 and 1921 destroyed any progress on the plans, testing the city's resolve. Some even suggested simply covering the river with concrete and using it as a sewer, an idea met with little enthusiasm. Then came the Big One. On September 10, 1921, while the city slept, an enormous flood swept through the area, killing 50 people, steeping downtown in 2 to 10 feet of water, and making it crystal clear to the entire city that water must first be managed before it can be enjoyed. So the Olmos Dam was constructed in 1926, and a cutoff channel, allowing excess water to bypass downtown, was completed in 1929—projects that together provided flood control. Then, a young architect, Robert H. Hugman, stepped forward with an ingenious plan. Designed specifically to showcase the river, his proposal of narrow pedestrian walkways, shops, and restaurants built to hug the bends and curves of the waters flowing 20 feet below street level was inspired by the old cities of Spain. Unfortunately, the Great Depression derailed this new plan, and only a few new flower beds were planted along the river instead.

In 1936, the 100th anniversary of the Republic of Texas, a rush of civic pride washed over the city; by 1939 construction had begun on Hugman's plan for the Paseo del Rio, the San Antonio Riverwalk. The Works Progress Administration (WPA) managed the project, and on March 13, 1941, the WPA gifted the

DETAIL FROM THE FRONT OF THE ALAMO

RIVERWALK ACCESSIBILITY

The Riverwalk is recessed below street level, and getting to it can be a challenge for anyone with restricted mobility. Strollers, wheelchairs, and walkers are simply impossible to manage on the steep, sometimes slippery steps. If you are planning some of the details of your trip in advance and online, consider printing a copy of the "Accessible Riverwalk" map found on the Disability Access Office's page of www.sanantonio.gov.

While elevators dot the Riverwalk, other particularly convenient locations include Crowne Plaza Hotel, Hawthorne Suites Hotel, Hilton del Rio, Holiday Inn Riverwalk, Hotel Contessa, the Hyatt, La Mansión Del Rio, Rivercenter Mall, the Westin, and in front of the Aztec Theater.

completed Riverwalk, with 17,000 feet of sidewalks, 31 stairways, and 4,000 plantings, to the city of San Antonio. Although 50,000 people came out to cheer for its dedication on April 21 of that year, the Riverwalk didn't come into its own until the 1968 Hemis-Fair, during which it finally became an icon of the city.

PRIDE AND PRESERVATION By 1930 both Houston and Dallas had surpassed San Antonio in population and economic clout. Geographically, San Antonio remained within the boundaries of its original Spanish charter until 1940, when the automobile hastened suburban growth.

Economically, San Antonio relies on military bases, educational institutions, and its medical complexes for stability. Good weather, access to health care, and a large veteran community, not to mention outstanding golf, have made San Antonio a popular

ENJOYING A BOAT RIDE ON THE SAN ANTONIO RIVER

WHO IS KING WILLIAM?

As the story goes, King William Street, once the main thoroughfare of the neighborhood, was originally christened Kaiserwilhelm Strasse—in honor of King Wilhelm I of Prussia—by the German immigrants who settled here. During World War I, political tensions between America and Germany boiled over, and the name was changed to Pershing Avenue. Several years after the war the name was restored, this time in its Anglicized form, King William Street. In 1967 the King William District was designated the first Historic Neighborhood District in Texas.

KING WILLIAM DISTRICT

retirement area. Another big segment of its economy is tourism, and San Antonio is well aware of the value of its many cultural and historic sites, neighborhoods, and festivals. With a rich history to care for, San Antonio has been a leader in preservation; the San Antonio Conservation Society, founded in 1924, has become a force to be reckoned with. Strict preservation codes, tempered by tax incentives for rehabilitation and preservation, have enabled individual buildings, even entire neighborhoods, to retain their unique features and identities. Festivals such as the San Antonio Annual Livestock Show and Rodeo in February, the wildly popular Fiesta San Antonio in April, the Tejano Conjunto Festival in May, and the Texas Folklife Festival in June bring out the city's best. A dynamic and diverse city with lots of personality and a river running through it, San Antonio is the pride and joy of Texas.

GETTING AROUND Public transportation offers an enjoyable way to get around in San Antonio. The city's public bus system, **VIA** (210-362-2020; www.viainfo.net), runs a network of routes throughout the city, and three are particularly useful to visitors. "VIVA" is a series of routes designed to connect San Antonio's most popular destinations. Route 11 travels among the city's cultural attractions, Route 40 ferries riders to and from the missions, and Route 301 includes stops in the city center. All VIA buses are handicapped accessible. Fare: $1.30 a ride or $2.75 for a convenient one-day pass.

Or try a water taxi! **Rio San Antonio** (210-244-5700; www.riosanantonio.com) provides both river taxi and tour services on the San Antonio River. You can purchase

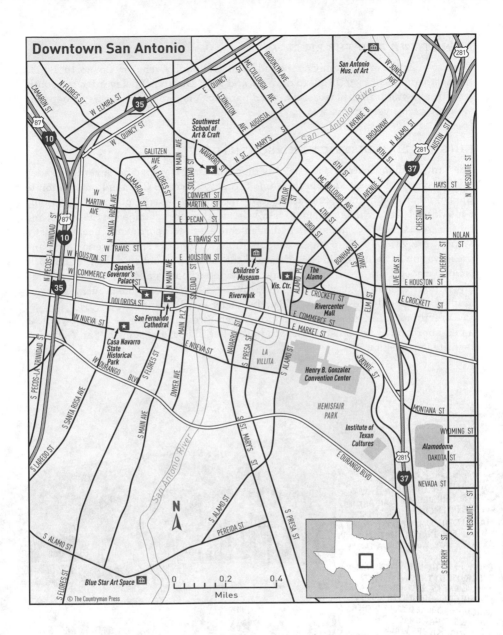

Downtown San Antonio

tickets from the drivers onboard, at a kiosk, or online. Fare: $10 for a one-way trip, $12 for a 24-hour pass, and $25 for a three-day pass.

NEIGHBORHOODS Many of San Antonio's sights, historic and cultural, can be found in the compact downtown surrounding the Riverwalk. Once you procure parking, this area is very easy to navigate on foot. Outside downtown, driving to and from the recommendations listed in this book is a nice way to explore the city's unique neighborhoods.

DOWNTOWN AND THE RIVERWALK

Downtown is the area roughly contained by McCullough Avenue to the north, I-35 to the north and west, I-37/US 281 to the east, and West Durango Boulevard to the south. It is urban, with traffic, noise, and limited parking. Visitors can easily eat, sleep, and sightsee exclusively in this area.

KING WILLIAM DISTRICT AND SOUTHTOWN

The King William District is the neighborhood south of Durango Boulevard, bounded by the river to the west and South Alamo Street to the east. German immigration to the neighborhood in the 1840s earned it the nickname "Sauerkraut Bend." Originally a fashionable area with large, single-family homes, the area slumped in the 1920s, and by the 1940s many of the homes had been converted to apartments. Located just a stone's throw from downtown, the neighborhood caught the spirit of renovation and preservation in the 1950s; in 1967 it earned the distinction of being the first Historic Neighborhood District in Texas. Today the neighborhood is a lovely mix of restored larger homes, more modest abodes, atmospheric B&Bs, several small businesses, art studios, and popular restaurants, all nestled under huge pecan trees.

Directly east, the area south of South Alamo Street is known as Southtown. It is a neighborhood of art galleries and studios, coffee shops, and some of San Antonio's favorite local restaurants.

PUBLIC ART ALONG THE RIVERWALK

MURAL ON A BUILDING IN SOUTHTOWN

MUSEUM REACH AND PEARL BREWERY

Completed in 2009, the Museum Reach section of the Riverwalk doubled the length of the famous walkway, extending it from the downtown core another 1.3 miles north to the San Antonio Museum of Art and the Pearl Brewery just beyond. Fairly quiet and calm, with plenty of lovely landscaping, parks, benches, and public art, this section of the walk is a wonderful connector of some of the city's most vital cultural institutions.

BRACKENRIDGE PARK AND ALAMO HEIGHTS

From downtown, Broadway heads north past Brackenridge Park on its way to Alamo Heights. While the area surrounding Brackenridge Park and its attractions maintains an urban feel, Alamo Heights, San Antonio's original suburb and now its own city, is much more residential. Its large homes, upscale dining, and shopping are clustered around the intersections of Broadway, North New Braunfels Avenue, and Austin Highway south of Northeast Loop 410 near the McNay Art Museum.

MONTE VISTA AND OLMOS PARK

Neighboring Alamo Heights to the west, this once-exquisite neighborhood has an uneven look and feel today, with lovingly restored mansions side by side with those that have fallen on hard times. A down-to-earth side of San Antonio, Monte Vista and Olmos Park are home to some well-loved restaurants.

✳ To See

Most of San Antonio's sights can be found in three neighborhoods of the city—the Riverwalk, King William District, and Brackenridge Park—but don't miss the Mission Trail, the route linking the four historic missions on the outer edges of the city.

HISTORIC PLACES Visitors may be surprised by the size of the **Alamo** (210-225-1391; www.thealamo.org). Rather than an imposing fort, the Alamo is a small structure whose architecture is indicative of its religious roots. Built from local rock, its intricately carved exterior is a light, sandy beige color that reflects the bright Texas sun. The Daughters of the Republic of Texas (DRT), women whose Texas roots run as deep as the Edwards Aquifer, began caring for the structure in 1892. By 1905, the state legislature had installed the DRT in the role of custodian of the structure, and thousands of the organization's volunteers dutifully dedicated over a century of hours of service to its upkeep. After several political twists and emotional turns, the Texas General Land Office assumed responsibility for the Alamo in 2011, collaborating with the Alamo Endowment (www.alamoendowment.org) to preserve and manage the complex. By 2015 the Alamo, along with the four missions in the San Antonio Missions National Historical Park, was designated a UNESCO World Heritage site.

To best understand the Alamo's significance, you must first understand its history. The Alamo began as an idea when Antonio de San Buenaventura y Olivares, a participant in the *entrada* to establish missions in Texas, visited a spot just west of the San Pedro Springs on April 13, 1709, and dreamt of building a mission there. That dream was realized nine years later, on May 1, 1718, when he erected a small hut of brush and grapevines, said Mass, and named his creation the Mission San Antonio de Valero. In 1719 the mission relocated to the east of San Pedro Springs; it was later uprooted and moved once more to the spot now occupied by St. Joseph's Church in San Antonio, where it was destroyed by floods in 1724. Finally, in 1744 the mission was built along the banks of the San Antonio River, only to be abandoned when Mexico secularized the missions in 1793. From these chaotic beginnings and amid rising tensions between area Anglos and Mexicans, the mission's function morphed from sanctuary for converts to an enclave of combatants. When the Mexican cavalry occupied the mission in the early 1800s, it was referred to as the *pueblo del alamo*— *alamo* being the Spanish word for cottonwood, so-called perhaps for the trees along the river—and the name stuck.

MARKET SQUARE/EL MERCADO

On October 2, 1835, turf wars between Mexicans and Anglos reached a boiling point when Mexicans demanded the town cannon from the nearby settlement of Gonzales, and were told, in no uncertain terms, "Come and get it." Needless to say, the Mexicans did, and promptly lost the first battle of the Texas Revolution. Emboldened by success, a hastily gathered group of barely 200 male colonists (and dozens of women and children), including the legendary Davy Crockett, Stephen F. Austin, William Travis, and the famous knife fighter Jim Bowie, seized San Antonio and settled into the

HEMISFAIR PARK

The HemisFair, held April through October 1968 and planned to coincide with the 250th anniversary of the founding of the city, was an international exposition celebrating the shared cultural heritage of San Antonio and Latin America, organized around the theme of "Confluence of Civilization in the Americas." Canada, Mexico, Italy, Spain, France, and Japan were quick to host large exhibits, but some effort, including securing sponsorship from local foundations, had to be made in order for exhibits representing Nicaragua, Honduras, Guatemala, El Salvador, and Costa Rica to be realized. The Institute of Texan Cultures (see below) was constructed for this event, and its exhibits highlighting the contributions of various ethnic groups to the formation of modern Texas were a huge hit.

The construction of the fairgrounds was mired in controversy, as the land used was part of the "old city," home to 120 buildings in various states of upkeep and residents with an attachment to their neighborhood. Fair planners were able to have the area designated an urban renewal site and secured federal funding for the project. In the end only 22 of the original structures survived and were incorporated into the park—the rest were destroyed and all the residents relocated. The Tower of the Americas, a technological feat at its time, was built for the fair, and the Riverwalk was extended a quarter mile to link the park to the greater downtown neighborhood. Though over 6 million visitors enjoyed the park during the HemisFair, the park failed to become the cultural or recreational center of the city, as planners had hoped. The Institute of Texan Cultures excepted, many of the buildings now serve functions that aren't recreational or cultural; for example, what was formerly the United States' exhibit hall is now a federal courthouse.

Today, the park consists of 5 acres of grass, trees, and gardens crisscrossed with paths and dotted with fountains, benches, and playgrounds. The Instituto Cultural Mexicano (210-227-0123; www.icm2.sre.gob.mx/culturamexsa/) hosts films, music, salsa, merengue, and tango dance classes and is home to the small Casa Mexicana Gallery, which displays works of contemporary artists from Mexico. The Tower of the Americas (210-223-3101; www.toweroftheamericas.com) has undergone an $11 million makeover designed to ignite more interest among both residents and visitors. The observation deck, Flags Over Texas, offers spectacular views of the city, and the 4-D theater, Skies Over Texas, will challenge your sensitivity to vertigo. At the deck's pinnacle, the rotating Chart House Restaurant (210-223-3101; www.toweroftheamericas.com) is run by Landry's, with a seafood-centric menu and panoramic views. The ground floor café is open for coffee or cold drinks.

TOWER OF THE AMERICAS, WITH A STORM BREWING

THE ALAMO

abandoned mission, the Alamo, to wait for the inevitable Mexican retribution.

On February 23, 1836, an estimated 4,000 Mexican troops, under the command of the formidable General Antonio López de Santa Anna, besieged the Alamo, capturing it after 13 days of constant battle and the deaths of all defenders. While the participants lost the Alamo and their lives (though some women and children were released), their actions became the stuff of legend. The event galvanized support for the ultimately successful revolution against Mexico, for which the phrase "Remember the Alamo" became a rallying cry. Or so the story goes. As with any historically significant battle, especially one as dramatic and pivotal as this, the facts are still debated. What remains is what the Alamo has come to represent: collective courage in the face of insurmountable odds.

Plans are in the works for a new visitor center and a museum that will showcase a remarkable collection of Alamo-related artifacts gathered over decades and donated by British drummer, Genesis frontman, and lifelong Alamo enthusiast Phil Collins. Introduced to the Battle of the Alamo as a young child by the 1950s TV series *Davy Crockett: King of the Wild Frontier*, Collins became hooked and went on to amass over 200 Alamo and Texana items, including Davy Crockett's rifle, several Mexican muskets and musket balls, and an IOU written by William Travis, who used the signed scrap of paper to settle his debt for supplies in the cashless Wild West.

MEMORIAL TO THOSE WHO DIED AT THE BATTLE OF THE ALAMO IN 1836

THE MISSIONS The **San Antonio Missions** (210-932-1001; www.nps.gov/saan), now a national park, were built in the 1700s as part of Spain's efforts to colonize Texas, which was then its northern frontier. The idea was to build self-sustaining communities, patterned after villages in Spain, that would provide support for continued colonization as well as formal education for Native Americans in the ways and religion of the country that now considered them subjects. While some Native Americans met the idea with resistance, others acquiesced, and construction began. The five expansive San Antonio missions were built in just 13 years, with *presidios*, or military outposts, established nearby for protection.

One of the extraordinary features of the missions are the *acequias*—aqueducts and irrigation ditches—running between them. While the Pueblo in New Mexico had already designed and built aqueducts, this technology would have been unknown to the nomadic Native Americans in Central Texas. Desperate to irrigate the arid land, the Franciscan missionaries, familiar with the aqueducts built by the Romans and the Moors, designed the system, part of which is still in use and can be seen at various locations along the Mission Trail, including Espada Park near Mission San José.

With housing, water, and farming in place, the missions functioned relatively well from 1745 to the 1780s. Over time, though, attacks and looting by Native Americans, lack of recruits, and disease took their toll; in 1794 a decree from the government ordered the secularization of all missions, disbanding their communal structure.

Throughout the years, the missions have endured the passing of time, weather, and some misguided attempts at restoration. Though many of the details you see today are actually painstaking reproductions, the sheer beauty and scale of the endeavor is impressive.

Today, the individual missions are active parishes, with many descendants of the original parishioners among their members. Though visitors are welcome to attend Mass, the Park Service reminds guests to be respectful of weddings, funerals, or other functions, which may temporarily close the venue for several hours.

Leaving San Antonio and following signs for the Mission Trail, the first property you'll come to along Missis Road is **Mission Concepción** (210-534-1540; www.nps.gov/ saan) at the corner of Felisa. A stone church bookended by a pair of bell towers, Mission Concepción is a spectacular example of Spanish Colonial architecture, with intricate details, artwork, and design adaptations that illustrate the close relationship between the Native American, Spanish, and Mexican artisans who built it. Colorful and detailed frescos once covered both the front and interior of the church. While only a handful have survived the 250 years since they were created, those that do remain are a testament to the craftsmanship and artistry of their makers. Mission Concepción hosted many religious festivals, celebrations, pageants, and processionals, all designed to school new Spaniards in the ways of Christianity.

MISSION SAN JOSÉ

A few miles south is **Mission San José** (210-932-1001; www.nps.gov/saan), home to the Park Service's **Visitor Center.** Founded in 1720 by Father Antonio Margil de Jésus, its complex of bastions, a granary, and a church, surrounded by stone walls, was completed in 1782. Elaborate design features, such as the intricately carved wooden doors, poignant statuary, and ornate Ventana de Rosa ("rose window"), earned Mission San José the reputation of "Queen of the Missions." A thriving community of 300 souls in its heyday, Mission San José was a model of success for the other missions.

It is still a very active parish, and visitors are welcome to attend Mass on Sunday. The noon "Mariachi Mass" is very popular; doors close once seats are filled, so plan on arriving early.

Next in line is **Mission San Juan Capistrano** (210-534-0749; www.nps.gov/saan), founded in 1716 in what is now East Texas and moved to its present location in 1731. This mission is best remembered for its remarkable productivity, with orchards and gardens in its adjacent *labores* (farmlands designated for the

MISSION SAN JUAN CAPISTRANO

mission's use) and herds of sheep and cattle. By the mid-1700s, Mission San Juan was a major supplier of produce not just to the local area, but to markets as far away as Louisiana and Mexico.

Duck under I-410 and make your way to **Mission San Francisco de la Espada** (210-627-2021; www.nps.gov/saan), the very first mission in Texas, originally founded in East Texas in 1690 and moved to San Antonio in 1731. The present-day building, completed in 1756, is clearly recognizable by its graceful *espadaña* (bell tower), with three bells, which rises above its unique arched doorway; be sure to ask a park ranger about the mystery of its design. The wooden cross beside the door, as the story goes, was borne by parishioners in procession while praying for rain. The diminutive and detailed chapel is intimate and tranquil. Mission Espada's *acequia madre* (the main aqueduct) and nearby Espada Dam, built in the 1730s, are both still in use.

Casa Navarro State Historic Site (210-226-4801; www.visitcasanavarro.com) is a complex of white limestone, clay, and adobe structures, once home to prominent Tejano businessman, statesman, and writer José Antonio Navarro, and of interest to anyone wanting to dig a little deeper into the complexities of Texas history. Navarro, who was born in 1795 and died in 1871, witnessed the most significant years in Texas history. He was one of the signers of the Texas Declaration of Independence in 1836 and a tireless defender of Tejano rights.

You can see the bell towers of the **San Fernando Cathedral** (210-227-1297; www.sfcathedral.org) a few blocks away. Established in 1731 by just over a dozen families from the Canary Islands, the cathedral that was designed to be in the center of town has certainly been the center of drama over the years. Jim Bowie was purportedly

MISSION SAN FRANSCISCO DE LA ESPADA

LA VILLITA

Perched above the San Antonio River is the city's first neighborhood, La Villita (210-207-8610; www.getcreativesanantonio.com), "little village." First, the Coahuiltecan Indians settled here. Later, Spanish soldiers built huts, which were washed away in a flood in 1819 and replaced with more substantial dwellings made of stone, adobe, and brick. In 1836 General Santa Anna used the area for his cannons in the Battle of the Alamo. In the late 1800s Germans and French immigrated to the area and brought with them their own architectural style, hence the Victorian elements still seen in La Villita. In the early 20th century the neighborhood fell into disrepair, but by the late 1930s talk of the Riverwalk project brought renewed interest in San Antonio's historic past, and La Villita was preserved as the urban center grew around it. These days, La Villita is called an artist community, though it feels more like one gift shop after the next. The area is pleasant, a welcome detour from the city's busy streets, and its Arneson Theatre (see page 108) is well known for hosting music and cultural performances.

married there. Santa Anna used it as a lookout post and from its walls raised the flag that signaled the start of the Battle of the Alamo. The huge Gothic Revival–style cathedral you see today, built in 1868, integrates the original structure into its plan. In 1871 the original massive dome ceiling collapsed to be later rebuilt. In the 1930s, human remains uncovered on-site, thought to be those of Bowie, Davy Crockett, and William Travis, were laid to rest in a marble casket at the back of the church. After Texas joined the US in 1845, the strong ties between San Fernando Cathedral and the community it served survived; they are still vital today, making the cathedral one of the most important, lasting Hispanic institutions in a rapidly changing city and state.

San Fernando Cathedral is host to music, concerts, and interdenominational events, and doubles as a community center and social services headquarters. In order to preserve the historic structure and add much-needed space for functions, San Fernando is currently raising funds for a massive renovation project scheduled to begin in the near future. A parish church, San Fernando conducts hundreds of baptisms, weddings, and funerals each year: If your visit coincides with one, the church respectfully asks that you return at a different time. The best way to visit just might be by attending Mass; see the website for details.

Across the street, the **Spanish Governor's Palace** (210-224-0601; www.spanishgovernorspalace.org), a National Historic Landmark, was actually the

THE DRAMATIC FACADE OF SAN FERNANDO CATHEDRAL

QUIRKY MUSEUMS

There are several museums in San Antonio that, depending on your interests, may intrigue.

Buckhorn Saloon and Museum and Texas Ranger Museum (210-247-4000; www.buckhornmuseum.com) If you're not into alcohol and taxidermy this place may not appeal, but if you are, it's neat. The entrance is at the bar, and from there you can wander, drink in hand, into the museum, where all sorts of Wild West memorabilia share billing with the mounted heads of a wide variety of animals. Just in case you didn't think it was odd enough, check out the Curio Store.

O. Henry House Museum (www.ohenryhouse.org) A glimpse into the world of William Sidney Porter, who lived in this 1886 Queen Anne–style cottage from 1893 to 1895; but die-hard O. Henry fans will find the O. Henry Museum in Austin more satisfying (see page 42).

residence and headquarters of the presidio captain who was to watch over the Mission San Antonio de Valero—the Alamo. Built in the early 1700s, the building is the only surviving example of a Spanish aristocratic home in the US. A small, white stucco building with very low ceilings and doorways, the abode is graceful in its simplicity; a small courtyard, fountain, and period furnishings lend themselves to the atmosphere, as does *La Compañía de Cavallería del Real Presidio de San Antonio de Béxar,* the living history group that gives performances on the final Sunday of each month.

SPANISH GOVERNOR'S PALACE

MUSEUMS The **Institute of Texan Cultures** (ITC) (210-458-2300; www.texancultures.com) was originally designed as a collection of exhibits for the Texas pavilion of the HemisFair held in San Antonio in 1968. The ITC is best described as an education center highlighting the contributions of the state's vastly diverse ethnic groups and, as their mission statement states, "the dynamics between cultural history and scientific discovery." Though it was supposed to have only a six-month run, the effort was so well received that the ITC remains open to this day, now under the auspices of the University of Texas at San Antonio. Its exhibits, while fairly low-tech and not particularly flashy, are engaging, thoughtfully put together, and rich with historical detail. The esoteric surprises are fun, such as the small exhibit on the Wendish immigrants who came to Texas from what is now the borderland between Germany and Poland. The staff is particularly knowledgeable and happy to answer questions. The institute hosts the fantastic Texas Folklife Festival every year in June (see "Festivals" on page 135).

INSIDE THE SOUTHWEST SCHOOL OF ART AND CRAFT

Stroll north along a more peaceful stretch of the Riverwalk, and you'll come upon the exquisite **Southwest School of Art and Craft** (210-224-1848; www.swschool.org), built in 1851 as the Ursuline Convent and Academy as part of an effort to renew Texans' interest in the Catholic Church. The Ursuline Academy remained until 1965, when it relocated and sold a portion of its property to the San Antonio Conservation Society, which in turn invited the Southwest School of Art and Craft to take up residency in the early 1970s. Possessing a creative appreciation of the property's beauty and significance, the school extensively renovated the complex while retaining its lovely sense of calm and quiet dignity. The school's gardens, courtyards, and chapel are serene. The graceful buildings were created using a technique known as *pisé de terre*, in which bricks are made by forcing clay, rock, and straw into wooden forms, allowing them to dry, and then skim-coating with plaster—it is the inspiration for modern-day rammed-earth construction. The resulting bricks are solid and thick so that they can resist the heat of the sun, and, when combined with creaky wooden floors, make for a very atmospheric interior. The structures are designated as a Texas Historic Landmark and are on the National Register of Historic Places. The Copper Kitchen Café (210-224-0123) serves simple, healthy meals, and its dining rooms have an austere beauty that harks back to convent days; the Gift Gallery (210-224-1848) has unique artistic gifts; the History Museum (210-224-1848) offers docent tours of the property on weekdays; and the annual Fiesta Arts Fair is a much-anticipated kickoff event for Fiesta San Antonio in April (see "Festivals" on page 135).

Tightly knit Southtown has a growing number of galleries and creative shops, all within easy walking distance of one another. The highly respected **San Angel Folk Art Gallery** (210-226-6688; www.sanangelfolkart.com), in the **Blue Star Arts Complex** (www.bluestarart.org), displays a very nice selection of folk art pieces created by artists living in the US, Mexico, and Europe. Also in Blue Star, **StoneMetal Press** (210-627-8170; www.stonemetalpress.com) displays works on paper, and **Garcia Art Glass** (210-354-4681; www.garciaartglass.com), nearby on South Alamo, sells vividly colored handblown art glass.

Continuing north and slightly east along the Museum Reach extension of the Riverwalk, the **San Antonio Museum of Art** (SAMA) (210-978-8100; www.samuseum.org) inhabits the large, industrial, almost fortress-like facilities of the former Lone Star Brewery. The bulk of the museum's holdings results from the combination of two major collections: the Stark-Willson Collection and another collection bequeathed by Gilbert M. Denman Jr. The SAMA is noted for its outstanding collection of ancient Egyptian, Near Eastern, Greek, and Roman art; it is the largest collection of antiquities in the US. Remarkable ivory carvings, detailed mummy masks, a flask with snake-shaped threads at its opening, and a camel cosmetic case are all good examples. The museum's Nelson A. Rockefeller Center for Latin American Arts has over 10,000 pieces in its collection. Pre-Columbian art, mostly from the first millennium A.D., is well represented, and there is plenty of Spanish Colonial art, particularly that which is religious in nature. For some, though, it is the pieces of folk art that really stand out—such as a fascinating display of colorful jaguar masks used in religious rituals from pre-Columbian days through the colonial era and still used in the villages of southern Mexico during certain celebrations. That it has endured for this long illustrates the staying power of imagery and its adaptability under outside influences and changing times. From the Riverwalk, take the #11 VIVA "Culture" bus (www.viainfo.net), a river taxi (www.riosanantonio.com), or rent a bicycle (sanantonio.bcycle.com).

INTERIOR OF THE SAN ANTONIO MUSEUM OF ART

Located on Broadway, at the edge of Brackenridge Park (see pages 114–115), the **Witte Museum** (210-357-1900; www.wittemuseum.org) has a story or two to tell. Remarkably, San Antonio's natural history museum was born through the perseverance of a local schoolteacher. Botanist and high school teacher Ellen Schulz managed to raise $5,000 in the 1920s and purchase a large group of specimens, which were then put on display at the high school. An appeal to the city for assistance in building a proper museum yielded public funding and a $65,000 donation from a local businessman, Alfred G. Witte, who requested that the planned museum be built in Brackenridge Park and named for his parents. The Witte Museum subsequently opened its doors in 1926. In the 1970s the museum hired an art historian as director, and its focus began to shift, leading to the purchase and renovation of an old brewery to house its rapidly expanding collection of art and culminating in 1981 in the formation of the San Antonio Museum of Art (see above), an entity that would become independent in 1994.

Refocused on its original mission, the Witte is now a museum dedicated solely to the history, cultures, ecology, and science of South Texas. The curious are rewarded by full-scale dinosaur skeletons (including the enormous Acrocanthosaurus, whose footprints were found at nearby Government Canyon State Natural Area—see page 116), life-sized re-creations and detailed dioramas depicting what life may have been like for Native Americans in the Lower Pecos region, and elaborate displays of the many habitats and ecological zones represented in the Lone Star state, including deciduous forest, grassland, desert, mountains, brushland, and the tropics. The museum has undergone a much-needed expansion and now encompasses several buildings and courtyards, and is separated from Brackenridge Park by a narrow section of the San Antonio River.

After a day of saying, "Please don't touch that, honey, this is a museum" and "Please don't climb on that; it is very fragile and of great historical significance," doesn't a museum for kids sound great? At the **DoSeum** (210-212-4453; www.thedoseum.org), San Antonio's children's museum, kids can be kids, and all you have to do is just sit back and watch. Even with plenty of high-tech exhibits illuminating math, music, and such scientific mysteries as light and sound, kids seem to gravitate to the tried-and-true thrills of operating the cash registers in the model grocery store, sitting in the real-life airplane, or splashing around in the outdoor water features. Conveniently located across the street from Brackenridge Park and other family-friendly attractions, the DoSeum is an engaging good time.

Broadway continues north, merging with New Braunfels Avenue at the location of the wonderful **McNay Art Museum** (210-824-5368; www.mcnayart.org). The first modern art museum in Texas, the McNay is located in the Spanish Colonial Revival–style mansion of art lover Marion Koogler McNay. Upon her death in 1950, she bequeathed the mansion, the gorgeous 23 acres on which it sits, the extensive art collection housed within it, and two-thirds of her fortune to the city of San Antonio, which opened the entire estate as a museum in 1954. A serious collector, Mrs. McNay had a wonderful eye; the museum houses some real gems, most of them American or European pieces from the 19th and 20th centuries. There are bold paintings by Paul Gauguin and Vincent van Gogh, watercolors by Mary Cassatt and Winslow Homer, and collections of pieces in various mediums that McNay acquired on trips to artist colonies in New Mexico in the 1930s. Over the years, gifts by various collectors have added major paintings by Georgia O'Keeffe and sculptures by Auguste Rodin and Alberto Giacometti, among others. In 1984 Robert L. B. Tobin donated a collection of 8,000 books, many on the theater arts, which are now part of a research library that bears his name. The Blanche and John Leeper Auditorium was completed in the early 1990s, paving the way for performances and concerts to be held at the museum. In many ways, the McNay is best known for the breadth and depth of the outstanding national exhibitions it is able to attract and host in its galleries in a given year. All told, it's a lovely museum, inside and out.

THE PERFORMING ARTS San Antonio's love of both the performing arts and urban revitalization is on display with the new **Tobin Center for the Performing Arts**

PENSIVE STATUE IN FRONT OF THE MCNAY ART MUSEUM

(210-223-8624; www.tobincenter.org). Voters approved a $100 million bond, the city donated the property—a derelict public auditorium valued over $40 million—and donors chipped in an additional $50 million to bring the project to fruition. Home to many of San Antonio's own performing arts organizations, the Tobin Center is also a tour stop for big names in music, dance, and comedy.

San Antonio is also home to a number of historic and atmospheric theaters and cultural centers; most are multipurpose performing arts centers.

Arneson Theatre (210-207-8610; www.getcreativesanantonio.com) The Arneson hosts events in its outdoor amphitheater on the banks of the Riverwalk at La Villita. Diverse offerings include the **Fiesta Noche del Rio** (www.fiestanochesa.com), a summer celebration of song and dance from Mexico, Spain, Argentina, and Texas, put on by the Kiwanis Club with all proceeds benefiting local charities.

ARTS San Antonio (210-226-2891; www.artssa.org) ARTS San Antonio brings an invigorating roster of dancers, musicians, poets, and performers to stages throughout the city.

The Blue Star Arts Complex (210-227-6960; www.bluestarart.org), or Blue Star for short, is both a building and a community. Blue Star the building is a historic 1920s warehouse that has been renovated, retrofitted, and readapted to serve as a residential, commercial, and art space, with lofts, studios, and several galleries. This effort was pioneered in 1985 by a community of artists and volunteers bound by their dream of providing exhibition space for contemporary artists; it made a big splash when it opened, and the ripple effects of revitalization were felt throughout its neighborhood, the King William District and neighboring Southtown. Though Blue Star has matured into a sophisticated and sought-after contemporary art venue, one now run by a professional staff, it retains much of the earnestness of its grassroots days. With local, national, and international artists represented across the gamut of painting, etching, photography, and performance art, Blue Star shines brightly in South San Antonio.

Carver Community Cultural Center (210-207-7211; www.thecarver.org) The Carver Center began as an African American public library in 1929, when segregation mandated separate facilities. The center soon grew into an epicenter of the arts, with performances by many of the greats, such as Ella Fitzgerald, Louis Armstrong, Charlie "Bird" Parker, and Cab Calloway. These days, the Carver is a historic venue that still hosts big-name national and international stars of dance and music, especially jazz.

Empire Theatre (210-226-5700; www.majesticempire.com) Nine feet of water poured into this theater during the flood of 1921, damaging much of its gilded 1890s interior. Over time, the Empire declined, and it closed in the 1970s. Rescued by the city with the help of the Las Casas Foundation, a nonprofit organization responsible for saving some of San Antonio's most historic and treasured cultural institutions, the

CONJUNTO MUSIC

As the Spanish moved across Texas in the early 1800s, they organized dances and concerts featuring the violins, guitars, and *pitos* (a wind instrument) specific to their musical traditions. By the 1860s, the rhythms of the waltzes and polkas of the European court had drifted from Maximillian-ruled Mexico north into Texas and were added to the developing style of *música tejana*, or Tex-Mex music. Then Germans arrived to live and work in South and Central Texas and northern Mexico, bringing with them the diatonic button accordion, the instrument that would revolutionize the music of the area.

Since the accordion allowed for a single musician to play both melody and harmony with one instrument, the popularity of the violins and *pitos* diminished. By the late 1880s, the *tambora de ranch* (goatskin drum) and the *bajo sexto* (12-string guitar) were added to the accordion to give more depth and complexity to the sound. By the 1900s, *música norteña* was played all over ranches and farms of South Texas and northern Mexico and at the *fandangos*—get-togethers featuring eating, dancing, and gambling—closely identified with working-class Tejanos.

In the early 1900s, as Tejanos moved to cities, they took their accordions with them and continued to play *conjunto* at home, parties, and neighborhood events. During the 1930s virtuoso Narciso Martínez, known as the father of modern *conjunto*, and San Antonian Santiago Jimenez popularized the genre through recordings and radio broadcasts. The legendary Tejana singer of this era, Lydia Mendoza, also known as the "queen of Tejano," sang her way to fame in the plazas of San Antonio.

In the 1940s and 1950s, singer Valerio Longoria layered lyrics over the accordion, playing what would become known as *canciones rancheras*. These "ranch songs" were nostalgic pieces whose lyrics of love, loss, and simpler times resonated deeply with listeners. As *conjunto* matured, it never strayed far from its Tejano roots. Touring and playing for large groups along the migrant trail between Mexico and the US in the 1950s and '60s, Tony de la Rosa added amplifiers to what had by then become the standard quartet: accordion, *bajo sexto*, bass, and drums.

In more recent memory, individual musicians have left their mark. Paulino Bernal, Roberto Pulido, and Rubén Vela each added his own innovations in the 1960s. Leonardo (Flaco) Jimenez, son of Santiago Jimenez, took the music to more mainstream audiences throughout the US and Europe, to much acclaim. The very open-minded Esteban Jordán stretched the limits of the genre, and his followers, such as Inocencia and Emilio Navaira and Río, have added saxophones, keyboards, and synthesizers, creating the new sounds of *conjuntos orquesta*.

San Antonio has long been the epicenter of *conjunto* music in Texas, and each May the Guadalupe Cultural Arts Center brings some of the biggest names and greatest talents to the city for the spectacular Tejano Conjunto Festival (see "Festivals" on page 135). The event draws crowds of thousands of fans and features an outstanding lineup of top-notch musicians, including such luminaries as Fred Zimmerle, Eva Ybarra, Lupita Rodela, and Laura Canales, as well as some of the musicians mentioned above. *Conjunto* music is sometimes referred to as *música alegre*, or happy music; after just a few notes you'll know why.

Empire reopened in 1998, restored to its original glory. Due to its outstanding acoustics, the Empire Theatre hosts mostly music.

Guadalupe Cultural Arts Center (210-271-3151; www.guadalupeculturalarts.org) The Guadalupe, as it is known, aims to "preserve, promote, and develop the arts and culture of the Chicano/Latino/Native American peoples for all ages and backgrounds" through the performing arts. And it certainly does. Among other things, the organization presents the city's annual CineFestival and Tejano Conjunto Festival (see "Festivals" on pages 134–136).

Josephine Theatre (210-320-0514; www.josephinetheatre.org) The Josephine is a small local theater with a lot of chutzpah. When the future of the theater company's 1947 art deco digs became uncertain in 2003, the spunky little company raised enough money to buy the building and continued right along, producing high-energy, feel-good musicals.

Jump-Start Performance Company (210-227-5867; www.jump-start.org) Jump-Start recently staged *The Return of the Shrew*, a contemporary takeoff on *Taming of the Shrew* that involved lots of outrageous outfits and madcap escapades, as do most of their productions. Each year, Jump-Start and writer Sandra Cisneros pair up to host a special event, always a mélange of entertainment, refreshments, and well-chosen words; see the website for details.

Magik Children's Theatre (210-227-2751; www.magiktheatre.org) This is a terrific theater for children and families. Daytime and evening shows change monthly, each production as free-spirited and whimsical as the next.

Majestic Theatre (210-226-5700; www.majesticempire.com) The impossibly ornate Majestic Theatre was built in 1929, sadly closed in the 1970s, then triumphantly renovated and reopened in 1989. The Majestic has an enticing roster, ranging from Broadway shows to ballet and classical to contemporary music.

San Antonio Dance Umbrella (210-212-6600; www.sadu.org) This city organization promotes, encourages, supports, and hosts all aspects of dance in San Antonio. Its comprehensive website lists all dance performances throughout the city.

San Antonio Living History Association (www.sanantoniolivinghistory.org) A group of dedicated volunteers performs action-packed reenactments of historic battles, including the one for the Alamo. The events are interesting, free, and infrequent.

San Antonio Symphony (210-554-1010; www.sasymphony.org) For many years after its inception in 1939, the San Antonio Symphony traveled a bumpy road fraught with financial difficulties and changing leadership. Today the path is smoother, and music lovers revel in the symphony's sharp performances of a wide-ranging repertoire at the Tobin Center for the Performing Arts.

San Pedro Playhouse (210-733-7258; www.sanpedroplayhouse.com) Actors at the San Pedro Playhouse have been onstage in this Greek Revival–style mansion in San Pedro Park for more than 70 years, putting on everything from *Hair* to *Hamlet*.

Sunken Garden Theater (210-735-0663; www.sanantonio.gov) Another abandoned quarry put to good use, the Sunken Garden Theater is located in Brackenridge Park, next to the Japanese Tea Garden. A lovely open-air venue for comedy, Shakespeare, and music performances.

Texas Talent Musicians Association (210-320-4200; www.tejanomusicawards .com) A nonprofit organization dedicated to promoting more understanding and appreciation of Tejano music, in part through its largest event, the Tejano Music Awards. The list of past winners reads like a Who's Who of the Tejano music scene.

CINEMA **Alamo Drafthouse** (210-677-8500: www.drafthouse.com) The San Antonio branch of this Central Texas–based cinema chain is every bit as fun as the ones in Austin. Great flicks, with great food brought right to your seat. Everything from Angus burgers to fried pickles.

Alamo IMAX Theater (210-247-4629; www.amctheatres.com) The larger-than-life drama of the siege of the Alamo comes alive on this six-story screen accompanied by six-track stereo sound. Highly recommended for those whose Texas history has gotten a little rusty.

✻ To Do

A tremendous online resource for all outdoor recreation in Texas is Texas Outside, www.texasoutside.com.

BICYCLING Bicycling, both road and mountain biking, is big in Central Texas, especially in the Hill Country; helpful websites include:

B-cycle (210-281-0101; sanantonio.bcycle.com)
San Antonio Wheelmen (www.sawheelmen.com)
South Texas Off-Road Mountain Bikers (www.storm-web.org)

BIRD-WATCHING San Antonio is a great spot to catch a glimpse of rare, migratory, and native birds. Online, Texas Parks and Wildlife (www.tpwd.texas.gov) and the Audubon Society of San Antonio (www.saaudubon.org) both offer a wealth of information. See "Suggested References" in the Information chapter for a selection of bird-watching guides.

CAMPING Camping around San Antonio is best accomplished in New Braunfels (see page 189).

FISHING Fishing in Central Texas is excellent, though your best bet is to head west to Medina Lake, north to Canyon Lake or the rivers in New Braunfels, or to a Texas state park where you don't need a license to fish from shore (check www.tpwd.texas .gov for details). See "Attractions, Parks, and Recreation" and "Texas State Parks" in the Hill Country chapter. Other online resources include www.texasoutside.com, www .txfishing.com, and www.austinkayakfishing.com.

GOLF Though Mark Twain once remarked that golf is just "a good walk spoiled," San Antonians seem to like the walk just fine. The dips and rises of the Hill Country lend themselves perfectly to the game, and some of the courses have been built in old, abandoned quarries, a nice reuse of land. With near-constant sunshine and courses ranging from the charming and historic municipal Brackenridge Golf Course to the breathtaking Palmer Course at La Cantera, it is no wonder that San Antonio has become a destination for serious and recreational golfers alike. The courses listed below rank as some of the best; expect to pay $50–$100 and up. For a complete interactive online listing of local courses, visit www.golfsanantonio.org, a nonprofit organization that uses golf to both educate children and enhance charitable giving in San Antonio, or go to www .visitsanantonio.com.

Brackenridge Golf Course (210-226-5612; www.alamocitygolftrail.com) With all the great golf to be had in greater San Antonio, one of the charms of this course is that it has that comfortable, well-worn, communal feel of an old-school municipal course. It was designed in 1915 by the fascinating and charismatic A. W. "Tillie" Tillinghast, who was also the mastermind behind a few of what are now considered classic courses across the country—Newport in Rhode Island, Quaker Ridge in Scarsdale, New York, and his triumphant Baltusrol in Springfield, New Jersey. Golf enthusiasts may enjoy reading about his legacy at www.tillinghast.net.

Canyon Springs Golf Club (210-497-1770; www.canyonspringsgc.com) Canyon Springs is situated on the site of an old homestead, and many of the current buildings are constructed using rocks that were originally part of the 50-mile dry-stack wall encompassing the property. The unique loop design of the course means the scenic views are completely unobstructed.

The Quarry Golf Club (210-824-4500; www.quarrygolf.com) The atmospheric back nine is situated inside an old quarry and surrounded by 100-foot-high walls of rock. Elsewhere there are terrific views of the city, particularly at dusk. From downtown take US 281 out of the city and exit right at Basse Road.

La Cantera Hill Country Resort and Spa (210-558-6500; www.destinationhotels .com) Built high on a hill on the site of the former *La Cantera* limestone quarry, this resort is 20 minutes from downtown but in a world all its own. A golfer's fantasy, the resort boasts two championship 18-hole golf courses that have earned it kudos from national magazines such as *GOLF Magazine* and *Condé Nast Traveler*.

PROFESSIONAL SPORTS **The Alamodome** (210-207-3663 or 800-884-3663; www .alamodome.com) hosts the high school Texas Football Classic in September and the Alamo Bowl in December (see "Festivals" on page 136).

The AT&T Center (210-444-5140; www.attcenter.com) is host to most sporting events in San Antonio. Texans love their sports; in San Antonio, the sport is basketball, thanks to the three-time NBA champion **San Antonio Spurs** (www.spurs.com) and the **San Antonio Silver Stars** (www.stars.wnba.com), the women's basketball team with an enthusiastic following. The **San Antonio Rampage** (www.sarampage.com), the minor league ice hockey team, keeps things chill.

SWIMMING **San Pedro Springs Park** (210-732-5992; www.sanantonio.gov), San Antonio's oldest park (and the second oldest in the nation after Boston Common), is popular today primarily for its swimming area, which consists of a natural spring-fed body of cool water lined with trees and stone walkways.

THEME PARKS One of the reasons Central Texas is such a popular family getaway is the proliferation of amusement, theme, and water parks just outside San Antonio that are also easily accessible from both Austin and the Hill Country. By March or April, all are open for the season; most cut back to weekends only after Labor Day. If possible, consider planning your trip early or late in the season, avoiding July and August, for a more manageable visit; in the summer months the parks can be crowded, their sidewalks sizzling hot, and their food, snacks, and cool drinks expensive. Arriving early in the day helps beat both the throngs and the heat, but some park-goers achieve the same result by arriving in the mid-to-late afternoon, once most everyone else has worn themselves out. Arriving early may also help you snag a decent parking spot, but it won't help you avoid the $10–$15 parking fee. All of the parks recommend you wear comfortable shoes and pack sunscreen, a hat, extra towels, and even a change of clothes. For swimming, proper swimsuits are essential; park-goers in anything else may be turned away. In all cases, purchasing tickets on the Internet tends to save both time and money.

German for "slippery road," **Schlitterbahn** (855-246-0273; www.schlitterbahn.com) is the place for soaking-wet, family-style fun. The park is consistently voted one of the best water parks in the country, and there are some obvious reasons why. The park is expansive, built on two different locations along the Comal River, with shuttle service in between. There are numerous chutes (some spring-fed from the river), beaches, slides, pools, tubs, and playgrounds, all very well designed for a variety of age-appropriate thrills. Adventurers may wait over an hour to ride the Master Blaster, a jet-propelled water roller coaster, while others are perfectly content to float along in tubes on the low waves and currents of The Torrent. While plenty of food and drinks are on sale inside

THE MISSION REACH

For decades, the San Antonio River south of the city languished, flowing along concrete channels through neglected urban areas. In 2008, the Mission Reach Ecosystem Restoration and Recreation Project (www.sanantonioriver.org) set its sights on changing the city's relationship with the southern portion of its river by restoring it to a more natural state. This multiphase project has created the section of the river now known as "Mission Reach."

In what became the nation's largest urban ecosystem restoration project, workers planted 20,000 trees and shrubs representing close to 100 varieties of native vegetation. They sowed wildflowers and native grasses, creating habitats and inspiring birds and butterflies to return by the thousands. They created the stable riverbanks required for flood control and freed the river from its restraints, letting it flow and meander along its natural route. They designed an 8-mile hike and bike path to follow alongside the shoreline, allowing residents and visitors to connect with the city's five historic missions, nature, and each other.

Allow at least three hours to visit the entire park: 1½ to 2 hours at Mission San José and the park's Visitor Center located there, then 30–40 minutes at each of the other three parks. See www.nps.gov for details and maps. The missions are approximately 2 miles apart, a short drive from one to the next. Bicycle rental is available through B-cycle (210-281-0101; sanantonio.bcycle.com), San Antonio's municipal bike sharing system. You can even rent a kayak at Mission Kayak (210-849-2958; www.missionkayak.com) and enjoy a paddle along parts of the river. Since the park is spread out over several sites, each with limited amenities, please plan accordingly—local advice is to bring along plenty of water, some sunscreen, and a hat.

the park, you are actually allowed to bring your own (no alcohol or glass containers, however) into the park, where picnic tables are thoughtfully provided. Schlitterbahn has on-site lodging, which, while modest and well used, is certainly serviceable, with kitchens and barbecue areas for do-it-yourself meals.

Part of the larger Busch Gardens group of Sea World parks across the US, **SeaWorld San Antonio** (210-520-4132; www.seaworldparks.com) is part amusement park, part water park, and part marine life education center. Smaller than the SeaWorld parks in Florida and California, the San Antonio park is more manageable, and tickets are somewhat less expensive. The amusement park includes water rides and roller coasters, all of which spin, drop, propel, twist, or lurch their riders in the name of fun. While Journey to Atlantis will leave you soaking wet, the Steel Eel might just leave you breathless. The water park section of SeaWorld—Aquatica—is tamer, with water slides and wave pools; it's an area easily enjoyed by family members of all ages. Marine life enters the picture, with rare opportunities to interact with the animals, or sit back and watch elaborate shows. Amid animal welfare concerns, SeaWorld has shifted its focus from theatrical shows to new experiences and presentations focusing on education and conservation.

The name says it all. This is **Six Flags Fiesta Texas** (210-697-5050; www.sixflags.com), not Disney, so expectations should be adjusted accordingly. The park is designed with rides for smaller children scattered in and among those for adults, making it easier for families to stay together and stay sane. Crowd-pleasers include the mile-long, super-smooth Superman Krypton roller coaster and the soaking wet Texas Tree House, with its cowboy and his ominous 1,000-gallon hat. Award-winning shows and music performances, many of which retain a Texas twang, are fun, as are the holiday-themed events. While it might be nice to have a little less Tweety Bird—who came to stay when Warner Brothers bought the Six Flags group—the park is still a Texas good time.

Much more low-key than its high-energy neighbors, **Splashtown** (210-227-1400; www.splashtownsa.com) is a small, fun, easygoing water park just a few minutes north of San Antonio. Perfect for preschool and young children, Splashtown has a wave pool, huge slides, a water bobsled, and the gently flowing Siesta del Rio waterway for tubing.

TOURS SegCity (210-224-0773; www.segcity.com) Tours on this self-balancing, motorized two-wheel contraption are rumored to be great fun, but be prepared for plenty of stares. Variety of tours daily.

Rio San Antonio Tours (210-244-5700 or 800-417-4139; www.riosanantonio.com) Narrated cruises lasting 35–40 minutes and covering 2.5 miles of Riverwalk. Tickets available online or at ticket booths at the Rivercenter Mall (Commerce Street and Bowie Street), Holiday Inn Riverwalk (St. Mary's and College Streets), and under the Market Street Bridge at Alamo Street. All ticket booths are near elevators for handicapped access. Rio San Antonio also runs a water taxi (see "Transportation" on page 93). Open: Daily 9 AM–9 PM.

Texas Trolley Hop (800-804-9486; www.sanantoniotours.net) Two 60-minute double-decker bus tours departing from the Alamo Visitor Center beside the Alamo. With the Hop Pass, visitors are allowed to use the trolley services all day.

TUBING Nearby New Braunfels and historic Gruene offer outstanding tubing on the pretty Guadalupe and Comal Rivers. See pages 188–189.

✳ Outdoor Activities

The **San Antonio Botanical Garden** (210-536-1400; www.sabot.org) and Lucille Halsell Conservatory are located north of the city, just a few blocks east of Broadway near the Witte Museum and Brackenridge Park and en route to the McNay Art Museum. The entrance to the 33-acre property is through the stone Daniel Sullivan Carriage House, which was built in 1896 and moved, stone by stone, to its present location in 1988. The building also houses a gift shop and a small, casual restaurant offering simple, healthful, and filling dishes, some of which come garnished with fresh, edible flowers.

The botanical garden is fascinating for flower enthusiasts, and though the variety and volumes of blooms you see will depend on the time of year you visit, there is something flowering year-round in the warm Texas climate. One of the most fascinating gardens here is the Garden for the Blind, centered on a gurgling fountain and planted with flowers and plants known for their smells and textures, such as the fragrant "root beer plant" and fuzzy lamb's ears, all labeled in braille on metal markers.

A highlight of any trip is bound to be the award-winning Lucile Halsell Conservatory, designed by the noted Argentinean architect Emilio Ambasz and opened in 1988. The conservatory is actually a complex of glass structures in which plants grow in their natural ecosystems; each is designed to re-create various climates from around the world. The building regulates the environments through the ingenious use of light and heat, and the results are wonderful to wander through.

San Antonio and Kumamoto, Japan, are sister cities, and gardeners came from Japan to San Antonio to help design the authentic and lovely Kumamoto En Japanese Garden, jam-packed with highly symbolic plants, structures, materials, and gestures. The double granite bridge clearly connotes mutual respect, understanding, and friendship.

Brackenridge Park (210-207-7275; www.sanantonio.gov) is a 343-acre urban park 2 miles north of downtown San Antonio, beside and behind the Witte Museum on

A WELCOME SIGHT ON A HOT DAY

Broadway. The park first opened in 1899, and it has aged gracefully since then. Home to the popular San Antonio Zoo, the tranquil Japanese Tea Garden and neighboring Sunken Garden Theater, and the Brackenridge Golf Course, the park is also dotted with play structures, picnic tables, and ball fields. The San Antonio River, which flows from an artesian spring just north of the park, meanders through, as do shady paved walking paths.

The **San Antonio Zoo** (210-734-7184; www.sazoo.org), like many zoos in America, is continuously restructuring both the physical space and the philosophy of keeping animals in captivity. The zoo's master plan will transform it into five zones, each representing a different continent and its respective ecosystems. While the zoo is still enacting this plan, and some of the facility feels old-school by today's standards, the new Africa Live! exhibit is quite dynamic and features animals in their natural habitat, surrounded by native plants and with much more room to roam; its "African Plains" extend around a man-made watering hole, from which various species come and go freely. Additionally, the barnyard-themed petting zoo is fun for tykes, and the butterfly exhibit, rebuilt after a 45-foot-tall red oak tree toppled over and destroyed it in 2005, is of particular local interest. Opened in 2000, Cranes of the World is a verdant environment for all sorts of cranes, including the endangered whooping crane. The *Brackenridge Zoo Eagle,* a replica of an 1863 Central Pacific Huntington steam engine, pulls a miniature train filled with children around a several-mile track through adjacent Brackenridge Park (210-735-7455; hours vary seasonally). Wear comfortable shoes for walking, and take a cue from the animals and drink lots of water.

The **Japanese Tea Garden** (210-212-4814; www.sanantonio.gov), situated in what was once an abandoned rock quarry, has been utterly transformed into one of the most lush and peaceful places in San Antonio. The park was the brainchild of City Parks Commissioner Ray Lambert, who about a hundred years ago came up with the wacky

ENTRANCE TO THE SAN ANTONIO ZOO

plan of creating a "lily pond" in a quarry. Turns out that where there's a will, there's a way—especially if you are a penny-pincher. Lambert used prison labor to shape the rocks into paths. He asked city residents and companies to donate supplies and plants. He used palm fronds from city trees to roof the pagoda. In the end, he had spent only $7,000 when the park opened in 1919. The park got a $1.5 million facelift in 2008, its year-round gardens, koi ponds, bridges, 60-foot waterfall, and shaded paths all restored to tip-top shape. Next door, the outdoor Sunken Garden Theater (see "The Performing Arts" on page 110) is known for its Shakespeare productions.

Five and a half miles of trails weave throughout the hilly and heavily wooded 232-acre **Friedrich Wilderness Park** (210-207-3781; www.sanantonio.gov), an oasis in otherwise rapidly urbanizing Bexar County. A nesting area for the endangered black-capped vireo and the golden–cheeked warbler, the park is a popular spot for both birders and hikers, and its paths are clearly marked and designated by difficulty levels 1–4. All grade 1 trails are accessible by wheelchairs and strollers. First Saturday Interpretive Hikes take place on the first Saturday of each month. Two additional natural areas offering trails and fresh air near San Antonio are Medina River Natural Area and Crown Ridge Canyon Natural Area. See www.sanaturalareas.org for details on all San Antonio natural areas.

Located just outside San Antonio, the **Government Canyon State Natural Area** (210-688-9055; www.tpwd.texas.gov) was purchased in 1993 and opened to the public for the first time in the fall of 2005. Trails are still being blazed through the park's 8,600 acres, but some are completed and ready for use, as are picnic areas and restrooms.

While you cannot swim in the 600-acre **Mitchell Lake** (210-628-1639; mitchelllake.audubon.org) you can spot, if you're lucky, more than 300 species of birds as you hike its protected wetland trails. Managed by the Audubon Society of Texas, the lake is somewhat off the beaten track, but worth the trip for birders and nature lovers.

Talk to a native of San Antonio and they'll say that while the amusement parks are fun, **Natural Bridge Caverns** (210-651-6101; www.naturalbridgecaverns.com) is really fascinating. A National Natural Landmark, this place will exercise your vocabulary, reminding you that stalactites hang down, stalagmites rise up, and a sluice is a series of troughs leading from a water-filled tower. The standard North Cavern Tour is an informative 75 minutes that will take you a half mile underground. The very challenging Adventure Tour is open to only the physically fit, who will enjoy the challenge of hours climbing, crawling, and rappelling in a room that is otherwise off-limits. Kids will love the Watchtower Challenge, a massive outdoor climbing wall with two zip lines, and the chance to pan for treasure.

TORCH OF FRIENDSHIP, CREATED BY MEXICAN ARTIST SEBASTIÁN AND DONATED TO THE PEOPLE OF SAN ANTONIO BY THE PEOPLE OF MEXICO IN 2002

✳ Lodging

Since much of the activity in San Antonio revolves around the Riverwalk, it is no surprise that many visitors spend the night as close as possible to the water. While the area is dominated by large chain hotels, boutique hotels just blocks away offer variety. One of San Antonio's best-kept secrets is its network of bed and breakfasts scattered throughout the historic neighborhoods, just minutes from the city center. The San Antonio B&B Association, or SABBA (www .sanantoniobb.org), is a self-regulating group that ensures standards are kept up. Unlike chain hotels, however, B&Bs frequently require a two-day minimum stay on weekends, possibly more during holidays. Prices tend to rise and fall with the seasons.

When choosing an area of town, keep in mind that the Riverwalk tends to stay open late for dining and drinking, and people like to visit San Antonio to have a good time. If you are used to city sounds, the resulting noise level may not bother you, but if you require silence to sleep, you might consider a hotel in a quieter neighborhood several blocks away or a B&B with strictly enforced quiet hours. In addition, downtown hotels often charge hefty parking fees; be sure to inquire when making your reservation.

Guests with limited mobility may find the larger hotels to be the best fit, especially those along the Riverwalk, where they may have elevator access to the walk itself. The city's B&Bs are located in older homes that cannot always be retrofitted appropriately, but that said, if a certain property catches your eye, by all means call and inquire, as special arrangements can sometimes be made.

DOWNTOWN AND RIVERWALK

La Mansión Del Rio (210-518-1000; www .omnihotels.com), 112 College St. The distinctive building, once a Catholic school, dates back to 1852, and its hacienda-style courtyards, lush vegetation, and bubbling fountains exude the charm of a bygone era. Details such as exposed ceiling beams and brick walls capture the look and feel of old San Antonio. As with all older hotels, room sizes vary, ranging from spacious to cozy. The on-site restaurant, Las Canarias, serves a memorable Sunday brunch buffet that you can enjoy outside on the tiled veranda or inside in the atmospheric dining rooms. $$$.

Mokara Hotel and Spa (210-396-5800; www.mokarahotels.com), 212 W Crockett St. This place impresses guests with a combination of luxury and a slow-down-and-smell-the-roses friendliness. The hotel is stylish and sophisticated, with plenty of thoughtful touches, great service, and attention to detail. Rooms are spacious and airy, with simple furnishings and comfortable beds. Bathrooms have a separate Jacuzzi tub and shower, with big, fluffy robes and slippers at the ready. There is a full-service spa for pampering, a pool for relaxing, and a bowl of fresh fruit in the lobby. Mokara is pricey, but guests claim it's worth the splurge. $$$$.

Hotel Valencia (210-227-9700; www .hotelvalencia-riverwalk.com),150 E Houston St. Modern and hip, this boutique hotel isn't just a building, it's architecture. The Valencia is stylish, sophisticated, dramatic, and dimly lit. The down comforters, pillows, and seven layers of Egyptian cotton linens on each bed are thick and luxurious, and the sparse, uncluttered decor feels refreshing and romantic. Outdoor space is limited, with no pool and a tiny "balcony" that may best be described as a ledge outside some rooms. The Valencia is on busy Houston Street, so be prepared for some noise. Have a drink at the bar and decide for yourself. $$$.

The Hotel Contessa (210-229-9222; www.thehotelcontessa.com), 306 W Market St. This 12-story, all-suite hotel and conference center is right on the Riverwalk. Each spacious room has a separate parlor (with sleeper sofa) and bedroom, with comfy mattresses and crisp linens, and flat-screen televisions. The Contessa is designed with lots of open space, and noise can travel throughout it, especially on weekends, so consider requesting a room on one of the upper floors if you're a light sleeper. The exercise room is small but adequate, as is the rooftop pool, which comes with super views. Prices vary depending on the view; one features Marriage Island, just behind the property, where San Antonio's first Catholic Mass was held in 1691 and couples still say their nuptial vows today. $$$.

Drury Plaza Hotel San Antonio Riverwalk (210-270-7799; www.druryhotels .com), 105 S St Mary's St. Once home of the Alamo National Bank, the building was completed in 1929 and is now listed on the National Register of Historic Places. The lobby gives you the best sense of the pre-Depression grandeur—travertine floors, bronze framework, marble walls, stained glass windows, and original chandeliers suspended from the 50-foot ceiling. Rooms now occupy what were once offices; strolling the wide hallways it's easy to imagine them bustling with workers. Neat, organized, clean, and family friendly, with a snack and breakfast buffet to boot, this Drury property is a good value on the Riverwalk. $$$.

The Emily Morgan (210-225-5100; www.emilymorganhotel.com), 705 E Houston St., has a coveted location directly across from the Alamo. This tall, wedge-shaped Gothic-revival building built in the 1920s—a former medical facility whose exterior is festooned with ailing gargoyles. While the hotel has been updated, older hotels such as these have idiosyncrasies, such as fickle showerheads, well-worn tiling, and noisy heating systems. Overall, the Emily is a slice of history and character for travelers who prefer homespun hotels to big chains and expect quirks, including, reportedly, ghosts. $$$.

Menger Hotel (210-223-4361; www .mengerhotel.com), 204 Alamo Plaza. On the other side of the Alamo, the Menger, built in 1859, which, like the Emily Morgan, is so steeped in history that there are tales of ghosts haunting its halls. As with most hotels of this vintage, the Menger's front entrance is grand while its rooms and bathrooms are small, especially by today's standards. On the plus side, the beds are comfy, the rooms cozy, the location fantastic, and the courtyard and poolside relaxing. Past guests include Mae West, Babe Ruth, and Teddy Roosevelt, so you can rest easy knowing you're in good company. Another perk is the Menger Bar (see "Drinks" on page 133), built in 1887 as a replica of the

LA MANSIÓN DEL RIO HOTEL ALONG THE RIVERWALK

THE MENGER HOTEL BESIDE THE ALAMO

taproom inside the House of Lords in London and the venue from which T. R. reportedly rustled up his Rough Riders; it's still a fun place for a drink. $$.

Hotel Havana (210-222-2008; www .havanasanantonio.com), 1015 Navarro St. Stylish and hip, this has an old-school vibe and plenty of panache. The hotel was built on a pretty piece of property overlooking the river in 1914 and has maintained its Mediterranean Revival charm ever since. Rooms are simple and serene, with well-worn wood floors, sparse furnishings, white bedspreads, and vintage Cuban artwork on the walls. Spend the night or just stop in for drinks at the Ocho Lounge (see "Drinks" on page 133). $$$.

Hotel Emma (210-448-8300; www .thehotelemma.com), 136 E Grayson St. The standout of the Pearl Complex, this hotel was built in 1881 as the Pearl Brewery's original brewhouse. The grand Second Empire hotel is the namesake of Emma Koehler, the woman whose clever business sense and resourcefulness enabled the brewery to survive both the death of her husband, the brewery's president, and Prohibition, the only San Antonio brewery to do so. Today, the sumptuously renovated hotel has soaring ceilings, wooden beams, exposed brick, wrought iron, and remnants of industrial brewery equipment that hark back to the building's utilitarian roots, but the bedding, bathrooms, sitting areas, and terraces are all luxuriously appointed for comfort. Gorgeous tile, touches, and fixtures—some original, some restored, and others replicas—give the building a seamless style. Bonus features include a rooftop pool, a library, Riverwalk access, and the culinary delights of the Pearl. $$$$.

KING WILLIAM DISTRICT AND SOUTHTOWN

The lovely King William District, just a few blocks' stroll from the river and lively South Alamo Street, is home to several delightful B&Bs.

Ogé House (210-223-2353; www .nobleinns.com), 209 Washington St. Pronounced "oh-jay," this place is nestled among the trees along the banks of the San Antonio River. Built in 1857, this lovely mansion is both listed on the National Register of Historic Places and designated a Texas Historical Landmark. Once the home of Texas Ranger, cattle rancher, and businessman Louis Ogé, the Ogé House embodies the grandeur of bygone Texas, with tall ceilings and windows, verandas on each of its three stories, and fireplaces in many of its rooms. The same owners operate several other luxurious, though much smaller, B&Bs throughout the area; see www.nobleinns .com for details. $$$.

The Brackenridge House (210-271-3442; www.brackenridgehouse.com), 230 Madison St. The neatly kept rooms in this historic home are individually decorated with cheerfully painted walls,

ARCHITECTURAL DETAIL IN THE KING WILLIAM DISTRICT

Eva's Escape at the Gardenia Inn (210-223-5875; www.evasescape.com), 307 Beauregard St. This stunning Greek Revival–style home was built in 1905. The interior features gleaming woodwork set against crisp white walls in rooms decorated with richly colored rugs, upholstery, and artwork. Rooms tend to be large, light, and airy, with lustrous wood floors, antique beds, and deep claw-foot tubs. The Desert Blossom Suite can sleep five guests in its two connected rooms, making it a good choice for families or friends traveling together, and children over 12 are welcome. $$$$.

King William Manor (800-405-0367; www.kingwilliammanor.com), 1037 S Alamo St. This pleasant bed and breakfast is in an 1892 Greek Revival–style mansion expanded in 1901 with a cottage addition. Rooms are casual, comfortable, uncluttered, and slightly modern, with clean lines and cheerful colors. The property includes a breezy veranda and pool, and breakfasts are provided by local eateries. $$.

OUTER SAN ANTONIO

The Hyatt Hill Country Resort and Spa (210-647-1234; www.hillcountry.hyatt .com), 9800 Hyatt Resort Dr. With amenities like a spa, a golf course, a 4-acre water park, pools, numerous restaurants, a slow-moving artificial river for tubing, and pristinely manicured grounds, this place is made for those who like to combine relaxation and recreation, especially families. With so much to do there, you may find you check in and never go out, spending day after day at the pool just lazing around. Once you've worn yourself out, retire to the guest room with its understated earth-tone fabrics, wooden furniture, and sumptuous beds to sleep off the experience. If you visit the Hyatt Hill Country Resort and Spa, be sure to wear pants with deep pockets; with all the additional fees, this place can get pricey. $$$$.

well-chosen antiques, and colorful carpets over hardwood floors. Some rooms have quilts, others have kitchenettes, but they are all cozy as can be. In the morning, breakfast is a three-course affair, served with fancy crystal and china in the dining room and including all sorts of treats to start the day off right, like strawberries with whipped cream, cherry scones, and zucchini, sausage, and cheese mini quiches. $$.

A Yellow Rose Bed and Breakfast (210-229-9903; www.ayellowrose.com), 229 Madison St. The home you see when you walk up is the owner's; the guest rooms are tucked back behind, each with its own door to the porches and garden. The rooms are large—especially the roomy Carriage House Suite, which has two separate beds—and are clean, entirely comfortable, and have an air of familiarity. With large bathrooms, comfy sitting areas, books to peruse, and large beds for lounging, A Yellow Rose feels private and relaxing. Breakfast is not included in the price but is available, so be sure to inquire when you book. $$.

THE TABLE, SET FOR BREAKFAST, AT A LOCAL BED AND BREAKFAST

Weston La Cantera Resort (210-558-6500; www.resortlacantera.com), 16641 La Cantera Pkwy. Built high on a hill on the site of a former limestone quarry—*la cantera*—this is 20 minutes from downtown but in a world all its own. The resort's two world-class golf courses, including the challenging and spectacular Palmer Course, are a big draw, and the patrons who come to play are quite serious about their game. Consequently, the mood doesn't feel quite as relaxed as at the Hyatt. Six pools, tennis courts, spa services, and three hot tubs round out the offerings. For accommodations, you can choose between a typical Westin guest room in the main complex or a *casita,* "little house," in Casita Village. $$$$.

✻ Where to Eat

In a culture of chain restaurants and fast food, San Antonio has a satisfying number of homegrown restaurants and old-time establishments that have been favorites forever, as well as exciting new eateries that diners are always eager to try. In general, the Riverwalk is a mix of high-end restaurants, some of which are real culinary gems, and more predictable eateries catering to out-of-town visitors. In an effort to preserve the historic nature of the Riverwalk, the city of San Antonio has recently sought to limit the number of chain restaurants that can operate on its famed waterside in favor of highlighting local eateries. And you certainly don't have to go far to find restaurants with character and history. Just blocks away, the business section of downtown San Antonio is home to some much-loved standbys, which pack in the locals on lunch breaks. Visitors looking for a memorable dining experience may want to travel the short distance to the artsy King William District or the Alamo Heights neighborhood, where a rise in diversity of both cuisine and clientele makes dining more interesting.

The restaurants below are either local favorites or are frequently and enthusiastically cited as "best of" citywide. San Antonians are justifiably proud of the uniqueness of their city, and they love frequenting the restaurants that contribute something special to the city's culinary scene.

DOWNTOWN AND RIVERWALK

The many convenient eateries lining the Riverwalk are perfectly enjoyable places to stop in; some are even destinations unto themselves. Several of the best downtown restaurants cater to the business lunch crowd.

Chef/owner Bruce Auden, four-time James Beard Award nominee, hit it big with **Biga on the Banks** (210-225-0722; www.biga.com),203 S St Mary's St. Auden's menu changes daily and features plenty of southwestern flavors. Start with the tempura shrimp, paired with chile lime glass noodles, watermelon, peanuts, and mint, and move onto the 11-spiced Hill Country venison and grilled quail, which is served with apple-braised cabbage, grilled eggplant, and juniper sauce. The popular sticky toffee pudding with English custard hints at Auden's roots in Britain. With all entrées averaging $35 and appetizers starting at $9, Biga isn't for everybody every day, but it is a boon for foodies, those celebrating special occasions, and anyone looking for a memorable meal. Reservations recommended.

Boudro's on the Riverwalk (210-224-8484; www.boudros.com), 421 E Commerce St., manages to keep both visitors and locals happy with its cheerful, modern atmosphere and tasty food. The flavors here are big and bold, with hot chiles and Cajun spices used liberally. The guacamole appetizer, made at your table, is as fresh as can be and always a big hit. The big, juicy steaks, Gulf Coast seafood, and the not-to-be-missed prickly-pear margaritas are all a taste of Texas, and the lime chess pie is a knockout. While dinner with drinks, dessert, and tip can easily put you over the $40 per person mark, the lunch menu will set you back just a fraction of that. Altogether, Boudro's is a predictably delicious local favorite for dinner as well as a solid value for a midday meal on the Riverwalk.

Upstairs on Presa Street you'll find Boudro's relative, **Zinc Bistro & Wine Bar** (210-224-2900; www.zincwine.com), 207 N Presa St. A polished bistro that's popular for late-night martinis and apps. The guacamole—assembled tableside from Boudro's recipe—is outstanding, the rustic, gourmet pizzas are fantastic, and the super juicy Zinc Burger, with melted smoky cheddar and spicy tomato aioli, tops the list of diners' favorites. Since Zinc is primarily a wine bar, don't be shy about asking for recommendations. Equal parts trendy and down-to-earth, Zinc's intimate, upscale atmosphere is paired with reasonable prices, making it a fantastic bargain.

Around the corner, you'll find **Schilo's Delicatessen** (210-223-6692; www.schilos.com), 424 E Commerce St. Serving the sort of food necessary to survive hard labor and cold German winters—hearty and economical pea soup, plump kielbasa, pungent krauts, plates of rye bread with butter, and thick, dark beers. In sunny, urban San Antonio an old-style German deli may seem out of place, until you learn that the Schilo family arrived in San Antonio via Poland and Germany in 1914 and has been feeding the good people of this city since 1917. In that time, many of the recipes have remained the same, and the prices seem barely to have matched inflation. In a part of town where a decent breakfast can be hard to come by, Schilo's is a real find, serving diner-style classics like two eggs, bratwurst, your choice of hash browns or grits, biscuits or muffins, and coffee for less than $7. If you are searching for a bit of historic San Antonio, step into Schilo's and split a pitcher of frosty homemade root beer in one of the well-worn wooden booths. In case you need to ask a local for directions, Schilo's is pronounced "she-lows," not "shy-lows."

Private and intimate, the **Fig Tree Restaurant** (210-224-1976; www

TEX-MEX IN SAN ANTONIO

San Antonio is known for its plentiful Mexican and Tex-Mex food. Compared to the established El Mirador, Mi Tierra, and popular Rosario's, the eateries listed below are located somewhat off the beaten tourist path and frequented mostly by locals. From the cloth tablecloths at La Fogata to the paper napkins at Guajillo's, the atmosphere varies widely, but the food is consistently delicious. While every San Antonian has a favorite, the restaurants below always seem to top the list; they are presented here in alphabetical order.

Los Barrios (210-732-6017; www.losbarrios1.com), 4223 Blanco Rd. Does everything so well, from predictably great enchiladas to the more obscure Argentinian *churrasco* steak with chimichurri sauce, that they've put it all in a cookbook.

La Fogata (210-340-1337; www.lafogata.com), 2427 Vance Jackson Rd. Offers fresh, home-made northern Mexican cuisine served in a refined tropical setting. The dessert empanadas are delicious.

La Fonda on Main (210-733-0621; www.lafondaonmain.com), 2415 N Main Ave. Feeding San Antonio since 1931. Tortilla soup, light and flavorful, with tender chicken, fresh avocado, and crispy tortilla strips, exemplifies the menu. An atmospheric dining room and hacienda-style patio make dinner special.

At Guajillo's (210-344-4119; www.guajillos.net), 1001 NW Loop 410, the green *mole*, made with chiles and pumpkin seeds, is a must. A clean, casual, no-nonsense place north of town.

La Hacienda de los Barrios (210-497-8000; www.lhdlb.com), 18747 Redland Rd. In a residential neighborhood north of Loop 1604, this is owned by the enterprising Barrios family (see Los Barrios, above), who bring their well-honed techniques and time-honored recipes to the upscale menu.

Jacala Mexican Restaurant (210-732-5222; www.jacala.com), 606 West Ave. Serves puffy tacos and spinach quesadillas, just as they've done since 1949.

El Jarro de Arturo (210-494-5084; www.eljarro.com), 13421 San Pedro Ave. Offers outstanding upscale Mexican food made with high-quality ingredients, which has made this place a local favorite for decades.

Picante Grill (210-822-3797; www.picantegrill.com), 3810 Broadway St. Across the street from the Witte Museum, makes fabulous fajitas and spicy hot salsa.

.figtreerestaurant.com), 515 Villita St., offers fine dining from its perch near La Villita, high above the noise and crowds of the Riverwalk. The restaurant is located in a graceful, mid-19th-century home, and the elegance continues onto the outdoor terrace, surrounded by lush landscaping and trees festooned with twinkling white lights. The menu matches the ambiance, with delicately seasoned dishes and lovely presentation. Though the filet mignon, New Zealand lamb rack, and wild Tasmanian salmon are fantastic, diners also single out the jumbo Gulf shrimp cocktail, the Gulf lump crab cakes, truffled mashed potatoes, and the bananas Foster for superlatives.

On a quieter stretch of the Riverwalk, **Bella on the River** (210-404-2355; www.bellaontheriver.com), 106 Riverwalk St., is about as charming as they come. This little grotto of a restaurant has stone walls, wooden ceiling beams, candlelight, live music in the evenings, and outstanding Italian cuisine. Dishes are deceptively simple and perfectly prepared. The goat cheese ravioli, butternut squash soup, pasta with sautéed Texas Gulf shrimp, and pistachio cake are all exceptional. Even the bread—served with a little plate of olive oil, rosemary, and sweet roasted garlic—is delicious.

While it may have a classic old-school steakhouse look and feel, **Bonahan's Prime Steaks and Seafood** (210-472-2600; www.bohanans.com), 219 E

Pico de Gallo (210-225-6060; www.picodegallo.com), 111 S Leona St. Owned by the same folks who keep Mi Tierra (see below) going all night long. This restaurant pleases crowds with its simple breakfasts, traditional Mexican dinners, accomplished mariachi band, and in-house bakery.

At **Taco Haven** (210-533-2171; www.tacohavenpresa.com), 1032 S Presa St., everything from the *migas* to the tacos are made delicious by their fresh, homemade tortillas.

Teka Molino (210-344-7281; www.tekamolino.com), 7231 San Pedro Ave. In business since the 1930s and makes up in food for what it lacks in atmosphere. Order at the counter, pick up your meal when it's ready, and dig in to the sort of Mexican food that makes San Antonio proud.

Hot hot sauce, meal-sized appetizers, and margaritas make **Tomatillo's** (210-824-3005; www.tomatillos.com), 3210 Broadway St., a popular happy-hour destination.

Houston St., serves a very modern product. High-quality, Texas-bred Japanese Akaushi beef, prepared and grilled with expert precision over flaming mesquite, takes center stage at Bonahan's, earning the steakhouse a reputation as one of the best in Texas. Outstanding seafood and cocktails play supporting roles on the menu. Pricey, but delighted diners are consistently happy to splurge.

Mi Tierra (210-225-1262; www.mitierracafe.com), 218 Produce Row. Demurely calls itself a café, but this Tex-Mex bakery and restaurant should be called Mi Tierra World. Festive hats and decorations stream from the ceiling, mariachi bands cycle through, and the waiters with overflowing trays of food weave their way in and out of the crowd.

The restaurant is open 24 hours a day, offering a slightly overpriced menu packed with Tex-Mex favorites, and is always bustling, which it has been since it opened in 1941. The bakery, on the other hand, is very reasonably priced, and the lines move quickly. In addition to baked goods such as the traditional pumpkin or sweet potato empanadas (turnovers) or churros (a fried stick of dough often dusted with sugar), there is a pineapple biscuit, which is best likened to a scone, and a pecan praline that is not to be missed. Take a minute to ogle the pastries, cookies, and treats at what feels like a mile-long counter, then order a wide selection to sample as you wander the nearby Market Square.

Branching out from the most touristy spots, stroll along Museum Reach to the **Pearl Brewery Complex** (www.atpearl.com) at the northern reaches of the Riverwalk, or head south to the **King William District** and **Southtown** for delightful—and delicious—dining.

KING WILLIAM DISTRICT AND SOUTHTOWN

King William District and Southtown have some much-loved restaurants that possess as much character and charm as the neighborhood itself.

From the minute you tuck into the chips and salsa, you'll notice something different about **Rosario's** (210-223-1806; www.rosariossa.com), 910 S Alamo St. For instance, instead of the ubiquitous red salsa, Rosario's serves a signature tangy chipotle version that rings true to its deep Mexican roots. Everything on the menu is super fresh and homemade, with a modern sensibility. The *enfrijoladas Santa Clara* (chicken enchiladas with a zippy cumin chile sauce) and the fish tacos are just two of the many favorites that have

diners returning again and again. The restaurant is usually hopping with professionals just off work, couples stopping in for drinks, families with children of all ages, and tourists and residents alike. While it can get a bit loud, Rosario's is also the sort of place where you can have a wonderfully intimate meal while surrounded by the din of happy diners. Consider arriving early to avoid a wait, and as the menu gently reminds diners, good food takes time, so allow for a leisurely meal; the outstanding results, at modest prices, will make you happy you did.

Nearby, **The Friendly Spot** (210-224-2337; www.thefriendlyspot.com), 943 S Alamo St., feels instantly familiar. Imagine a neighbor's backyard get-together—kids running loose, dogs lying around, cold beer, plenty of brightly colored, well-worn, mismatched metal tables and chairs, maybe a game projected on the big screen, and a whole bunch of folks you've just met laughing away the evening—because that's exactly what this "ice house" feels like. You can order chips and guacamole, pulled pork sliders, fish tacos, and beers from a menu as

TREATS AT MI TIERRA CAFÉ

large and diverse as the crowd lounging under the shady trees in this friendliest spot in the city.

Azúca Nuevo Latino (210-225-5550; www.azuca.net), 709 S Alamo St., offers an indoor/outdoor experience of the food, music, and drinks of Central and South America and the Caribbean. While entrées can be pricey, some of the simplest menu offerings are the tastiest. The black bean soup with pico, crunchy chicharrones, and sour cream is delicious, as is the yellowfin tuna with a lime, *aji amarillo*, and green onion marinade. With fresh mojitos and salsa and merengue dancing into the evenings, Azúca is a fun place to spend an evening in Southtown.

La Frite Belgian Bistro (210-224-7555; www.lafritesa.com), 728 S Alamo St. Marries European bistro-style dining with the charm of the King William District, offering a full menu of Belgian cuisine. Belgian cuisine. Who knew? Turns out there are crisp salads, savory crepes and tarts, and a variety of seafood, including succulent mussels. The *mussels marinieres*—with onion, garlic, and white wine—are out of this world, served with a pile of wonderfully crispy fries that are the best of Belgium on a plate. The menu changes seasonally; the $39 prix fixe menu changes daily.

Just a few years ago, the **Liberty Bar** (210-227-1187; www.liberty-bar.com), 1111 S Alamo St., was located on a nondescript street, tucked under an elevated highway, and leaning quite literally and rather dramatically to the left as a result of flood damage. Somehow this suited it just fine, since, while the setting was casual, the food itself was refined—not expensive, fussy, or extravagant, just very simply inspired and wonderfully cooked—and its quirky building was part of its charm. Flash forward, and the Liberty Bar is now happily ensconced in a bright, coral-colored former convent, with the words St. Scholastica inscribed on the lintel over the front door. Again, this suits the Liberty Bar just fine. Diners

haven't missed a beat in the move, arriving for delicious dishes like roasted hazelnut with prosciutto, apples, and Pecorino cheese, *chile relleno en nogada* (a poblano pepper in walnut sauce), lamb burgers, mesquite-grilled smoked pork sausages, pot roast sandwiches, and homemade fettuccine with garlic. The weekend menu is light and delightful, and the wine list at all meals is particularly well considered. Proving you can always "bloom where you're planted," the Liberty Bar is in full blossom on South Alamo Street.

Madhatters Tea House and Café (210-212-4832; www.madhatterstea .com), 320 Beauregard St. A lovely spot for tea and a tête-à-tête, either outside at a bistro table under shade umbrellas or in the armchairs dotting the cheerfully painted and eclectically decorated interior. The inventive menu includes grilled bacon-wrapped artichoke "lollipop" appetizers and entrée salads, including the tea-smoked chicken breast salad with chile roasted pecans and tea vinaigrette and the warm pork tamale salad with a creamy chipotle dressing. Don't be fooled by the humdrum name of the grilled spinach and chicken salad sandwich—it is a signature dish and a favorite of devotees. Saturday breakfast is especially popular; they often run out of the eggs Benedict early. Not surprisingly, Madhatters loves tea parties, and you can order high tea, afternoon tea, or kids' tea served on a three-tiered tea service.

Carl Hilmar Guenther came to America seeking fortune and found it when the flour mill he built in the mid-1800s, Pioneer Flour Mills, prospered. **Guenther House** (210-227-1061; www .guentherhouse.com), 205 E Guenther St. The home Guenther built for his family in the 1860s, a popular restaurant and gift shop live here today. Guenther House serves a lovely lunch, including its champagne chicken enchiladas, but diners are also milling about outside waiting for a table because of the baked goods on the all-day breakfast menu. The

A SIDE OF CHIPS AND SALSA

buttermilk biscuits with sausage gravy, the sweet cream waffles—served with or without strawberries and whipped cream—and the enormous cinnamon rolls and sticky buns are a big draw. Guenther House's art nouveau interior and outdoor garden seating are both special and casual, making it a crowded, family-friendly favorite; you may want to consider eating here off-hours to avoid a long wait.

MUSEUM REACH AND PEARL BREWERY

San Antonio's newest addition to the Riverwalk, **Museum Reach**, was completed in 2009, successfully connecting the downtown portion with the **Pearl Brewery Complex** (www.atpearl.com), a little under a mile and a half to its north. Stop by the **Pearl Brewery Farmers' Market** for fresh produce, flowers, food, and treats every Saturday from 9 AM to 1 PM and Sunday from 10 AM to 2 PM.

Interrupt your stroll along the Riverwalk with a detour to **Ocho Lounge** (210-222-2008; www.havanasanantonio .com) in the Hotel Havana (see page 133), 1015 Navarro St. For breakfast, evening drinks, or anytime tapas-style snacks, try dishes like their Havana papas bravas—roasted poblano peppers, caramelized onions, queso fresco, aioli, and fruita mixta (a mixture of juicy fruits sprinkled with jalapeños , agave nectar, chile powder, and mint). Pretty and chic with great Riverwalk views, Ocho's atmosphere can't be beat.

A French-inspired bakery with a global twist, **Bakery Lorraine** (210-862-5582; www.bakerylorraine.com), 306 Pearl Pkwy #110, has gained national recognition for deliciousness. The husband and wife chefs behind this beloved pâtisserie and viennoiserie in the heart of the Pearl have perfected their signature macarons—Earl Grey, dark chocolate lavender, and lemon—and won over diners with such items as banana, curry, and dark chocolate torte, matcha and black cherry cake, and jasmine crème brûlée, each as gorgeous as it is delicious. Sweet and savory comingle on the menu, and the breakfast pastries, salads, tartines, and quiche make Bakery Lorraine a popular spot from the minute the doors open in the morning.

Chef Steven McHugh, having travelled from a small Wisconsin town to the Culinary Institute of America and from there to acclaimed restaurants in New Orleans and San Antonio, has landed in a wonderfully rustic, refined charcuterie of his own creation: **Cured** (210-314-3929; www.curedatpearl.com),1900 Blanco Rd. Ensconced in the Pearl's original Administration Building, a distinguished brick structure constructed in 1904, Cured carries on the tradition of being all business. Pure, fresh, and local ingredients are stored with scientific precision (behind glass in a humidity-controlled partition in the dining room), handled with expert care, and beautifully presented. A wonderful place for craft cocktails, the charcuterie is a must. Dinner standouts include dishes like pork cheek poutine or roasted bone marrow with escargot, pickled shallots, and hedgehog mushrooms. Don't overlook brunch, which includes chicken and donuts, a delicious riff on a southern classic, dusted with lemon sugar and drizzled with jalapeño syrup. Vegetarians shouldn't be put off; Cured has wonderful vegetable dishes and substantial salads.

Green Vegetarian Cuisine (210-320-5865; www.eatatgreen.com), 200 E Grayson St #120, has made a name for itself as one of the healthiest, tastiest, and friendliest eateries in the city, winning over vegetarians, vegans, and omnivores alike with salads, sandwiches, reworked soul food, and pared-down Tex-Mex favorites. Crowd-pleasers include cauliflower "hot wings" and the portobello "steak" with caramelized onions and mashed potatoes. Be sure to leave room for a cupcake.

Il Sogno Osteria (210-223-3900; www.atpearl.com), 200 E Grayson St #100, pairs upscale Italian cuisine with the trendy Pearl Brewery vibe. While the restaurant itself is a newcomer, owner Andrew Weissman isn't—he has two James Beard Award nominations to prove it. Rustic favorites like osso buco, delicate homemade pastas, and wood-fired pizzas seem elegant at Il Sogno Osteria. The antipasto selection—available in three- or five-dish options—is wonderful, and they have a wine to go with everything; just ask for a recommendation. Save room for the dreamy Nutella tart. Reservations recommended.

On a bluff atop a lovely, quiet stretch of the northern reach of the Riverwalk, between the San Antonio Museum of Art and The Pearl, **The Luxury** (210-354-2274), 103 E Jones Ave., has created a casual hang-out spot from repurposed shipping containers, corrugated metal, wood, and large stone end tables, with white lights strung throughout. Chef Andrew Weissman has stocked the menu with casual favorites. Everyone loves the buttermilk fried chicken sandwiches with jalapeños and coleslaw, the seasoned french fries, and the long craft beer list.

COWGIRL HAT IN SAN ANTONIO

BRACKENRIDGE PARK AND ALAMO HEIGHTS

Just a short drive from downtown, Brackenridge Park is less urban, yet home to several one-of-a-kind restaurants with a city feel. Farther north, Alamo Heights is even more polished.

Cappy's (210-828-9669; www.cappysrestaurant.com), 5011 Broadway St. Located in a brick building dating from the 1930s in the Alamo Heights neighborhood, serving an upscale menu at fairly modest prices. One dish is so popular it is served for both lunch and dinner: the Mustang Chicken, which packs a punch with fresh horseradish and Dijon cream. The casual, cheerful interior and leafy patio only enhance the dining experience and keep Cappy's a neighborhood favorite.

For classic—and classy—Tex-Mex, leave the Riverwalk behind and head a short way up Broadway into the Alamo Heights neighborhood to **Paloma Blanca Mexican Cuisine** (210-822-6151; www.palomablanca.net), 5800 Broadway St. Start with the basics: homemade chips and salsa and a side of guacamole made with a spritz of orange. Move on to something as simple as a chicken enchilada, which comes with your choice of *crema de chipotle, crema de cilantro, salsa de mole,* or a tangy tomatillo sauce, and prepare to be impressed. The menu is extensive, filled with all sorts of combinations and a wide variety of vegetarian and gluten-free options. The lush patio is a delight, and the dining room strikes the perfect balance between rustic and refined. Paloma Blanca is worth both the drive and the price.

MONTE VISTA, OLMOS PARK, AND BEYOND

Monte Vista and Olmos Park are distinct historic neighborhoods, organized around the north–south thoroughfare of McCullough Avenue. Some eateries in this section are literally within these boundaries and some are nearby; all are north of I-35.

Everyone likes to slip into **The Cove** (210-227-2683; www.thecove.us), 606 W Cypress St. The funky spot near San Antonio College has become known as much for its great food, friendly service, and outstanding live music as for its odd mix of additional offerings. The Cove has an extensive, healthy, and affordable menu; eating a grilled fish taco served with cilantro coleslaw and a signature poblano cream sauce is a terrific way to pass the time while doing your laundry. That's right, laundry. The Cove's 34 washers and 30 dryers get lots of use—almost as much use as the basketball court out back, or the child-friendly playscape, or the self-serve, four-bay car wash. The Cove has everything you've never thought of, plus a pool table, video games, art on the walls, and wine and cheese tastings. At night, the nice long beer list takes center stage and things heat up around 8, when music lovers show up for the live blues, jazz, and acoustic folk concerts. The Cove is a San Antonio classic; stop in for some hospitality and go home full, clean, and satisfied.

Chris Madrid's (210-735-3552; www.chrismadrids.com), 1900 Blanco Rd., is the place to go for burgers in San Antonio, and people do, all day long. Choose from their many topping combinations, which include Porky's Delight, with cheddar and bacon, and the Flaming Jalapeño, with mustard and piles of jalapeños that will clear your sinuses for a week. The Tostada Burger, with mounds of refried beans, chips, onions, and cheddar cheese, is a crowd-pleaser despite its dubious reputation. The freshly made burgers come in two sizes—regular and macho—and are served in a casual, no-frills atmosphere.

Continue north on Blanco Road, veering east onto West Avenue, to **Magnolia Pancake Haus** (210-496-0828; www.magnoliapancakehaus.com), 606 Embassy Oaks. There you'll find hot and fluffy buttermilk, blueberry, chocolate chip, and pecan pancakes, and even a hot apple *munchener apfel pfannekuchen,* a Bavarian puffed pancake served with powdered sugar and whipped cream, for breakfast and lunch.

Pressing farther north still you'll come to **Silo Elevated Cuisine** (210-483-8989; www.siloelevatedcuisine.com), 1133 Austin Hwy. Enter this old farmers' market on the ground floor, now a martini bar, and take the elevator up to the main dining room. Menu mainstays include chicken-fried oysters served with applewood bacon, sautéed spinach, and apples with a mustard hollandaise sauce, and the Asian-inspired mango-wasabi crab cakes, both of which are crowd-pleasers. Embellishments such as the mint marigold béarnaise, a cognac cream sauce, foie gras port sauce, and a spicy dried cherry sauce bump the dishes up to new heights. Even though the restaurant is located on North Loop, on the outer edges of the city, the prix-fixe lunch is very popular.

Pizza lovers make a beeline for the northern reaches of Olmos Park, where **Dough Pizzeria** (210-979-6565; www.doughpizzeria.com), 6989 Blanco Rd., serves hot, gourmet pies fresh from the wood-fired oven. Dough's Neapolitan-style pizza features a thin but still chewy crust, bright tomatoey sauce, housemade mozzarella, and any number of toppings. The popular "Pork Love" is a medley of spicy sausage, soppressata salami, and pancetta. Supplement your meal with an Italian wine or a decadent dessert. Located in an unassuming commercial area, Dough can be a little hard to find, but persistence pays off.

Located well outside the tourist loop, **The Big Bib BBQ** (210-654-8400; www.thebigbib.com), 104 Lanark Dr., is a local favorite. No frills here, just basic 'cue and plenty of it. Try the brisket, ribs, or rib tips, or branch out to the chicken, fried catfish, or jalapeño sausage. Pair with the signature standout side—the sweet potato casserole topped with plenty of brown sugar and pecans—and

finish up with a serving of cobbler. Don't be fooled by the nondescript strip mall facade and unremarkable neighborhood. The Big Bib consistently earns high marks for its warm welcome and friendly service.

✳ Entertainment

Nightlife in San Antonio is quite tame; simple pleasures such as sitting out under the stars, sipping a drink on the patio of just about any restaurant along the Riverwalk, are sure to make for a relaxing evening. Strolling the sidewalks of the historic King William District, gallery hopping on First Fridays, or just lingering over dessert at a local bistro are activities San Antonians enjoy on nights out. Visitors will find that the city offers a nice selection of live music, from jazz ensembles to *conjunto* music, energetic performing arts organizations, and dynamic festivals whose exuberant celebrations can last well into the evening. For variety's sake, locals don't think twice about driving the 30 miles north on I-35 to historic Gruene for dinner and dancing in Gruene Hall (see page 187). For up-to-the-minute information on San Antonio's nightlife, pick up a copy of either the *San Antonio Current* or *San Antonio Express-News,* or access the information online at www.sacurrent.com and www.mysanantonio.com.

MUSIC **Bella on the River** (210-404-2355; www.bellaontheriver.com) is a tiny Italian restaurant that provides the perfect backdrop for the jazz combos who frequent its small stage and the perfect foil to the noisy, wide-open patios of the Riverwalk. A cozy place to spend a rainy evening or a sticky summer night.

Built in 1902 as a Southern Pacific Railroad depot, **Sunset Station** (210-222-9481; www.sunset-station.com) is located in the St. Paul Historic District near the Alamodome. The structure has been extensively renovated and is now a multipurpose entertainment venue, with an old-time saloon and plenty of space for the wide-ranging, big-name concerts it is known for hosting. Check the website for event details.

With a very '40s feel, **Luna Fine Music Club** (210-804-2433; www.lunalive.com) pairs top-notch musicians with a slightly more upscale ambience than other area clubs. The acoustics of the club benefit blues, jazz, Latin, soul, swing, and world music equally, making it a music lover's delight. A classic mix of music, dancing, and cocktails in north central San Antonio, Luna is a local favorite.

The **Bonham Exchange** (210-224-9129; www.bonhamexchange.net), located near the Alamo, is known for over-the-top celebrations, booty-shaking contests, and hot dancers. This LBGTQ-friendly bar and club is popular with anyone looking for a fun night out.

Rosario's (210-223-1806; www.rosariossa.com) anchors the Southtown social scene. Arrive early, order dinner, eat at your leisure, and then join the margarita-fueled throngs on the dance floor for live salsa, pop, or contemporary Latin music. The combination of free live music every Friday night, a great Southtown location, and fantastic food all week long are just some of the many reasons to stop in at Rosario's.

Just off Broadway and just south of Brackenridge Park, **Sam's Burger Joint** (210-223-2830; www.samsburgerjoint.com) kicks off Monday with swing dancing and mixes it up all week with a wide range of singer-songwriters, blues, rock, and a little bit of country. No need to eat before you go; Sam's sells enormous, juicy burgers.

Cowboys Dancehall (210-646-9378; www.cowboysdancehall.com), a warehouse-sized combination dance hall and indoor rodeo, is country western through and through. From the George Strait and Dwight Yoakam concerts to the live professional bull-riding shows, Cowboys is the place to go for dancing, cold beer, and a Texas-sized good time. Check the website for concert and event schedule. Tucked beside Loop 410 at I-35.

MUSICIANS ON THE RIVERWALK

A dance hall northwest of town, **John T. Floores Country Store** (210-695-8827; www.liveatfloores.com) has had patrons singing, dancing, and whooping it up with folks like Willie Nelson and Patsy Cline for over 60 years. Floore's isn't as old as the historic dance hall in Gruene (see page 187), but it is much bigger and the boot scootin' is every bit as fun. Take Bandera Road northwest to Helotes, just past Loop 1604.

DRINKS You can duck into anyplace on the Riverwalk for a beer and a view, but if you are looking for character, history, or just a place the locals love, give these a try.

For history's sake, take a break from the margaritas on the crowded Riverwalk and duck into the dimly lit **Menger Bar** (210-223-4361; www.mengerhotel .com) for a stiff shot of whiskey in the shadow of the Alamo. Rumor has it that here Teddy Roosevelt offered free drinks to men who would, after throwing back a few, readily join his Rough Riders and head off to fight in the Spanish-American War. Built in 1887, with a design based on the taproom in London's House of Lords, the bar is quiet and relaxed, with dark cherry-wood paneling, beveled glass mirrors from France, and other Victorian embellishments.

Established in 1933, the **Esquire Tavern** (210-222-2521; www.esquiretavern-sa .com) is still a local haunt, with a nice little patio overlooking the river and a jukebox full of Texas tunes. Located near the corner of Commerce Street and St. Mary's, the Esquire is a great place to enjoy drinks and a burger while sitting elbow-to-elbow with anyone from anywhere.

Located at street level—just a stone's throw from the Riverwalk, but easily missed on Presa between Commerce and Market—**Zinc** (210-224-2900; www .zincwine.com) is a casual wine bar that's consistently a local favorite. Share appetizers over martinis, split the juicy Zinc Burger (topped with smoky cheddar and

spicy tomato aioli), or enjoy a gourmet pizza and a bottle of something special.

Head to the King William neighborhood for a casual drink and an evening stroll. Stop by **Rosario's** (see page 126) for a margarita; **The Friendly Spot** (see page 126) ice house for a cool one; or the **Liberty Bar** (see page 127) for spectacular cocktails, half-price appetizers daily from 5 to 7 PM, and half-price late-night pizzas daily from 10 PM to midnight.

Farther north, the **Ocho Lounge** (210-222-2008; www.havanasanantonio.com) in the Hotel Havana exudes a sophisticated, old world, Latin-inspired vibe. The decor looks the part, with antique sofas and armchairs, tiled floors, marble counters, and a dramatic, almost vaulted, glass ceiling soaring above. Candlelight, glowing chandeliers, and a peek at the river add romance.

✳ Selective Shopping

There are plenty of knickknack and souvenir shops in the neighborhood surrounding the Riverwalk and **Market Square/El Mercado** (210-207-8600; www

.marketsquaresa.com), with plenty of Mexican imports for sale.

For clever and quirky gifts, try the gift shops at any of the area museums; **Southtown** is a good neighborhood for gallery gazing. Other good options include:

Alamo Quarry Market (210-824-8885; www.quarrymarket.com)

Crossroads of San Antonio (210-735-9137)

Ingram Park Mall (210-864-9570; www.ingramparkmall.com)

North Star Mall (210-340-6627; www.northstarmall.com)

River Center Mall (210-225-0000; www.shoprivercenter.com)

The Shops at La Cantera (210-582-6255; www.theshopsatlacantera.com)

✱ Special Events

FESTIVALS San Antonio is bursting at the seams with festivals, cultural events, market days, and music. Some may be worth planning a trip around, and others may just happen to coincide with your visit. These events always bring out the best in vivacious and community-minded San Antonio.

January: **Martin Luther King Jr. March** (210-444-2315; www.dreamweek .org) While most cities have special events on the weekend of Martin Luther King Jr. Day, San Antonio has one of the largest, longest, and most uplifting. Free.

San Antonio Cocktail Conference (210-472-2211; www.sanantoniococktail conference.com) A newcomer to the festival scene, the Cocktail Conference has stirred things up. While open to the public—the schedule is packed with "paired dinners" matching cocktails and cuisine, tastings, and seminars on the ins and outs of mixology—tickets sell out quickly.

February: **San Antonio Stock Show and Rodeo** (210-225-5851; www.sarodeo .com) A 16-day extravaganza of food, music, and rodeo performances. Admission charged.

HATS FROM MEXICO FOR SALE IN MARKET SQUARE/EL MERCADO

Mardi Gras (www.thesanantonioriver walk.com) Colorful barges and a variety of music along the river are the hallmarks of Mardi Gras in San Antonio. Held the weekend before Ash Wednesday. Free.

CineFestival (210-271-3151; www .guadalupeculturalarts.org) The longest-running Latino film festival in the country, featuring Chicano/Latino/ indigenous films at the historic Guadalupe Theater, with panels, workshops, retrospectives, and sidebar programs offered in conjunction. Admission charged.

March: **Remember the Alamo Weekend** and **Dawn at the Alamo** (210-273-1730; www.mysalha.org) Reenactment and interpretation of the events at the Alamo, both commemorative and educational. Free.

St. Patrick's Day (210-227-4262; www .thesanantonioriverwalk.com) Various events, including parades on both street and river, and the "Dyeing o' the River Green." Free.

Watercolor Month (www.texaswatercolorsociety.org) Watercolors of all sizes, styles, and subjects on display in galleries, museums, and other venues throughout town. Free.

April: **Fiesta San Antonio!** (210-227-5191; www.fiesta-sa.org) One of the country's oldest traditions of sheer cross-cultural fun, and the city's signature event. Food, art, fireworks, carnivals, sports, and music you can't help but dance to bring out some 3 million revelers to this weeklong, citywide party. Admission charged.

King William Fair (210-271-3247; www.kwfair.org) Held at the end of April, this fair encompasses several blocks of Madison, King William, and Washington Streets. The fun includes food booths, juried arts and crafts vendors, a children's area with pony rides and blow-up bouncy structures, and a parade. A great way to spend some time in the lovely King William District. Free.

May: **Cinco de Mayo** (210-207-8600; www.visitsanantonio.com) Commemoration and celebration of the Mexican army's victory over the French at the Battle of Puebla on May 5, 1862. A joyous cultural festival featuring events in Market Square and throughout the city. Free.

Tejano Conjunto Festival en San Antonio (210-271-3151; www.guadalupeculturalarts.org) A week of live music from traditional *conjunto* to progressive *Tejano* and everything in between, played by extremely talented musicians, in some cases living legends. Food, games, and dancing. Admission charged.

June: **Texas Folklife Festival** (210-458-2224; www.texancultures.com) A major four-day cultural extravaganza representing more than 40 ethnic groups, with plenty of food, dancing, music, and crafts to go around. The 2006 celebration had nine performance stages booked solid for the duration of the festival, with such acts as Scottish bagpipe bands; Lebanese, Flemish, and German folk dancers; Mexican ranchero songs; Latin jazz; and Chinese dragon dancers, all from groups with strong Texas roots. Food is as wide ranging, from Czech *kolaches* to Polish *pierogi* to homemade flour tortillas. A truly amazing display of diversity. Admission charged.

Juneteenth (210-843-7805; www.juneteenthsanantonio.com). Remembering June 19, 1865, the day that slaves in Texas first received word of the Emancipation Proclamation. A spirited citywide celebration of freedom. Admission charged.

July: **Fourth of July** (210-227-4262; www.thesanantonioriverwalk.com) In San Antonio, Independence Day festivities center on Market Square, the Riverwalk, and blow-out celebrations at the local theme parks. Admission and free.

San Antonio Conjunto Shootout (210-207-8600; www.visitsanantonio.com) A *conjunto* battle of the bands, held in Market Square, with food, refreshments, and dancing. Free.

Contemporary Art Month (210-630-0235; www.contemporaryartmonth.com) The only monthlong contemporary arts festival in the nation, with more than 400 exhibitions in galleries, museums, neighborhoods, and studios. Admission and free.

Cactus Pear Music Festival (210-838-2218; www.cpmf.us) A chamber music festival in San Antonio and the Hill Country towns that steps in where the San Antonio Symphony leaves off in the summer. Admission charged.

Pridefest (www.pridesanantonio.org) Local gay/lesbian groups celebrate this nationally recognized event with a block party and parade in HemisFair Park.

San Antonio Film Festival (210-885-5888; www.safilm.com) A filmmaker's and film fan's film festival.

August: **Ford Canoe Challenge** (210-227-4262; www.thesanantonioriverwalk.com) Participants race canoes from the Chamber of Commerce, around the Convention Center lagoon, through the

River Center mall lagoon, and back to the Chamber of Commerce. Free.

September: **FotoSeptiembre USA** (www.safotofestival.com) One of the largest photography festivals in the country, with exhibits, workshops, and multimedia presentations. Admission and free.

Jazz'SAlive (210-212-8423; www .saparksfoundation.org) Outstanding performances from the nation's top jazz entertainers and local talent. Travis Park. Free.

Diez y Seis Events (210-207-8600; www.visitsanantonio.com) A celebration of Mexico's independence from Spain on September 16, 1821. Three days of parades, dance, and rodeos. Free.

Valero Texas Open at La Cantera (www.valerotexasopen.com) One of the oldest professional golf tournaments and an official PGA tour event. Admission charged.

October: **AT&T Championship** (210-698-3582; www.pgatour.com) An official Senior PGA Tour golf tournament at the Oak Hills Country Club (210-349-5151; www.oakhillscc.com). Admission charged.

November: **Día de los Muertos** (210-207-6700; www.visitsanantonio.com) "Day of the Dead" is the ancient cultural tradition in which families "welcome back" departed loved ones, commemorating them through special altars and cemetery visits. Poetry readings and *calavera* processions, in which participants dress as skeletons, are especially moving. Admission and free.

Culinaria Wine & Food Festival (210-822-9555; www.culinariasa.org) A celebration of food, wine, and San Antonio's position as culinary and cultural gateway to Mexico and Latin America. Admission charged.

Holiday River Parade and Lighting Ceremony (www .thesanantonioriverwalk.com) Held the day after Thanksgiving, this twilight river parade lights up the Paseo del Rio. The more than 122,000 lights stay on until New Year's Day. Admission charged.

December: **Alamo Bowl** (210-226-2695; www.alamobowl.com) Post-season college football game featuring teams from the Big 12 and Big 10 conferences at the Alamodome. Admission charged.

Celebrate San Antonio (210-212-8423; www.saparksfoundation.org) New Year's Eve fireworks, live music, food, and family activities. South Alamo Street between Durango and Market Streets, La Villita, and HemisFair Park. Free.

Hecho a Mano/Made by Hand (210-271-3151; www.guadalupeculturalarts .org) An arts and crafts market featuring ceramics, jewelry, woodwork, fiber arts, clothing, metalwork, and more. Admission charged.

ALTARS FOR DÍA DE LOS MUERTOS, DAY OF THE DEAD

THE HILL COUNTRY

■

BANDERA

BLANCO

BOERNE

COMFORT

FREDERICKSBURG

JOHNSON CITY

KERRVILLE

LUCKENBACH

MARBLE FALLS

WIMBERLY

THE HILL COUNTRY

The Hill Country occupies the eastern portion of the Edwards Plateau and is bounded by the Balcones Fault to the east and the granite domes of the Llano Uplift to the north and west. The green grazing terrain is textured with limestone rocks and boulders and pierced by outcroppings. The region is the perfect habitat for deer, coyotes, squirrels, foxes, raccoons, skunks, and armadillos, as well as migrating birds and butterflies, and its many caves and caverns are home to millions of bats. Numerous state parks offer ample opportunity to view nature close-up. You could spend the day or a week in these hills, winding your way from town to town, past wildflowers, vineyards, and fields of lavender, watching the sun move across the enormous Texas sky.

Bandera

The self-proclaimed "Cowboy Capital of the World," little Bandera has got some big boots to fill. Located approximately 50 miles northwest of San Antonio on TX 16, Bandera is named for nearby Bandera Pass, the natural V-shaped access point that allowed Native Americans, the Spanish, the US Army, Texas Rangers, and even cattle during

BANDERA GENERAL STORE

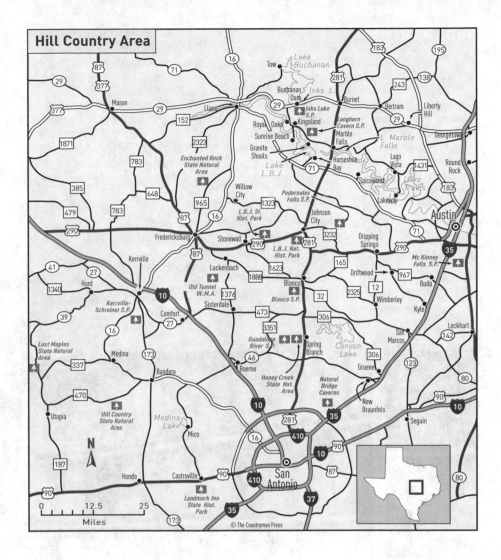

Hill Country Area

the cattle drives of the 19th century to pass through the rocky ridge separating the Medina and Guadalupe River valleys. Founded in 1852, Bandera was settled by Polish immigrants and was also home to a Mormon colony. Since the 1920s, Bandera and its surrounding countryside have played host to summertime visitors who enjoy the area's ranches, campgrounds, dance halls, and rodeos. Bandera is known for its dude ranches, twice-weekly rodeos from Memorial Day to Labor Day, summertime water fun in the Medina River and nearby Medina Lake, and scenic trails in the two state natural areas located nearby.

✴ To See

Opened in 1933, the **Frontier Times Museum** (830-796-3864; www.frontiertimes museum.org) you see today is the result of decades of collecting; its eclectic mix of

DUDE RANCHES

Out here in Bandera the itch to slide into a pair of jeans, put on cowboy boots, and start wrangling begins to need scratching. Below are some ranches where you can be a cowboy for a day.

Rates are roughly the same, approximately $120 per day per adult and $80 per day per child, plus or minus, depending on the season. Limited horseback riding, use of the ranch swimming pool, and participation in ranch-organized events tend to be included, though three meals may not. Often there is a minimum stay of two or three nights. Details vary; check websites and don't hesitate to call for clarification. Day visitors are welcome at some of the ranches for horseback riding at rates of approximately $30 per hour; call to inquire.

Dixie Dude Ranch (830-796-7771; www.dixieduderanch.com)

Mayan Ranch (830-796-3312; www.mayanranch.com)

Flying L Guest Ranch (830-460-3001 or 800-292-5134; www.flyingl.com)

Hill Country Equestrian Lodge (830-796-7950; www.hillcountryequestlodge.com)

Rancho Cortez (830-796-9339; www.ranchocortez.com)

Silver Spur Guest Ranch (830-796-3037; www.silverspur-ranch.com)

Twin Elm Guest Ranch (830-796-3628 or 888-567-3049; www.twinelmranch.com)

BOOTS FOR SALE

western memorabilia, artifacts from frontier times, and oddities such as a stuffed, two-headed sheep are sure to intrigue.

Polly's Chapel (www.pollytexaspioneerassociation.org), a lovely little house of worship with a remarkable history, stands off TX 16, approximately 6 miles southeast of the city near Privilege Creek. Situated on a pretty piece of land in what feels like the middle of nowhere, the chapel is unexpected, to say the least. It was built entirely by hand by José Policarpo "Polly" Rodriguez more than 120 years ago. Polly was born in Mexico, moved to Texas as a child, and became a scout with the U.S. Army and eventually a Methodist minister. His spiritual awakening prompted Polly's desire to build the chapel, a labor of love he completed in 1882. The doors are usually left unlocked.

Once the sight-seeing's done, join the local tradition of live music, mostly country and western and honky-tonk, and dance your boots off. Though hours may vary, there is always a dance hall open Wednesday through Sunday nights, with mellower bring-your-own-guitar jam sessions Sunday afternoons.

Beside the general store and down a flight of stairs, **Arkey Blue's Silver Dollar** (830-796-8826; no website, but you can find 'em on Facebook) is one of the last of its kind, a honky-tonk with sawdust floors, a pool table, lots of neon, live music, and cold Shiner longnecks all night long. Boot scoot to Arkey Blue and his Blue Cowboys, who play live every Saturday night. Quintessential Bandera.

A block away is the **11th Street Cowboy Bar** (830-796-4849; www.11thstreetcowboybar.com), a creaky watering hole with fantastic live country and western and country swing music. These folks know how to throw a party, with dozens of themed dances, concerts, rallies, and celebrations a year, many spilling into the streets: New Year's Eve, Cowboy Mardi Gras, Spring Fling, Bandera "Stompede" Memorial Day Celebration, Celebrate Bandera, Thunder in the Hill Country and Chili Cook-Off, and Hunters Weekend, just to name a few. Wednesday nights are extra fun since they fire up the barbecue pits and invite guests to bring their own meat to grill over the communal flames. Patrons sometimes arrive on horseback.

RODEOS In Bandera, summertime is rodeo season; the big kickoff event is the **Cowboy Capital PRCA Rodeo** (830-796-7207; www.banderarodeo.com), held during Memorial Day weekend in Mansfield Park. Featuring cowboys competing for points to qualify for the National Rodeo Finals, this event always brings out some top-notch riders. Contact the Bandera Convention and Visitor Bureau (800-364-3833; www.banderacowboycapital.com) for more information.

LAVENDER

The Hill Country has several burgeoning lavender farms, thanks to growing conditions tailor-made to the herb and the insight of photographer Robb Kendrick, who noticed, while on a photo shoot in Provence, France, in the late 1990s, the similarities of that region and the Hill Country where he lived. Robb solicited advice from French farmers and went home to experiment with the rocky limestone soil around Blanco. He and his wife, Jeannie Ralston, found that Provence lavender grew beautifully, and they started Hill Country Lavender, which sold lavender and offered seminars on lavender farming. At the same time, Richard and Bunny Becker, owners of Becker Vineyards, also returned from a trip to Provence and noticed the very same similarities. The Beckers planted a 3-acre field of the fragrant herb behind their winery. The Hill Country Lavender seminars made an impression on the locals; soon farms were taking root, growing both plants and the region's identity as the newly anointed "Lavender Capital of Texas." In fact, so many farms participated in the hugely successful, first annual Blanco Lavender Festival (www.blancolavenderfestival.com), held in June 2005, that the event has become a Hill Country favorite. Visitors are welcome to stop by the farms during the lavender blooming season—May, June, and July—and doing so makes a nice complement to the Texas Hill Country Wine Trail (www.texaswinetrail.com). Growing, blooming, and harvesting times vary, as do hours of operation, so call ahead to the farms you hope to visit.

Becker Vineyards (830-644-2681; www.beckervineyards.com) Behind its main winemaking operation in Stonewall, this lovely vineyard and winery has a 3-acre field of lavender that guests are invited to wander through, drink in hand, especially during their Lavender Festival each May.

Hill Country Lavender (830-833-2294; www.hillcountrylavender.com) The first commercial lavender farm in Texas, Hill Country Lavender has a farm and store on US 281, and you can purchase their lavender-themed products at Brieger Pottery, located between the post office and the bank on the north side of the square in Blanco.

Hummingbird Farms (830-868-7862; www.hummingbirdlavender.com) Five lovely acres of organic lavender located 9.5 miles west of Johnson City.

Rough Creek Lavender (512-847-2888; www.roughcreeklavender.com) Rough Creek Lavender has 5,000 lavender plants, with alighting butterflies, for picking and frolicking among during blooming season. Located in Wimberley.

✳ Outdoor Activities

In town, the cypress-lined Medina River is an irresistible spot to cool off, though heavy rainfall can cause it to become temporarily hazardous. Rent tubes and kayaks from the **Medina River Company** (830-796-3600; www.themedinarivercompany.com).

To the southeast, **Medina Lake** is a recreational lake with plenty of cabins and cottages for rent; check the Bandera Convention and Visitor Bureau's website, www.banderacowboycapital.com, for links to individual properties. Farther south, the 5,500-acre **Hill Country State Natural Area** (see "Texas State Parks" on page 162), makes for terrific horseback riding, hiking, and views. To the west, the **Lost Maples State Natural Area** (see "Texas State Parks" on page 162) is just gorgeous in the fall and has nice hiking all year-round. The **Love Creek Orchards** (830-589-2202; www.lovecreekorchards.com) makes a nice lunch or apple pie stop en route to Kerrville along lovely TX 16.

✳ Where to Eat

Brick's River Café (830-460-3200; www
.bricksrivercafe.com), 1205 Main St.,
may not win you over with its location—
beside a hotel on the northern edge of
town—or decor, but one bite of the sweet
potato fries, hot ham and cheese sandwich on sourdough bread ("The Brick"),
or coconut cream pie and you'll soften.
Farther south, **Busbee's BBQ** (830-796-
3153), 319 Main St., smokes up hard-to-
resist brisket, sausage, ribs, ham, and
chicken, all served on red-checkered
tablecloths. The homemade pecan pie
and peach cobbler provide the perfect finish. Nearby, **Old Spanish Trail**
(830-796-3836), 305 Main St., known to
everyone as "OST," takes the cowboy
theme to new heights, placing diners
high in the saddles that double as lunch-
counter stools. Chicken-fried steaks
and enchiladas are menu mainstays, the
chuck wagon buffets are filling, and even
the simple breakfast tacos hit the spot.
With spurs on the wall, wagon wheels on
the ceiling, and an entire room devoted
to John Wayne, you'll never forget you're
in the Cowboy Capital of the World. **Dogleg Coffee** (830-796-8080), 315 Main St.,
has free Wi-Fi, great coffee concoctions,
and a wonderful lavender lemonade that
really hits the spot on a steamy day.

✳ Special Events

FESTIVALS Spice things up in April
with the annual **Silver Sage Corral Benefit Chili Cook-Off,** hosted by the 11th
Street Cowboy Bar, then cool off at the
Riverfest (830-796-4447; www
.banderariverfest.com) and its popular
Everything But a Boat River Regatta,
held in May.

Blanco

A small ranching and trade town, Blanco got its start in 1858 and almost immediately
entered into a power struggle with nearby Johnson City for the title of county seat, a
distinction it held until 1890, when Johnson City prevailed. Blanco is a typical small
town in the Hill Country, with a courthouse in the middle, shops all round, and hillside surrounding. Tubing in **Blanco State Park** and pie at the **Blanco Bowling Club**
are mainstays, but what really puts Blanco on the map today is the **Blanco Lavender
Festival** (www.blancolavenderfestival.com) and the proliferation of lavender farms
sprouting up all around.

✳ Outdoor Activities

After a meal, consider stretching your legs at **Blanco State Park** (830-833-4333; www
.tpwd.texas.gov). With over 100 acres of land on either side of a bend in the Blanco
River, Blanco State Park is one of the oldest in the state, known for great trout fishing,
shaded campsites, and river tubing—a favorite Central Texas pastime—on warm Texas
days. You'll find Blanco State Park located an easy four blocks south of the Blanco town
square on Park Road 23. Inquire at the park store about tube, canoe, and kayak rentals
and water safety tips. There are several other state parks within striking distance of
US 281, and each offers a close-up look at a piece of the Texas landscape. A complete
listing and maps can be found online at www.tpwd.texas.gov.

❋ Lodging

Blanco County Inn (830-833-4502; www
.blancocountyinn.com), 902 Main St. The
clever owners managed to take a run-of-
the-mill motor court motel and turn it
into something pleasant. The rooms have
been renovated, each neat and clean,
with personal touches such as quilts.
Flowerbeds, tidy landscaping, and comfortable chairs scattered on the massive
deck and underneath the property's huge
shade trees beckon guests to come out
of their rooms for a little sunshine and
socializing. $.

❋ Where to Eat

It would be easy to drive straight past
the nondescript **Blanco Bowling Club**
(830-833-4416; www.blancobowlingclub

.com), 310 4th St. This very informal
and friendly spot is popular with locals,
and you can just walk on in and plop
down at one of the formica tables in the
wood-paneled dining room. While the
hamburgers, hot roast beef sandwiches,
chicken-fried steak, and various Mexican
dishes are all tasty, leave room for a slice
of the famous meringue pie, an essential
part of the dining experience. The glazed
donuts and cinnamon rolls served hot in
the mornings are a perfect pairing for a
cup of coffee. And, yes, there is ninepin
bowling.

Nearby, the delightful **Redbud Café
Market and Pub** (830-833-0202; www
.redbud-cafe.com), 410 4th St., is located
across from the courthouse in the center of town and owned and operated by
local potters Jon and Jan Brieger. In fact,
their pottery shop (830-833-2860; www
.briegerpottery.com) is right next door.
On the menu, you'll find hot pastrami

STOP BY A FARM STAND FOR A TASTE OF HOMEGROWN TEXAS

Reubens on marble rye, pimento cheese sandwiches, homemade soups, quiches, and several delicious vegetarian options. The restaurant is open late Friday and Saturday evenings, featuring Real Ale on tap, several Hill Country wines, and live music; check website for details.

Speaking of Real Ale, **Real Ale Brewing Co.** (830-833-2534; www.realalebrewing.com), 231 San Saba Ct., is just a short jaunt up US 281. The brewery offers beer tastings Wednesdays through Sundays—the Fireman's #4 is often cited as a must-try—and free brewery tours on Friday and Saturday afternoons.

Before heading out of Blanco, stop at the only street light in town and set your odometer to zero. Drive exactly 3.5 miles north and you will find yourself at **McCall Creek Farms** (830-833-0442; www.mccallcreekfarms.com), 4524 US-281, located on the east side of the highway. (If you are coming from the north, look for the farm 4 miles south of the US 281/US 290 intersection.) This small farm stand sells locally grown produce, cheeses and eggs, and locally made jams and preserves. They also make their own delicious homemade custard-based ice cream in vanilla, chocolate, and peach. Hill Country Lavender (see page 142) is located in the fields behind the farm.

Boerne

Located in the San Antonio metropolitan area approximately 30 miles north of downtown, Boerne (pronounced BURN-ee) was settled in 1849 as a small agricultural community and maintains a small-town atmosphere with distinctly German roots. Its population fluctuated until the 1960s, when the completion of I-10 made it a bedroom community for growing San Antonio. Located on the banks of Cibolo Creek, Boerne makes a nice day trip from San Antonio or a jumping-off point into the Hill Country.

✳ To See

German-themed festivals such as the **Berges Fest** (www.bergesfest.com)—held on Father's Day weekend and featuring watermelon-eating contests and dachshund races—**Oktoberfest-Wurst Braten** in October, and **Weihnachts (Christmas) Fest Parade Weekend** in December celebrate the town's heritage, while **Cowboy Christmas** festivities exemplify the region's distinctly Texas twang. Check www.boerne.org for details of the city's festivals.

✳ Outdoor Activities

While the aboveground geography of the Hill Country is fascinating, the eerie subterranean landscapes of the region's caves and caverns can be an interesting and fun diversion. The natural area in and around Boerne offers both.

Cascade Caverns (830-755-8080; www.cascadecaverns.com) is located approximately 3 miles south of Boerne; take Exit 543 off I-10. Home to the endangered albino Cascades Cavern salamander, Cascade Caverns is 140 feet deep and a half mile long. The highlight of the 45-minute tour is a peek at the 100-foot waterfall for which the cavern is named.

Naming was an issue from the beginning for the **Cave Without a Name** (830-537-4212; www.cavewithoutaname.com). In 1939, when a contest was held to name this

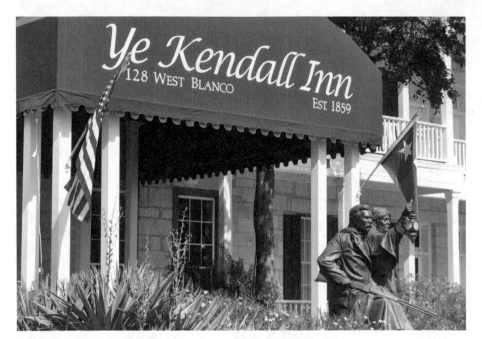

HISTORIC YE KENDALL INN IN BOERNE

cave, a boy remarked that it was "too pretty to name," and it is. To see for yourself, take FM 474 northeast for approximately 5 miles, then a right onto Kreutzberg Road.

From town, travel east on TX 46 for 1 mile to City Park Road, turn right, and follow to the **Cibolo Nature Center** (830-249-4616; www.cibolo.org). The four distinct ecosystems represented in the center's 100 acres make its pedestrian-only trails interesting and educational. Picnic tables and outdoor concerts invite visitors to stay the day, and the center's Mostly Native Plant Sale in April draws gardeners from near and far.

NEARBY

From Boerne, travel north along FM 1376 approximately 13 miles to Sisterdale, stop in at Sister Creek Vineyards (see "Hill Country Vineyards" on page 154) for a wine tasting, then head on to Comfort. Or head east on TX 46, then north on US 281 to Guadalupe River State Park (see "Texas State Parks" on page 161). Alternatively, take TX 46 westward to pretty TX 16 and head north to Bandera and Kerrville, or, from TX 16 take CR 337 farther west to Lost Maples State Natural Area (see "Texas State Parks" on page 162).

✳ Lodging

Ye Kendall Inn (830-249-2138; www .yekendallinn.com), 128 W Blanco Rd. Once a stagecoach stop, this is now a destination and a Texas historic landmark. Built in 1859, the solid limestone inn has a charmed atmosphere, with details such as a galvanized metal tub in the Texas Suite and rustic primitive decor in the Waco Cabin, a structure dating from the mid-1800s. Each of the inn's 34 very individualized guest rooms and cabins are well documented on its website, which is worth perusing before making your reservations. $$$. The on-site **Peggy's on the Green** (830-572-5000; www.peggysonthegreen.com) offers a sophisticated menu, including cheese grits topped with Andouille sausage and Gulf shrimp.

✷ Where to Eat

Heading south along Main Street, you'll come to the **Cypress Grille** (830-248-1353; www.cypressgrilleboerne.com), 170 S Main St., where everything from the pecan smoked bobwhite quail to the perfectly grilled prime rib is delicious. The decor is not as "fancy" as the food, but the atmosphere is very relaxed and enjoyable.

Several blocks farther, **The Creek Restaurant** (830-816-2005; www.thecreekrestaurant.com), 119 Staffel St., occupies several historic buildings—one was the baggage depot for the train station—along the banks of Cibolo Creek. The Creek serves fresh, healthy soups, salads, and sandwiches for lunch and steaks, seafood, and pasta dishes for dinner. The menu and the atmosphere are refreshingly simple and slightly elegant.

Follow River Road a few blocks east to the **Dodging Duck Brewhaus** (830-248-3825; www.dodgingduck.com), 402 River Rd. A popular place to unwind creekside with a home-brewed beer, some fried green tomatoes, a jumbo pretzel and sausage bites, or spicy stuffed mushroom caps.

The Hungry Horse (830-816-8989; www.hungryhorsehillcountry.com), 109 Saunders St., doesn't look like much, but folks say the chicken-fried steaks, creamy, bright yellow macaroni and cheese, fried onion rings, and corn muffins hit the spot. Portions are huge here; the "pony" size is a good fit.

Another casual eatery is the **Bear Moon Bakery** (830-816-2327; www.bearmoonbakery.com), 401 S Main St. You can have breakfast and lunch—diners love the chipotle grilled cheese and the Reuben—or simply enjoy an enormous cinnamon roll or slice of cake and a cup of coffee.

Two of Boerne's most popular restaurants are on its outskirts. **PO PO Restaurant** (830-537-4194; www.poporestaurant.com), 829 FM 289, a roadside classic since 1929, is widely known for its crispy yet juicy fried chicken, catfish, and shrimp. You haven't seen a big group of souvenir plates until you've seen the display at PO PO's. Located 6 miles north of Boerne off Exit 533/Welfare; reservations recommended. Though technically in Boerne, the **Welfare Café** (830-537-3700; www.welfaretexas.com) is located approximately 10 miles north of town, 223 Waring-Welfare Rd. (SR 1621), just off I-10/US 87. Irresistible

GIFT SHOPS IN BOERNE

gourmet food served in an irresistibly charming 1920s general store and post office. The *kartoffelpfannekuchen*—potato pancakes served with apple sauce or sour cream—and the crispy sausage and sauerkraut knödel served with spicy poblano sauce are clear references to the region's German heritage.

Comfort

Located near the intersection of TX 27, US 87, and I-10, Comfort is a lovely Hill Country hamlet nestled along the banks of gentle Cypress Creek. Settled by educated, free-thinking Germans who arrived via New Braunfels in 1852, Comfort has always marched to the beat of its own drummer. Opposed to slavery, the town was sympathetic to the Union in the Civil War, and it lost many men to the cause at the Battle of the Nueces in 1862. To commemorate their bravery, the Treue der Union ("Fidelity to the Union") Monument stands on High Street between Third and Fourth Streets. Averse to central authority, the settlers organized a communal form of self-governance and didn't get around to building a church until 1892. Comfort has several examples of traditional *fachwerk* (half-timber construction) and Victorian buildings, and much of the town is listed on the National Register of Historic Places. Comfort has weathered its share of tragedy. In 1978 a flood destroyed many historic buildings in town, and in 2006 a fire leveled the beloved Ingenhuett Store (834 High Street), a general store owned and operated by the same local family since 1867 and very much the anchor of the town. Despite these losses, tiny Comfort is sweet comfort indeed. The business part of town is only a few blocks long and takes in several restaurants, cafés, and antiques shops, all with varying business hours. See the town website at www.comfortchamber.com.

HOTEL FAUST, COMFORT

WILDFLOWERS

Springtime in Central Texas is lovely. The sun is out, the birds are singing, and the humidity has yet to arrive. Making an appearance are the millions upon millions of wildflowers that dot pastures and highway medians, line fences and riverbanks, and rise up with their colorful blooms turned sunward. By April, sometimes as early as March, these little native flowers—bluebonnets, Indian paintbrushes, and Mexican hats—seem to appear out of nowhere. In May, this first magical spray disappears and other, less well-known but equally exquisite natives bloom in their place. And so it goes, through summer, fall, and even a mild winter. In fact, in Texas the careful observer can find something in bloom all year long.

The sheer abundance of wildflowers along the state's roadways is courtesy of the Wildflower Program of the Texas Department of Transportation (TxDOT). In 1932, after noticing the persistent proliferation of wildflowers beside newly paved roads, TxDOT officials hired a landscape architect to assess how best to cultivate the native flowers and grasses along the public byways and back roads. The recommendation was simple: help them thrive. So the department developed a schedule of delayed mowing to allow flowers to seed and native grasses to grow. Not only were the results beautiful, but gently encouraging the natural landscape went a long way toward conserving water, controlling erosion, and preserving wildlife habitats. Today, TxDOT annually sows 30,000 pounds of wildflower seeds throughout the state for all to enjoy.

Scenic driving routes in the Hill Country include the well-traveled roads between Marble Falls, Burnet, Lampasas, Llano, Johnson City, and Fredericksburg. Some day-trippers like to press on as far north as San Saba and west as Mason, or poke around the roads alongside the Highland Lakes (see individual listings below). The Willow City Loop outside Fredericksburg, rural TX 16 South between Kerrville, Medina, and Bandera—even as far west as Utopia—and the meandering route along the Devil's Backbone heading out from Wimberley each offer back road beauty.

Remember, it's Mother Nature's show, so call local wildflower hotlines for advice; the **Lady Bird Johnson Wildflower Center** (512-232-0100) and TxDOT (800-452-9292) both have frequently updated recordings describing particularly colorful routes. To learn more about wildflower viewing and identification, visit the following websites: Lady Bird Johnson Wildflower Center (www .wildflower.org), Native Plant Society of Texas (www.npsot.org), TxDOT (www   .texas.wildflowersightings .org), and **Wildseed Farms** (www .wildseedfarms.com). Please don't pick the wildflowers, take care not to trample them, and if you pull off the highway and plop your children down for a photo amid the petals, be sure to watch your step; wildflowers and fire ants seek the same habitat: a sunny, dry, hot field.

TEXAS BLUEBONNET

✳ Lodging

Meyer Bed and Breakfast (830-995-2304; www.meyerbedandbreakfast.com), 845 High St. This congenial B&B is a complex of buildings dating from the 1800s to the early 1900s, each with clean and comfortably worn rooms. Sizes range from snug to spacious, making Meyer a good choice for families and friends traveling together. The lovely common breakfast area is lined with windows overlooking Cypress Creek. $$.

Camp Comfort (830-221-6090; www.camp-comfort.com), 601 Water St. This circa 1860s German social club has been repurposed as a stylish modern retreat. A strong sense of design and a laid-back vibe make this "camp" a popular choice for a feel-good getaway. Accommodations are unique and range from attached rooms, fashioned from the club's original bowling alley, to freestanding cabins, some with sleeping lofts. All have rough-hewn details, including shiplap, wainscoting, and wood floors, paired with sunny windows, high ceilings, and luxurious bedding. A tire swing out back, fire pit in the courtyard, and muffins when you wake in the morning complete the charm. $$$.

Hotel Faust (830-995-3030; www.hotelfaust.com), 717 High St. At the center of town, this collection of antique buildings has been restored and renovated and is ready to host visitors in comfort. The large two-story historic hotel on High Street was built to last; constructed of 21-inch limestone blocks, it is now over 130 years old. Wood floors, white trim, simple furnishings, and homey linens and spreads make the rooms welcoming. The deep porches with rocking chairs and the fireplace in the parlor are inviting places to relax any time of year. Guests can also choose to stay in a pioneer log cabin relocated from Kentucky, a two-bedroom cottage which was once the innkeeper's residence, and a carriage house which contained the hotel's original kitchen and dining room. A voucher for breakfast at High's across the street included. $$.

✳ Where to Eat

Most of Comfort's restaurants are located in a little cluster along High Street, the nexus of which is **High's** (830-995-4995; www.highscafeandstore.com), 726 High St. It feels like everyone stops by High's at some point during the day: to grab a muffin and coffee for breakfast, maybe a turkey sandwich with pepper Jack cheese and cilantro-or-ange-chipotle cabbage slaw for lunch, or a homemade key lime tart with a graham cracker crust in the middle of the afternoon. The food at this casual eatery is outstanding, but the friendliness of

HIGH'S ON HIGH STREET IN COMFORT

TEXAS PEACHES

Gillespie County, which includes both Fredericksburg and Stonewall, grows 40 percent of Texas's peach crop annually, making it the largest peach-producing county in Texas. Though the crop is susceptible to variable weather conditions—a late frost or spring hail can wreak havoc—when the conditions are right, the peaches are perfect and sun-ripened to a golden juicy sweetness.

To find a farm stand or an orchard that allows you to pick your own peaches, this 35-mile route is suggested: From Fredericksburg head east along US 290; in approximately 13 miles turn left onto Gellerman Lane, the site of the largest concentration of peach trees in Texas; continue to FM 2721, where you turn west back toward Fredericksburg. Continue to FM 1631 and follow it the 7 miles back to Main Street. Allow 45 minutes for the drive. Check www.texaspeaches.com for orchards and ripening dates, which fall anywhere between early May and late July.

HILL COUNTRY PEACHES FOR SALE AT A ROADSIDE STAND

High's lovely owners and staff is just as big a draw.

With service from a little restored gas station with a wood-fired oven out back and a collection of seating under trees and red umbrellas, **Comfort Pizza** (830-995-5959; www.comfortpizza.com), 802 High St., is a casual spot to spend an afternoon with a slice or two. Pies here have thin and crispy crusts and zesty sauce, and are piled high with toppings and cheese. Open for lunch and dinner, but when they are out of dough, you're out of luck. Closed Monday and Tuesday.

For a special night out, try the cozy **814 A Texas Bistro** (830-995-4990; www.814atexasbistro.com), 713 High St. The bistro specializes in such delicious gourmet dishes as grilled molasses-marinated Bandera quail and New York strip steak, served in the casual setting of the former Comfort post office, which was originally street number "814." The bistro comes complete with exposed brick walls and creaky wooden floors. Open for dinner Thursday through Sunday and weekend brunch; reservations recommended and BYOB.

NEARBY

The outstanding meals at the Welfare General Store and Café (see "Boerne"), a 15-minute drive south, are worth every mile, and the road to Sister Creek Vineyards is a treat unto itself.

Fredericksburg

Fredericksburg, named for Prince Frederick of Prussia, was founded in 1846 by John O. Meusebach and a group of 120 German immigrants. The founders came to the area from New Braunfels as participants in the Adelsverein, the planned German settlement of Texas. At the time, as was the case in most of the Pedernales Valley, the area that would become Fredericksburg was inhabited by Native Americans, in this case the Comanche. In 1847, Meusebach and the Native Americans hammered out the details of the Meusebach-Comanche Treaty, establishing peace in their shared valley—a remarkable feat given the times and circumstances.

The town, patterned after villages in Germany, was laid out with one long, wide road, Main Street, running parallel to Town Creek, and residents set about building the *fachwerk* homes that are now synonymous with Hill Country architecture. The Vereins-Kirche, a multipurpose building, served as school, church, fortress, and gathering place. Crops were planted, stores opened, and the town prospered.

The Civil War challenged the immigrants to square their communal beliefs with those of their new home country. Many were opposed to slavery and secession, with most supporting the Union, but all endured the hardships of Confederate martial law in 1862. The experience galvanized the German sense of self-determination; many residents spoke only German for decades afterward in an effort to distance and insulate themselves from national issues.

At the turn of the century, Fredericksburg was a manufacturing center, with various factories, quarries, and plants, but in the 1930s the town's reputation as a resort

FOURTH OF JULY PARADE IN FREDERICKSBURG

SUNDAY HOUSES

Devoutly religious, German settlers on farms and ranches outside Fredericksburg were determined to journey to town for church services, but the long distances, road conditions, and weather made this difficult. The solution was to build "Sunday houses." These tiny houses were built on small parcels in town and used by families coming to town for shopping on Saturday and church on Sunday. The houses were of frame construction, with steeply pitched roofs and decorative millwork. The lean-to kitchen was tacked on the back and sometimes the staircase was built on the outside of the home to save precious space indoors. Sunday houses were wildly popular between 1890 and 1910, and the ones that survive today are sprinkled throughout Fredericksburg and the Hill Country; many are used as B&Bs. In Fredericksburg, small groups of Sunday houses can be seen on West San Antonio Street, near St. Mary's Church on West Main Street, and on South Milam Street.

area began to grow. Today, Fredericksburg is known as a weekend getaway spot, with restful B&Bs, gourmet dining, and historic sites surrounded by parks, wineries, and wildflowers. At times it can feel a little kitschy, but head off the beaten path and there's plenty of genuine Hill Country to be enjoyed.

✳ To See

To get a sense of the region's pioneer past, visit the **Pioneer Museum** (830-990-8441; www.pioneermuseum.com), a dozen historic buildings spread out over 3 acres and tended by the Gillespie County Historical Society. The museum includes a one-room schoolhouse, a bath and barber shop, and the distinctive octagonal Vereins-Kirche, a replica of Fredericksburg's first social building—home to a permanent historical display and a gallery with changing photography exhibits. The Historical Society has over 300,000 artifacts within its rich and diverse collection, offering a fascinating look at pioneer life in the mid-1800s. On the outskirts of town, you'll find **Fort Martin Scott** (830-997-9895; www.fortmartinscott.org), "Guardian of the Texas Frontier." This was a U.S. Army frontier outpost between 1848 and 1853, though various groups, the Texas Rangers among them, have been cycling in and out ever since. In fact, you can pay your respects to the Rangers next door at the brand new **Texas Rangers Heritage Center** (830-990-1192; www.trhc.org). While the center is in the middle of a multiphase construction process, the completed Rangers Tower and the Ranger Ring of Honor are worth stopping in to see.

The **National Museum of the Pacific War** (830-997-8600; www.pacificwarmuseum .org) encompasses 9 acres and includes the George H. W. Bush Gallery, Admiral Nimitz Museum, Plaza of Presidents, Veterans' Walk of Honor, Japanese Garden of Peace, *Pacific Combat Zone* exhibit, and the Center for Pacific War Studies. The National Museum of the Pacific War leads visitors through both the chronology and the emotions of World War II in the Pacific through restored artifacts such as a South Pacific PT boat, Avenger dive-bombers, and pieces of battleships, photographs, and personal effects. From the scary sounds of mortar fire to the distressing reports of casualties, the only respite seems to be the reverence of the commemorative Veterans' Walk of Honor or the calm of the Japanese Garden of Peace. Honoring Admiral Chester Nimitz, the war icon and native of Fredericksburg, the museum that bears his name is located in the old Nimitz Hotel, once his family's business. A must for military-history buffs.

HILL COUNTRY VINEYARDS

The similarities between Texas and Tuscany are striking. Sure, you have to look past the cowboy hats and longhorn cattle to really notice them, but the distinct qualities of the limestone outcroppings, the berries growing wild along the roadsides, and the hot, hot sunshine shared by the regions are notable. And those similarities are not lost on Texas winemakers, who toil year-round to create a little bit of Italy in the Lone Star State. The region's rich alluvial soil is mixed with limestone, flint, and shale chips from rivers past and provides ideal conditions for growing grapes. For the past 40 years, vintners have coaxed their vineyards to take root in the Hill Country, and consumers and connoisseurs are now drinking the fruits of their labor.

All wineries offer tastings; some are complimentary and others charge a small fee, usually between $1 and $5. Those new to the experience of wine tasting will enjoy any of the wineries listed below, as they all have their individual strengths, charms, and personalities. Those with a more discerning palate might enjoy perusing the vineyards' comprehensive websites for specific labels or vintages before planning their trip. **Texas Hill Country Wineries** (872-216-9463; www.texaswinetrail.com) comprises over 50 member wineries, several of which are listed alphabetically below. For up-to-the-minute information regarding festivals, special events, and the Wine and Wildflower Trail, a coordinated effort of all the vineyards, please check the website. Additionally, the wineries along US 290 have organized themselves online at **Fredericksburg Wine Road 290** (www.wineroad290.com), and the **Texas Department of Agriculture** (www.gotexan.org) curates a comprehensive list of wineries across the state.

Becker Vineyards (830-644-2681; www.beckervineyards.com) Becker Vineyards has acres of grapes and fields of lavender.

Dry Comal Creek Vineyard (830-885-4076; www.drycomalcreek.com) The rooster you see on the roof is also featured on this vineyard's labels.

Fall Creek Vineyards (325-379-5361; www.fcv.com) Started in 1975, Fall Creek Vineyards is known for its signature Meritus wine, which is a blend of cabernet sauvignon, merlot, and petit verdot.

Flat Creek Estate (512-267-6310; www.flatcreekestate.com) Located on former pastureland just west of Austin, Fall Creek Estate is a sophisticated yet casual 80-acre vineyard with endless views.

Fredericksburg Winery (830-990-8747; www.fbgwinery.com) This winery is right on Main Street in Fredericksburg.

Grape Creek Vineyards (830-644-2710; www.grapecreek.com) Take a tram tour of vines, a crush pad, and a tank room to see how wine is made, and enjoy a taste in the barrel room.

Sister Creek Vineyards (830-324-6704; www.sistercreekvineyards.com) These friendly folks make European-style wines aged in oak barrels.

Torre di Pietra (830-644-2829; www.texashillcountrywine.com) Patios, live music, and wine-filled chocolates only enhance the tasting experience.

Woodrose Winery (830-644-2539; www.woodrosewinery.com) A wonderful winery that's been growing by leaps and bounds.

❋ Outdoor Activities

Though it is a commercial nursery, **Wildseed Farms** (800-848-0078; www.wild seedfarms.com) feels like an education center, botanical garden, or nature preserve, with its winding paths through fields exploding with color. This is a must-stop wild-flowers photo op. Wildseed Farms has seeds of both native and nonnative plants, workshops, tips for growing and identifying native plants, and a "Butterfly Haus" filled with butterflies. While there is a fee to stroll "The Meadows," the distant view is free, and you are welcome to meander to your heart's content through the rows and rows of plants for sale. A small *biergarten* serves sandwiches, grilled bratwursts, and other refreshments.

NEARBY

Located at the western edge of the Hill Country, Fredericksburg is a great home base for exploring the surrounding area. From Fredericksburg, TX 16 heads north to **Enchanted Rock State Natural Area** or south to **Kerrville**; US 87 travels a particularly scenic stretch on its way south to **Comfort**, and a short trip east along US 290 takes in both **Stonewall** and **Johnson City**, deep in historic LBJ country, and the legendary **Luckenbach**. The **Wine Trail** swings past Fredericksburg, and wildflower lovers might enjoy driving the picturesque **Willow City Loop**—take US 16 north for 13 miles, turn right on FM 1323, follow it to Willow City, and turn left, staying on FM 1323, to begin the loop.

❋ Lodging

The locus of Fredericksburg is Main Street, and the nearby neighborhoods are just teeming with B&Bs, guest houses, and boutique hotels. Alternatively, the usual roster of chain hotels can be found along US 290 on the outskirts of the city. Fredericksburg is such a popular weekend destination that it's essential to book a room in advance, particularly during festivals.

Most of the establishments listed below are independently owned and operated by the very folks you'll meet when you call or visit. Another useful way to book a room is to use the following reservation services, which handle a wide variety of B&Bs and guest houses: **Gästehaus Schmidt** (866-427-8374; www.fbglodging.com); **Main Street Bed and Breakfast Reservations Service** (830-997-0153 or 888-559-8555; www .travelmainstreet.com). Most reservations require a two-day minimum.

Das Garten Haus (800-416-4287; www.dasgartenhaus.com), 604 S Washington St. Kevin and Lynn operate this spotlessly clean guesthouse with three private suites, each with a kitchen or kitchenette, and perks such as fresh flowers, homemade cookies, and popcorn. The delicious breakfasts, sometimes made with produce from the owners' gardens, are delicate and delicious yet healthy and filling. Spend a minute poking around the lovely gardens, planned and nurtured by Kevin, a professional horticulturalist. $$.

Magnolia House (800-880-4374; www .magnolia-house.com), 101 E Hackberry St. Full of 1920s charm, Magnolia House is expertly managed by gracious owners who woo guests with homemade cookies and delicious breakfasts from locally sourced ingredients. Warm, homey, and neat as a pin, this Prairie-style Craftsman B&B is tucked away on a quiet side street several blocks from the center of town. Magnolia House has plenty of repeat guests, and once you've experienced a relaxing getaway here it's easy to imagine why. $$$.

Two Wee Cottages (830-990-8340; www.2weecottages.com), 108 E Morse St. Granny Hein House and My Little House are tucked in a little garden behind the host's home on Morse Street, eight blocks north of Main Street. The cottages have their own individuality; the Granny Hein House feels a tad more formal, with dark wood and an adorable old-fashioned kitchen, while My Little House is light and cheerful. Both cottages have hot tubs on private screened-in porches, hammocks large enough for two, and breakfast fixings in the fridge. The fresh baked goods make a lasting impression. Skip and Kate, the on-site hosts, are happy to offer recommendations for dining and entertainment. $$$.

Hoffman Haus (830-997-6739; www .hoffmanhaus.com), 608 E Creek St. The individualized rooms each have wood floors, high ceilings, luxurious linens, and several well-chosen pieces of antique or reproduction furniture, are both rustic and sophisticated. Rough-hewn beams, chinking, whitewash, and simple window treatments give the rooms a historical feel. Have breakfast in bed, then stroll the spacious gardens or rock in the rockers on the porch. $$$.

Hangar Hotel (830-997-9990; www .hangarhotel.com), 155 Airport Rd. Adjacent to the small Gillespie County Airport, it isn't just for aviation buffs. The appealing decor is reminiscent of the 1940s South Pacific, a theme that is carried through in the mahogany and rattan furniture, the armchairs covered in bomber-jacket leather, the hexagonal white floor tile in the bathrooms, and music playing in the common areas. The on-site Officers' Club serves drinks, while the Airport Diner has the classic curved ceiling and cozy booths, with a menu of burgers, malts, and onion rings to match. $$$.

Settlers Crossing (830-997-2722; www.settlerscrossing.com), 92 Settlement Dr. On the way to Luckenbach,

B&B IN FREDERICKSBURG

this 35-acre spread includes seven 19th-century cabins, some relocated from Indiana, Missouri, and Pennsylvania. The country antiques, wood-burning fireplaces, and period touches throughout breathe life into these historic gems. Most have fully equipped kitchens, some have Jacuzzi tubs, and all have outdoor grills. Far more than just spending the night, staying at Settlers Crossing is like living in pioneer times, albeit much, much more luxuriously. $$$.

✳ Where to Eat

As in many "tourist towns," eating establishments in Fredericksburg cater to their captive—and hungry—audience with little impetus to alter the menu or force a direct correlation between quality and price. You can get a burger anywhere, pay more than you'd like, and walk away full; but if you know where to look, there are plenty of really special and memorable meals to be had in Fredericksburg. I've also included recommendations for treats, snacks, and samplings. Many restaurants are closed on Mondays, and some are open only for lunch; check websites before you go.

Housed in a little cottage, **Sunset Grill** (830-997-5904; www.sunsetgrillfbgtx.com), 902 S Adams St., is a charmer for breakfast and lunch. The colorful dining room is open and bright, and the shaded patio is pleasant. The smoked salmon Benedict is a creamy, smoky, salty, fluffy wonder atop a toasted English muffin, sprinkled with capers and bits of red onion and then covered with an herb-infused hollandaise—a menu standout. Panini, burgers, and enormous salads are on the menu for lunch. Closed Wednesdays.

Considering the region's German roots, **Otto's** (830-307-3336; www.ottosfbg.com), 316 E Austin St., fits right into Fredericksburg. The charming bistro is known for its farm-to-table German cuisine, and the Wurst Platte—a sampling of sausages and sauerkraut—the duck schnitzel with spätzle, and even the earthy homemade German bread, served with butter, salt, pepper, and beet jam, are all standouts. Tucked into a little house a block or two off Main Street with patio dining out front, Otto's has an air of Continental sophistication coupled with the warmth of the Texas Hill Country.

Part boutique, part gallery, part bistro, **Vaudeville** (830-992-323; www.vaudeville-living.com), 230 E Main St., brings French-inspired dishes to the table using homegrown Texas ingredients. Examples include venison Reubens; fried chicken served with corn bread, collard greens, and mashed potatoes; and braised pork belly tacos, served on homemade corn tortillas with charred eggplant purée, Asian slaw, and an avocado vinaigrette. Meals are pricey, but you can always stop in just for a cookie and coffee.

Off-beat burgers are on offer at **Hondo's** (830-997-1633; www.hondosonmain.com), 312 W Main St. Hondo, the "clown prince" of Luckenbach (see page 170), was a local character with a capital "C." Though he passed away in 1976, his legend, humor, and free-spirited approach to life live on in this part of the Hill Country. The burgers here are tailored to your whims. Made in the form of a donut and grilled over a mesquite fire, you can customize yours with irreverent ingredients like chipotle chiles and chopped jalapeños. The backyard picnic tables and live music concerts make Hondo's a vibrant, informal place to kick back.

With over 40 years of service and several cookbooks under its belt, the **Peach Tree Restaurant** (830-997-9527; www.peach-tree.com), 210 S Adams St., tastes as fresh as ever. Savory quiches, soups, and tasty, dainty sandwiches such as ham and Swiss on raisin pecan bread or the fried green tomato BLT make the Peach Tree a terrific option for lunch. Several child-friendly items and a relaxed atmosphere make this an enjoyable rest stop for families. The refreshing peach ginger tea is everyone's favorite. Peach Tree is located on Adams Street, just south of its intersection with Main, which cleaves the thoroughfare into East and West.

One mile south of Main Street, far from the crowds, **The Nest** (803-990-8383; www.thenestrestaurant.com), 607 S Washington St., strikes a nice balance between relaxed and sophisticated. Housed in an old bungalow, the restaurant has homey wood floors and window trim, a soothing wall color, and simple decor. The refined menu features items such as rack of lamb with a pecan pesto, quail stuffed with bacon, spinach, goat cheese, and sun-dried tomatoes, and a signature lightly grilled escargot

ENJOY A MEMORABLE MEAL AT THE HILL TOP CAFÉ

seems scattered, the Hill Top is very focused when it comes to service and hospitality. From the breadbasket of warm, crusty, homemade sourdough bread that greets you at your table to the "Come back and see us again" sign that ushers you out the door, the Hill Top Café is a pure delight. The menu description of the fried oysters could be used to describe this entire enterprise—"cornmeal-breaded and fried with love." Then there's the live music. Bluesman, musician, and transplanted Rhode Islander, owner Johnny Nicholas hosts live blues, jazz, and boogie-woogie at his joint when he's not on the road performing with his band, Johnny Nicholas and the Texas All-Stars. See the website for details.

There are plenty of treats and snacks to be had along Main Street, and a good place to start sampling is **Rustlin' Rob's** (830-990-4750; www.rustlinrobs.com), 121 E Main St. Hankering for pickled quail eggs? Jalapeño peanut butter? Chowchow relish? Rob's rustled a huge variety of Texas-made sauces, salsas, jams, jellies, and preserves and put them up for sale in this condiment emporium.

A stone's throw away, the **Clear River Ice Cream, Bakery, & Deli** (830-997-8490; www.icecreamandfun.com), 138 E Main St., has ice cream, shakes, malts, coffee, and a ridiculous number of baked treats fresh from the oven; a great place for families to unwind over sugar.

Stroll over to the **Fredericksburg Pie Company** (830-990-6992; www .fredericksburgtexasshopping.com), 108 E Austin St., where you can enjoy a slice of bourbon orange pecan, fresh peach, German chocolate cream, or any number of other flavors of pie and a cup of coffee on the delightful patio. They tend to sell out fast, so plan on pie for a morning snack.

✳ Special Events

FESTIVALS Fredericksburg loves its festivals, and the city seems to be in a

appetizer. The Nest is a popular place for celebrating special occasions or a romantic night out.

Sitting on a hilltop overlooking the scrubby countryside a few minutes' drive outside of town, the **Hill Top Cafe** (830-997-8922; www.hilltopcafe.com) has the look and feel of a well-worn honky-tonk: creaky wooden floors and walls jammed with old signs, license plates, posters, and memorabilia to which there seems very little rhyme or reason. The same could be said of the menu, where *kefalotiri saganaki* (an appetizer of flaming Greek cheese), southern fried Mississippi catfish, and pan-seared oysters are all on offer. Though the atmosphere

Leaving Fredericksburg now, take the scenic route—east on US 290 for 3 miles, then south on Old San Antonio Road (a.k.a "Old No. 9"), traveling for 10.5 miles and following signs to "Old Tunnel State Park"—to the **Alamo Springs Café** (830-990-8004). Known for its outstanding, old-fashioned burgers, Alamo Springs is the real deal. Try one of the enormous green chile cheeseburgers served with grilled onions and avocado, or order their most popular burger, a massive patty with cheddar cheese, grilled onions, and mushrooms on a jalapeño cheese bun. The café is located beside the **Old Tunnel State Park** (see page 163), whose caves, from March through October, are home to some three million bats that funnel into the sky and fan out over the Hill Country each night at dusk; an amazing spectacle.

perpetual state of celebration. The biggest is **Oktoberfest** (830-997-4810; www.oktoberfestinfbg.com), a weekend extravaganza of German food, music, and beer held at the beginning of October. At the end of the month, a great way to sample area cuisine is the **Fredericksburg Food and Wine Festival** (830-997-8515; www.fbgfoodandwinefest.com). The **Easter Fires Pageant**, held the Saturday evening before Easter, commemorates the Meusebach-Comanche Treaty. As the story goes, during the tense moments before the treaty was announced, a pioneer mother told her anxious children that the fires they saw in the hills—the fires belonging to Comanche families awaiting news—were those of the Easter Bunny boiling eggs for Easter. To this day, Easter fires are lit Easter eve, the story is retold, and peace cherished. Throughout the spring and summer, festivals of peaches, lavender, wildflowers, and wines abound; details online at www.visitfredericksburgtx.com.

TEXAS WILDFLOWERS

TEXAS STATE PARKS

Texas' state parks preserve the natural icons of Texas, the sunsets that stretch for miles, the springtime fields of bluebonnets, the earnest roadrunners, and pokey armadillos. In the Hill Country, the limestone ravines, extensive caverns, wooded trails, and gurgling streams showcase the diversity of the region's plant life and wildlife. The Hill Country is home to the gray fox, white-tailed deer, armadillo, coyote, opossum, raccoon, bobcat, rock squirrel, and javelina, as well as rarer species such as the golden-cheeked warbler, who is partial to nesting in the region's Ashe junipers, the Cagle's map turtle, the Guadalupe bass, the Texas salamander, and the Honey Creek Cave salamander.

Given that over 96 percent of the land in Texas is privately owned, the state park system really is a gift to the public. The parks of the Hill Country are a popular recreation destination, particularly for those making day trips from Austin and San Antonio for hiking, biking, climbing, birding, or fishing. Since the parks are so popular, many have capacity limits in an effort to reduce wear and tear on the environment, and it is not unusual for those parks to close because that number has been reached. Scheduling a visit for early morning, after 5 PM, or weekdays is a good way to beat the crowds.

Unfortunately, Texas' state parks, like many around the country, are experiencing serious financial troubles. Belts are so tight that many have scaled back hours, cut unnecessary services, and even closed amenities such as restrooms rather than repair them. To avoid disappointment, consider calling your destination in advance of your visit. Despite cutbacks, the staff and rangers remain as helpful, informative, and energized as ever and are more than happy to chat about the wonders of their respective parks; visit them in person or online at www.tpwd.texas.gov. Help support America's natural heritage, and get your boots dirty in a Texas state park. Listed alphabetically:

BLANCO STATE PARK (see "Outdoor Activities," under Blanco, on page 143).

PICNIC AT A STATE PARK

ENCHANTED ROCK STATE NATURAL AREA

ENCHANTED ROCK STATE NATURAL AREA (830-685-3636; www.tpwd.texas.gov)

It is easy to imagine how Enchanted Rock might have gotten its name. Amid the scrubby woods of oak, cedar, and mesquite, and the prairielike grasslands, the enormous, pink-granite dome gleams in the sun and emits mysterious creaking and groaning sounds that have astounded human visitors for thousands of years. The Tonkawa Indians attributed the noises to ghosts, but scientists now say they are due to the expansion and contraction of the rock in the heat of the day and the cool night air. The rock itself, covering 640 acres, is a batholith, an underground rock formation that has been partially exposed by erosion. The surrounding area is home to abundant wildlife and birds; a bird checklist is available at the office. Hiking, primitive camping, and rock climbing are all options, though campers will need reservations and climbers must check in at headquarters. A much-loved, natural Hill Country wonder, Enchanted Rock is on the National Register of Historic Places and tops many locals' lists of rural day-trip destinations and sights to show visitors. Due to the fragility of its environment, the park limits the number of visitors per day and must close when it reaches capacity. It is best to arrive early in the morning or after 5 PM; in both cases consider calling ahead.

GUADALUPE RIVER STATE PARK (830-438-2656; www.tpwd.texas.gov)

Hugging an idyllic, 9-mile stretch of the river, Guadalupe River State Park is a favorite nature retreat for day-trippers from San Antonio and a popular place for camping, picnicking, and hiking. Depending on the time of year and rainfall, the river can be placid or powerful, making tubing, swimming, and fishing along the bald-cypress-lined river an adventure. This park is also a favorite of canoeists. The 5-mile equestrian trail (you'll need to bring your own horse!) is also open to mountain bikers. Nature enthusiasts may enjoy the adjacent Honey Creek State Natural Area (www.honeycreekfriends.org), which is open only for guided interpretive tours offered Saturday at 9 AM; call Guadalupe River State Park to confirm. Located approximately 30 miles north of San Antonio.

HILL COUNTRY STATE NATURAL AREA (830-796-4413; www.tpwd.texas.gov)

This 5,300-acre park is minimally developed, making it a good choice for more experienced hikers, backpackers, and campers who enjoy primitive sites. The 40 miles of trails are terrific for horseback riding and mountain biking. The water in the park is not potable, so be sure to bring your own. From Bandera take TX 173 south, across the Medina River to CR 1077, and turn right. Follow the paved road for 10 miles, continuing along the unpaved road and following signs to the park.

INKS LAKE STATE PARK (See "Highland Lakes" on page 173).

LONGHORN CAVERN STATE PARK (830-598-2283; www.tpwd.texas.gov)

A natural landmark, Longhorn Cavern is an amazing formation with a history to match. Years ago, a drop in underground water levels dissolved, bit by tiny bit, the solid limestone rock, slowly carving a subterranean streambed and cavern with soft, undulating curves. The Comanche used the cavern for shelter, and with the temperature inside a constant 68 degrees, it is easy to speculate why. Legends surround the cavern—for instance, there has been talk of Sam Bass's hidden treasure of $2 million in stolen bills—but the big draw is its beauty. Located on Park Road 4, approximately 6 miles west and 6 miles south of Burnet, off US 281.

LOST MAPLES STATE NATURAL AREA (830-966-3413; www.tpwd.texas.gov)

Lost Maples State Natural Area covers more than 2,000 acres of craggy limestone canyons with the clear-running Sabinal River, grassy plateaus, and one very dramatic and lovely stand of unusual Uvalde bigtooth maples, whose fall color is by far the brightest in the area. During the last two weeks of October and the first two weeks of November, visitors descend on the park to catch a glimpse of the glowing red and yellow leaves. The bigtooth maple can stand 50 feet tall, is drought tolerant, prefers the local limestone and igneous soil, and has a fragile root system that is easily damaged by foot traffic—visitors are urged to remain on the 11 miles of marked trails. It is possible to drive 1 mile into the park to a scenic viewing location, a particularly helpful option for those with limited mobility. Lost Maples is home to many birds, including the rare green kingfisher and the endangered golden-cheeked warbler, making the park a boon for birders. Located on FM 187, approximately 20 miles north of Vanderpool.

LYNDON B. JOHNSON STATE PARK AND HISTORIC SITE (830-644-2252; www.tpwd.texas .gov)

Dedicated to President Lyndon B. Johnson, the state park and historic site are located across from the LBJ Ranch. The park offers fishing, swimming, and picnicking, and, in spring, its many, many acres are dotted with wildflowers. Visitors have a chance to see the buffalo, longhorn cattle, wild turkey, and white-tailed deer that roam in grassy enclosures, and the visitor center contains exhibits of memorabilia from President Johnson's time in office (see "LBJ's Texas" on page 165). The Sauer-Beckmann Living History Farm, just east of the visitor center, brings to life daily existence on a Texas farm in the early 1900s. Located on US 290 near Stonewall.

OLD TUNNEL STATE PARK (866-978-2287; www.tpwd.texas.gov)

The Old Tunnel State Park occupies a snug 16 acres, but up to 3 million Mexican free-tailed bats (*Tadarida brasiliensis*) and 3,000 cave myotis bats (*Myotis velifer*) call this old and abandoned railroad tunnel home from April to October. As the story goes, when the railroad moved out in 1942, the bats moved in, and they've been here ever since. They emerge from their tunnel each night in a spectacular vortex of flapping wings, heading toward either the Guadalupe or Pedernales River in search of food—moths and other insects—and return to the tunnel sometime after midnight. Bat viewing is possible from either the upper viewing areas, which are open daily and free of charge, or from the lower viewing area, which is part of a guided tour. Located on Old San Antonio Road between Fredericksburg and Comfort.

PEDERNALES FALLS STATE PARK (830-868-7304; www.tpwd.texas.gov)

The Pedernales River runs through this 5,000-acre park, at one point gently tumbling down a series of stepped layers of limestone known as the Pedernales Falls, the park's main attraction. Depending on the time of year and amount of rainfall, the current can be brisk, slight, or even nonexistent. Those unfamiliar with the Hill Country's rivers and streams should always be on alert for any change in water level, which may indicate imminent, and quite possibly immediate, flooding, even in pleasant weather. The park features opportunities for camping, picnicking, swimming, and tubing. Additionally, there are close to 20 miles of hiking and mountain-biking trails. For birders, this park has an enclosed watching station, which is wheelchair accessible, with feeders providing lots of close-ups of the area's many birds. Located off US 290, approximately 12 miles east of Johnson City.

GOIN' FISHIN'

Johnson City

Johnson City was established in 1876 and named for James Polk Johnson, an ancestor of the town's most famous native son, President Lyndon Baines Johnson. A rural ranching center and county seat, Johnson City did not have modern utilities as late as the 1930s. When President Franklin D. Roosevelt established the Rural Electrification Administration in 1935, the 28-year-old Lyndon Johnson, by then a congressman, lobbied hard for services in the sparsely populated Hill Country, succeeding in 1938.

Located at the intersection of US 281 and US 290, Johnson City makes a convenient stopover and is the destination of LBJ devotees who come to visit his childhood home in town and the family's ranch in nearby Stonewall. Johnson City is also the site of the **Blanco County Fair and Rodeo** (www.bcfra.org), held at the end of August and showcasing livestock, arts and crafts, food, and country music.

✱ To See

LBJ National Historical Park is in Johnson City, and the **LBJ State Park and Historic Site** is in nearby Stonewall; taken together, they offer insight into both LBJ, the man who was president, and LBJ, the little boy who grew up in rural Texas, an upbringing that affected and informed his domestic policies. See "LBJ's Texas" on page 165.

✱ Lodging

Rose Hill Manor (877-767-3445; www.rose-hill.com), 2614 Upper Albert Rd. Though reminiscent of a Charleston-style plantation home, the wide porches and large windows seem well suited to the Hill Country. All four rooms in the main house are thoughtfully decorated with a restrained use of floral prints and appointed with queen-size beds, sun porches, sitting areas, or access to the veranda. The cozy cottages have king-size beds, simple, white beadboard walls, vaulted ceilings, warm wood floors, and small front porches for lounging. $$$.

✱ Where to Eat

Johnson City itself has some folksy restaurants to stop in for a laid-back meal. Across from the courthouse, the **Pecan Street Brewing** (830-868-2500; www.pecanstreetbrewing.com), 106 E Pecan Dr., brings new life to an old building, winning over diners with very reasonably priced, freshly brewed beers, wood-fired pizzas, and juicy burgers. Pecan Street also serves up breakfast, live music, and Texas wines and has a pleasant patio out back for enjoying it all. **Bryan's on 290** (830-868-2424; www.bryanson290.com), 300 E Main St., is a treat on TX 290 in Johnson City. Diners are pleasantly surprised by this dynamic restaurant, where half a chicken with smoked Gouda macaroni and cheese shares the menu with pork belly pineapple fried rice. A delicious detour.

Housed in an old lumber yard, the **East Main Grill** (830-868-7710; www.theoldlumberyard.weebly.com), 209 E Main St., is a welcome stopping point for both classics like chicken-fried steaks and creative dishes like pork rib eye with chipotle plum sauce, both served with a heaping scoop of homemade garlic mashed potatoes.

The tables at the **Hill Country Cupboard** (830-225-1491; www.hillcountrycupboard.com), 101 US-281, are covered with disposable, checkered tablecloths, and iced tea is served in

LBJ'S TEXAS

Johnson City and nearby Stonewall are each home to significant sites from the life of President Lyndon Baines Johnson. There is no entrance fee for the parks, though donations are accepted, and there is a charge for the 90-minute bus tour of the LBJ Ranch.

In Johnson City, the **National Park Service Visitor Center** (830-868-7128; www.nps.gov/lyjo) is located in the former Pedernales Hospital. It displays exhibits, photographs, and videos pertaining to President Johnson's life and times. Behind the center, visitors can take a free guided tour of **Johnson's boyhood home**, which has been restored to the look and feel of the 1920s. To the west, a short, 10-minute walk away, the **Johnson Settlement** includes original buildings built by President Johnson's ancestor, James Polk Johnson. The barn, windmill, water tank, and cooler house help to illustrate the pioneer ranching life of the 1800s.

Located on US 290 about 14 miles west of Johnson City, near Stonewall, is the **Lyndon B. Johnson State Park & Historic Site Visitor Center** (830-644-2252; www.tpwd.texas.gov). LBJ spent so much time at his beloved ranch during his administration that it became known as the Texas White House. These days it remains a working ranch, with an operating Head Start preschool started during Johnson's administration. It is the final resting place of the president, who was buried here, in the family's cemetery, on January 25, 1973.

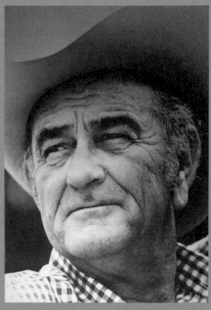

PRESIDENT LYNDON BAINES JOHNSON

battered plastic tumblers. Then again, there's no need for niceties when your specialty is chicken-fried steaks the size of dinner plates.

NEARBY

Leaving Johnson City and heading east on RR 2766, you can stop in for a glass of wine at **Texas Hills Vineyard** (830-868-2321; www.texashillsvineyard.com) before continuing on to **Pedernales Falls State Park**.

Kerrville

Established in the early 1850s, Kerrville has always depended on water for its success and prosperity. In 1857 a German miller and millwright duo built a large gristmill and sawmill here that transformed the town into a regional economic center and supplier of lumber and other goods to growing San Antonio, 62 miles to the southeast.

Water is still important here, with the clean, cool Guadalupe River running right through town and the surrounding parks. A quiet county seat, Kerrville is the largest town in the area and perhaps best known these days for its highly acclaimed music marathon, the Kerrville Folk Festival (see page 169).

✲ To See

A dozen galleries and museums in Kerrville have organized the **Second Saturday Art Trail** (www.artinthehills.com), hosting afternoon receptions and special events in their respective establishments on the second Saturday of every month.

Schreiner Mansion (830-895-5222; www.caillouxfoundation.org), formerly the Hill Country Museum, is housed in Captain Charles Schreiner's home, a massive native-stone structure built between 1879 and 1896. A native Frenchman, Schreiner moved to San Antonio with his family in 1852 and joined the Texas Rangers in 1854 at the age of 16. Schreiner fought in the Civil War, opened a mercantile establishment, excelled in banking, ranching, and marketing wool and mohair, and, in 1880, purchased the Y. O. Ranch. As Schreiner's wealth grew, so did his philanthropic interests, and he established the Schreiner Institute, now Schreiner University, in 1917. This museum, with its creaky hardwood floors, period furnishings, and quirky details, such as the trapdoor leading to a tunnel the captain used to safeguard money, tells the story of his bygone era and his lasting effect on Kerrville. Open for special events throughout the year; check website for details.

THE PACE SLOWS DOWN IN THE HILL COUNTRY.

MEDINA

Midway between Bandera and Kerrville, along a picturesque stretch of TX 16, is Medina, a blink-and-you'll-miss-it gem of a town. Spend the night at Koyote Ranch, slurp an apple cider slushy at Love Creek Orchards, and savor a little bit of Texas that's off the beaten path.

Love Creek Orchards (830-589-2202; www.lovecreekorchards.com) If you aren't hungry when you arrive, the smell of fresh hot apple pie wafting through Love Creek Orchards will have you salivating for a snack in no time. The Patio Café serves big, juicy burgers and sandwiches, with a side of chips and apples daily for lunch, and the country store sells all things apple, from ciders to jams and ice cream.

Medina Highpoint Resort (800-272-0183; www.rvcoutdoors.com/medina-highpoint-resort) Medina Highpoint Resort is a collection of cabins, campsites, and RV sites hugging the lovely green hillside outside Medina. With heated and air-conditioned bathrooms in the campground, a pool, and a camp store complete with a reasonably priced grill and deli, this is easy-does-it "roughing it" with family-friendly amenities.

The **Kerr Arts and Cultural Center** (830-895-2911; www.kacckerrville.com) is right at home in Kerrville's historic former post office, exhibiting works from photography to quilting, basketry to ceramics, all created by the center's 600 member artists.

In a limestone building designed by Texan architect O'Neil Ford, the **Museum of Western Art** (830-896-2553; www.museumofwesternart.com) pays homage to the West and its inhabitants. The artwork depicts western life from a wide range of perspectives, with images of the hardworking cowboy, Native Americans, and pioneer women figuring prominently. The interior of the museum is a juxtaposition of elements—mesquite wood floors and Saltillo tiles, crisp-white display walls, and bronze statues—with as much rough-hewn gracefulness as the artwork adorning it.

✳ Outdoor Activities

The 500-acre **Kerrville-Schreiner State Park** (830-257-7300; www.kerrville.org), on the banks of the Guadalupe River 3 miles southeast of Kerrville, offers picnicking, boating, and camping. There is tent camping along the water, two dozen air-conditioned cabins, and one large cabin that sleeps six. This stretch of the river is known for its fishing, and swimming is allowed, though there are no lifeguards on duty.

Another natural area to explore is the **Riverside Nature Center** (830-257-4837; www.riversidenaturecenter.org), which began to take shape in 1992 when a parcel of land was purchased and its native plants and habitat were restored through great community effort and volunteerism. The center opened in 1999, and its trails, which meander past native trees, wildflowers, birds, and butterflies, are as educational as they are relaxing.

✳ Lodging

It is essential to book a room in advance, particularly during festivals. Reservations may be made directly or through the following reservation services (the reservation services in Fredericksburg book rooms in Kerrville as well): **Main Street Bed and Breakfast Reservations Service** (888-559-8555; www.travelmainstreet.com) and **Gästehaus Schmidt** (866-427-8374; www.fbglodging.com). If you are looking for the charm of a B&B, you may want to stay closer to Fredericksburg, 25 miles north on TX 16. Kerrville does, however, have several conference centers that are happy to rent rooms to individuals, families, and groups.

Inn of the Hills Resort and Conference Center (830-895-5000; www .innofthehills.com), 1001 Junction Hwy. This inn has stood up to hundreds of family reunions, business conferences, and the stampede of children's feet racing through the courtyard to the tree-shaded, Olympic-size pool. While the rooms can feel somewhat dated, they are all clean and serviceable, with native-stone walls and ironwork details; ask for one of the pleasant poolside rooms on the ground floor. Annemarie's Alpine Lodge, the on-site restaurant, is known for its buffets, especially Sunday brunch, with its prime rib and abundant desserts. The Inn Pub features drinks and country and western music for dancing. $$.

Y. O. Ranch Resort and Conference Center (803-257-4440; www.yoresort .com), 2033 Sidney Baker St. Spacious rooms, two-room suites with bunk beds, a children's playground, swimming pool, and tennis, basketball, and volleyball courts, coupled with fairly reasonable rates and a convenient location near town, have made this resort a family favorite for years. Of course, this has also meant years of gentle wear and tear, but while it could use some updating or a fresh coat of paint, the Y. O. Ranch currently has a comfortable, well-worn feel that is right at home in the Hill Country. The weekday lunch buffet at the Branding Iron, their on-site restaurant, is very popular with locals. $$.

Mo Ranch Conference Center (800-460-4401; www.moranch.com), 2229 FM 1340. Located near the town of Hunt, west of Kerrville, this Presbyterian-affiliated ranch is known for hosting conferences, youth groups, and Road Scholar events, but there is also plenty of room for individuals and families who would like to enjoy swimming, horseback riding, a ropes course, and other recreational activities. Accommodations range from simply furnished two-bedroom apartments to tent camping sites, with hotel rooms and cabins in between. Since Mo Ranch is in a remote, rural area, all guests are required to purchase the modestly priced meal plan served in the communal dining hall. $$.

❋ Where to Eat

Though there aren't a lot of options, dining in Kerrville ranges from gourmet to grab-and-go, so you're sure to find something to suit your tastes.

Kerrville welcomed its very first train in 1887, and the entire town celebrated with music and barbecue. When the original wooden depot burned down in 1912, they built a masonry building to replace it in 1914, the current home of **Rails Café at The Depot** (830-257-3877; www .railscafe.com), 615 E Schreiner St. Now known for its elegant dining room, lovely patio, and delicious food, diners single out the salads, osso buco, and the shrimp Creole for praise.

For Mexican dining in Kerrville, folks head to **Francisco's** (830-257-2995; www .franciscos-restaurant.com), 201 Earl Garrett St., where the tortilla soup and *chile rellenos* are tops.

Nearby, fish tacos, outstanding antelope sliders with goat cheese, an extensive selection of beer and wine, and a slightly upscale but still casual atmosphere make **Grape Juice** (830-792-9463; www.grapejuiceonline.com), 623 Water St., popular with foodies. Of all the offerings, including tacos, burgers, sandwiches, and salads, the fried brussels sprouts topped with bacon are definitely a favorite. A pleasant patio adds to the ambiance.

If a burger is what you're after, stop in at **Classics Burgers and More** (830-257-8866; www.classicsburgers.net), 448 Sidney Baker St. S, for an enormous patty, massive onion rings, and a side of country charm.

Not surprisingly, the menu at **Cowboy Steak House** (830-896-5688; www.cowboysteakhouse.com), 416 Main St., is all meat. Stick with a porterhouse or try some quail. Sample shish kebab sirloin chunks or branch out into buffalo steak. Choose between rack of lamb, chicken breast, and whole catfish. While any entrée is served with soup or a salad, vegetables are available only "on request."

Conchita's on Main (830-895-7708), 810 Main St., is a humble spot serving the small town with pride and enthusiasm. Theresa, the owner, cook, and baker who named her little restaurant for her grandmother, Conchita, is in the kitchen every day, cooking fresh and tasty dishes of her own creation. The menu runs the range from Tex-Mex to café-style sandwiches. There are tacos, burgers, wraps, and the ever-popular chicken avocado eggrolls. Finish off your meal with a slice of her homemade cake. Open for lunch only.

Hill Country Café (830-257-6665; www.hill-country-cafe.com), 806 Main St., has been around forever, serving eggs, toast, bacon, and hot coffee to Kerrville's early risers. Cash only.

The Lakehouse (830-895-3188; www.hillcountrycookin.com), 1655 Junction Hwy., is known for its all-you-can-eat fried catfish and bite-size shrimp served with pinto beans, coleslaw, french fries, and hush puppies. This is a comfortable, no-nonsense place right on the water.

✱ Special Events

FESTIVALS The nationally acclaimed **Kerrville Folk Festival** (830-257-3600; www.kerrville-music.com) is held on an outdoor stage at the Quiet Valley Ranch RV Park and Campgrounds (830-257-7474)

in the peaceful Hill Country 9 miles south of Kerrville on TX 16. When the festival began, in 1972, it was centered on folk music, but it has grown to include acoustic rock, bluegrass, blues, country, and jazz. Many major-label artists played "Kerrville" on their way up, and some frequently return. The event takes place in May, starting the Thursday before Memorial Day, and lasts for two weeks.

Kerrville celebrates Easter weekend with an event that includes lots and lots of food and exercise, the **Annual Kerrville EasterFest and Cook-Off** (www.kerrvilletx.com). With a 5K Easter Run, egg hunts, children's games, washer pitching (akin to the game of horseshoes), armadillo races, and copious amounts of steaming hot chili, this one's fun. At the same time, the Easter Hill Country Bike Tour draws cyclists from throughout the region to the back roads of the Hill Country.

At the end of September, the Texas Heritage Music Foundation hosts the **Texas Heritage Living History Weekend** (830-792-1945; www.texasheritagemusic.org), a three-day event devoted entirely to Texas music and heritage. An impressive and eclectic lineup of talent includes gospel choirs, storytellers, trick ropers, *vaqueros* (cowboys), square dancers, and cloggers, all performing on the Schreiner University campus.

The Kerr County Fair (830-257-6833; www.kerrcountyfair.com) in October features a parade, carnival, 4H livestock exhibits, chili and barbecue cook-offs, dancing, and music.

Kerr County Market Days (www.kerrmarketdays.org) and the Hill Country Swap Meet are held together at the Hill Country Youth Event Center on the first Saturday of each month, April through December, except in August. A mix of handmade treasures and flea market finds.

Luckenbach

If you really want to slow down, grind to a halt in Luckenbach, where the only movement is tapping feet and guitar picking in the shade of surrounding oak trees. A tiny cluster of rustic wooden buildings, including the multipurpose General Store, make up this little community, which is worth a trip for the music and dancing alone.

Immortalized in Waylon Jennings' song "Luckenbach, Texas (Back to the Basics of Love)," little Luckenbach came into being in the 1840s and 1850s when several German-speaking families decided to settle along the banks of Grape Creek. The population fluctuated from 150 in 1896 to 492 in 1902, but by the 1960s it had leveled off to 25. In 1971, John Russell (Hondo) Crouch purchased the settlement, declared himself mayor, and set its spirit free. Live music on holidays brings out the locals, visitors, and Harley riders, who queue up for pulled-pork sandwiches and beer. Offbeat and good-natured events, such as the annual Hug-In held in February, capture the character of the hamlet beautifully. As the town slogan goes, "Everybody is somebody in Luckenbach." And if you're lucky enough to go, you will be too.

Open for business since 1849, the **General Store** (830-997-3224; www .luckenbachtexas.com) is old and creaky, with a sloping front porch, a bar in the

STATUE OF JOHN RUSSELL "HONDO" CROUCH, FORMER "MAYOR" OF LUCKENBACH

back, and spaces in between the floorboards that let in the draft. Folks here just love it to death. With live music every night at 7 and plenty of Hondo-style cowboy hats for sale, what's not to love? The store's sleek website has all the details.

✳ Lodging

There aren't many options for lodging in Luckenbach. **Full Moon Inn** (830-997-2205; www.fullmooninn.com), 3234 Luckenbach Rd. A log cabin from the 1800s, an old smokehouse, and a replicated Sunday house form a little compound of accommodations on 12 grassy acres with a creek. Soft sheets, Jacuzzi tubs, and sweet potato pancakes more than make up for the lack of television. While the mailing address for the Full Moon Inn is Fredericksburg, it is a half mile from Luckenbach. $$$$.

Marble Falls

Marble Falls, so named for the marble outcroppings over which the nearby Colorado River flows, was founded in 1887. Located just north of town on RM 1431, Granite Mountain was once a huge dome of pink and red granite; it was quarried in the 1880s to construct the Texas Capitol in Austin. These days, there is not much granite to see; a plaque at the picnic area across the road tells the story. Located on US 281 between Johnson City and Burnet, and within striking distance of many of the Highland Lakes, Marble Falls is a good place to stop for a bite to eat.

✳ Where to Eat

The **Blue Bonnet Cafe** (830-693-2344; www.bluebonnetcafe.net), 211 US-28, is not much to look at. In fact, you just might miss its red and white sign when rounding the curve over the bridge in Marble Falls. One thing you're sure to notice is the line of people snaking out the front door, particularly on weekends. Consistently crowded since it opened in 1929, this very casual diner has pot roasts, chicken-fried steaks, fried okra, catfish, an all-day breakfast menu, and all kinds of pie.

In the mood for a pint? Swing by the **Double Horn Brewery** (830-693-5165; www.doublehornbrewing.com), 208 Ave. H, and wash down overstuffed sandwiches, burgers, shrimp and grits, and appetizers—try the fried avocado with lump crab—with a brew. The spacious dining room and patio out back are both light and bright.

Stop by **Noon Spoon Cafe** (830-798-2347; www.noonspooncafe.com), 610 Broadway St., for lunch. The colorful café has healthy salads, sandwiches, wraps, hot baked potatoes, breakfast tacos, casseroles, and quesadillas galore.

NEARBY

From Marble Falls, you can easily visit the Highland Lakes, Spicewood Vineyards, and Sweet Berry Farm (830-798-1462; www.sweetberryfarm.com), with its mazes, hayrides, picnic tables, and U-pick fruits and vegetables—strawberries and blackberries in the spring, tomatoes in the summer, and pumpkins in the fall.

CHOCOLATE CREAM PIE AND COFFEE AT THE BLUE BONNET CAFE

HIGHLAND LAKES

The Colorado River passes through the northern part of the Hill Country, picking up the spring-fed Pedernales, Llano, San Saba, and Concho Rivers as tributaries before flowing through the city of Austin. The river then continues over the flat, alluvial land of the Coastal Plain and into the Gulf of Mexico. Throughout the early 1800s, the Colorado was prone to impassable logjams and periodic flooding that threatened riverside settlements. The need for irrigation, a reliable water source, and flood control prompted the Lower Colorado River Authority (LCRA) to construct six dams along the river between 1935 and 1951, creating a chain of six lakes known as the Highland Lakes. The Highland Lakes and their 25 waterside parks are favorite spots for boating, fishing, camping, and ecotourism. The lakes and their shorelines also provide habitat for rare, endangered, and migratory birds, including the American bald eagle, and support a large variety of wildlife.

Area websites—www.highlandlakes.com, www.lakesandhills.com, www.lcra.org, and www.texasoutside.com—provide details of the region's lodging, dining, and recreation.

LAKE BUCHANAN

Lake Buchanan, some 30 miles long, is the largest, oldest, and northernmost of the Highland Lakes; it is located approximately 75 miles north of Austin. The eastern shoreline is rocky, with granite cliffs, waterfalls, and deep, cold water, while the western shore has beaches for swimming. The majestic American bald eagle nests in the area surrounding the lake during the winter and early spring. The closest large towns are Burnet to the east and Llano to the west.

BURNET

Designated as the Bluebonnet Capital of Texas, Burnet stages the **Bluebonnet Festival** (512-756-4297; www.bluebonnetfestival.org) during the second weekend in April, complete with a parade, carnival, food, live music, and a good-natured Wild West–style shoot-out.

Austin Steam Train (512-477-8468; www.austinsteamtrain.org) The *Hill Country Flyer* travels from Cedar Park to downtown Burnet and loops back again. While the train does not have air-conditioning, it makes up for it with plenty of vintage details such as wood window moldings, upholstered seating, and an old-time concession stand. The train is operated by the Austin Steam Train Association, a local nonprofit whose mission is to preserve, interpret, and re-create the firsthand experience of historic steam-era railroading.

Canyon of the Eagles Resort and Nature Park (512-334-2070; www.canyonoftheeagles.com) This lodge, complete with fairly basic accommodations, cabins, campground, restaurant, and a tiny swimming pool, is located within the confines of an LCRA-owned, 940-acre public park, most of which is a nature preserve. The park includes 14 miles of hiking trails (maps available at the main lodge), an educational nature center, and boat rentals. Day-use passes are available.

Vanishing Texas River Cruise (512-756-6986; www.vtrc.com) The boat leaves from the Canyon of the Eagles Resort and Nature Park for ecological cruises on Lake Buchanan; vineyard tours and wildflower and dinner cruises are also offered.

Eagle Eye Observatory (800-977-0081; www.austinastro.org; Austin Astronomical Society) This observatory houses a 16-inch Ealing "Educator" Cassegrain telescope and hosts monthly stargazing parties; see website for details.

LLANO

Cooper's Old Time Pit Bar-B-Que (325-247-5713; www.coopersbbq.com) Pick your meat at the outdoor pits, watch the pit master submerge it in sauce, and proceed inside to pick out your sides. Cooper's may be slow-cooked, but the pizzas from **Tommy's Mesquite Flamed Pizza** (325-247-0388) are baked hot and fast over a hot mesquite fire in a steel drum oven Tommy made himself. This is a simple, no-frills spot with plenty of personality and outdoor seating, just north of the bridge and beside the Llano County Historical Museum. Day-trippers say Tommy's hits the spot after a trip to Enchanted Rock (see page 161).

TOW

Fall Creek Vineyards (325-379-5361; www.fcv.com; see "Hill Country Vineyards" on page 154) Situated at the northwest end of the lake, Fall Creek Vineyards makes a good destination for wine lovers.

INKS LAKE

Inks Lake State Park (512-793-2223; www.tpwd.texas.gov) Formerly ranchland, Inks Lake State Park is now a recreational facility on the eastern shores of Inks Lake, whose water levels remain constant throughout the year, regardless of drought, making it a reliable spot for swimming (be aware, the beach is unsupervised), fishing, and boating. Tent and primitive backpack camping are available, and limited-use cabins are equipped with two bunk beds, air conditioning, electricity, an outdoor grill, and a water spigot. Two of the cabins are handicapped accessible. Canoes and paddleboats are also available for rent, as are golf clubs and carts for the waterfront nine-hole golf course. Nearby **Longhorn Cavern State Park** (see "Texas State Parks" on page 162) is a geological wonder.

LAKE LBJ

The shoreline of Lake LBJ is very developed, with large homes along the resort town of Horseshoe Bay and particularly Applehead Island. A popular spot for boating, the lake can get crowded on weekends. Nearby, Longhorn Cavern State Park makes an easy side trip. The closest large town is Marble Falls to the east. Part of the **Texas Wine Trail** winds through the region, with **Lost Creek Vineyard** near Sunrise Beach on the western shore of Lake LBJ and **Spicewood Vineyards** just a short drive south along TX 71. **Lake LBJ Resort, Marina, and Country Club** (325-388-9393; www.lakelbjfun.com) rents condos and watercraft year-round.

LAKE MARBLE FALLS

The smallest of the Highland Lakes, this narrow, almost riverlike lake is surrounded by mostly steep, rocky, and privately owned land, though there are three modest city parks on the north shore of the lake just west of US 281. In August, the **Marble Falls LakeFest** (www.marblefallslakefest.com) brings ear-splitting speedboat drag racing to the lake. The nearby town of Marble Falls (see page 171) offers several tasty restaurants, all of which are local favorites.

LAKE TRAVIS

A party lake, Lake Travis is often swarming with motorized watercraft on weekends. Numerous parks allow day-trippers to get a little closer to nature on the outskirts of Austin, and a variety of eateries make this Highland Lake a sophisticated stopover for drinks or a meal.

PARKS Hippie Hollow (www.hippiehollow.com) A favorite spot along the rocky shores of Lake Travis for folks who like to swim and sunbathe in the buff. From MoPac (Loop 1), Capital of Texas Highway (Loop 360), or I-35, take 2222 west to Ranch TX 620 and follow the signs.

BOAT RENTALS Daybreak Boat Rentals (512-266-2176; www.daybreakboatrentals.com)
    Just for Fun (512-266-9710; www.jff.net)

DINING The Oasis (512-266-2442; www.oasis-austin.com) With multiple levels of decks jutting over Lake Travis, each dotted with dozens of colorful umbrellas, The Oasis has a very casual, come-as-you-are atmosphere; just the sort of place to relax and unwind over drinks. Splendid views of Lake Travis and the stunning Central Texas sunset.

LAKE AUSTIN

Located within the city limits, Lake Austin is an aquatic playground of parks, boats, cruises, plenty of casual, family-friendly spots to grab food and drinks, and lots of live music.

PARKS Emma Long Metropolitan Park (512-346-1831; www.austintexas.gov) Biking, camping, hiking, and swimming.

BOAT RENTAL Sun & Fun Watercraft Rentals (512-306-1820; www.sunfunrental.com) Rents Jet Skis and pontoon and ski boats.

CRUISES Lake Austin Riverboats (512-345-5220; www.austinriverboats.com) Enjoy a leisurely cruise aboard an authentic stern-wheel riverboat.
    Austin Duck Adventures (512-477-5274; www.austinducks.com) Drive around Austin in an amphibious British Alvis Stalwart before splashing into Lake Austin.

LODGING Lake Austin Spa (see page 60).

DINING The County Line (512-346-3664; www.countyline.com) The place to go for great barbecue with a great view.
    Hula Hut (512-476-4852; www.hulahut.com) A favorite spot for drinks, Hula Hut specializes in Mexico-meets-Polynesia cuisine with guacamole salads served beside pupu platters, seating overlooking the water, and a fun, breezy vibe. Owned by the creators of the local Tex-Mex chain restaurant Chuy's (www.chuys.com) and the Shady Grove (www.theshadygrove.com) in Austin.
    Mozart's Coffee Roasters (512-477-2900; www.mozartscoffee.com) Coffee and chocolate treats on the banks of Lake Austin, a few minutes' drive from downtown Austin. Stellar views of Lake Austin, outdoor seating on a spacious deck, and nightly live jazz, folk, or classical guitar.

Wimberley

Along the banks of Cypress Creek, just 30 minutes south of Austin or 15 minutes west of San Marcos along RR 12, Wimberley is a small but thriving town of artists and other folks who just like living "not in Austin." With a creek lined with bald cypress and pecan trees, the town is beautifully scenic. The dramatic Devil's Backbone (see "Outdoor Activities" on page 177) is visible from certain lookout points.

Founded in 1856, when a Mr. Winters built a small gristmill along the creek, the tiny settlement was first known as Winters Creek. The Cude family then bought the mill, and the community became known as Cude's Mill. In 1874 Pleasant Wimberley took over the mill, and the town's moniker changed again, this time to Wimberley's Mill. In 1880, on a petition for a post office, the town was referred to as Wimberleyville. The name stuck and was shortened over time to simply Wimberley. The mill continued operating, as a lumber mill, gristmill, flour mill, molasses mill, and cotton gin, before being razed in 1934. The community that had built up around the mill remained, and starting in the 1930s Wimberley became a tourist destination. Thematic events such as Market Days, held the first Saturday of each month, Second Saturday Gallery Trail, and Third Thursdays of evening music and shopping are popular. Each is hosted when the weather is pleasant, roughly March through December. Wimberley has a culture, community, and charm all its own and is enjoyable as a day trip or as an overnight retreat.

✳ To See

An enclave of artists, Wimberley has some galleries and cultural events of particular note and a full calendar of festivals; see www.wimberley.org for details. The **EmilyAnn Theatre** (512-847-6969; www.emilyann.org) is an outdoor community theater that stages, among other productions, a summerlong Shakespeare under the Stars, performed entirely by children and young adults no older than high school seniors (the only accredited high school Shakespearean theater in the United States). The theater also hosts a number of family-friendly events, such as a holiday tree lighting in December and a Butterfly Festival in April. The outdoor movie theater, the **Corral Theatre** (512-847-5994; www.corraltheatre.com), invites guests to enjoy a show under the stars. This local favorite, originally built in downtown Wimberley to show reel-to-reel films and host community meetings, relocated to Rocky River Ranch, a nearby girls' summer camp, in 1966. The camp has changed over the years, but the Corral continues to charm. For locals, it's a summertime tradition to catch first-run movies shown here on the "big screen" of white painted wood. The Corral is open May through September; doors open at dusk and the movie starts at dark. Moviegoers are welcome to bring their own food, drinks, and chairs. Wooden bleachers catch overflow and kids. Popcorn and candy for a dollar.

Opened by Tim de Jong in 1992, the **Wimberley Glass Works** (512-213-4148; www.wgw.com) rose quickly to become one of the region's foremost art glass studios and galleries. While the gallery space here is filled with exquisite handblown glass in every imaginable shape, size, and color, the best part of the Wimberley Glass Works is the live demonstrations, where you can see artists coaxing vases, pitchers, stemware, and art out of molten glass. After many years in Wimberley, the Glass Works is now located on RR 12 halfway between Wimberley and San Marcos, with a San Marcos address.

✳ To Do

A tremendous online resource for all outdoor recreation in Texas is **Texas Outside**, www.texasoutside.com.

BICYCLING Bicycling, both road and mountain biking, is big in Central Texas, especially in Austin and the Hill Country. Rentals are available through Hill Country Bicycle Works (830-990-2609, www.hillcountrybicycle.com), which has shops in both Kerrville and Fredericksburg.

> Helpful websites include:
> **Cycle Texas** (www.cycletexas.com)
> **Hill Country Bicycle Touring Club** (www.hcbtc.org)
> **Texas State Park System** (www.tpwd.texas.gov)

BIRD-WATCHING The Hill Country is a great spot to catch a glimpse of rare, migratory, and native birds. Online, Texas Parks and Wildlife (www.tpwd.texas.gov) and the Travis County Audubon Society (www.travisaudubon.org) both offer a wealth of information. See "Suggested References" in the Information chapter for a selection of bird-watching guides.

BOATING, CANOEING, AND KAYAKING Boat rentals are available at the Highland Lakes and Kerrville-Schreiner State Park in Kerrville.

CAMPING The state parks dotting the Hill Country offer a variety of camping opportunities. There is a state park with camping on Inks Lake in the Highland Lakes and another in Blanco (see "Outdoor Activities" on page 143). Kerrville's city park has camping. A terrific online source for all camping in the region—private or public, tent or RV—is www.texasoutside.com.

CLIMBING **Texas Climbing Adventures** (512-590-2988; www.texasclimbing adventures.com) offers weekend classes at Enchanted Rock State Natural Area near Fredericksburg.

FISHING There is plenty of fishing in the Highland Lakes and state parks, and you don't need a license to fish from shore in a Texas state park. See www.tpwd.texas.gov for details. Other online resources include www.texasoutside.com and www.txfishing .com.

GOLF **Lady Bird Johnson Municipal Golf Course** (830-997-4010; www.golf fredericksburg.com)
Scott Schreiner Golf Course (830-257-4982; www.golfkerrvilletex.com)

SWIMMING Swimming is available at the beaches of the Highland Lakes and several of the state parks (see separate listings).

TOURS **The Bluebonnet Trail, Texas Lavender Trail,** and **Texas Wine Trail** are self-guided. The **Austin Steam Train** (512-477-8468; www.austinsteamtrain.org) runs vintage trains through the Hill Country, and boat cruises are available on the Highland Lakes. (See separate listings on all the above.)

GO TEXAN

As part of a marketing campaign by the Texas Department of Agriculture, when you travel in Texas you may see the GO TEXAN sticker or stamp on agricultural products such as food, wine, and beef, indicating that the item was grown or processed in Texas. For a list of statewide farmers' markets, wineries, native plant nurseries, restaurants, products, or even recipes with a uniquely Texas twist, visit www.gotexan.org and shop with Lone Star pride.

BIG LOCAL FLAVOR

TUBING Probably the best spot to tube in the Hill Country is Blanco State Park (see page 143).

ZIP LINING **Cypress Valley Canopy Tours** (512-264-8880; www.cypressvalley canopytours.com) Tour participants use steel zip lines to travel between treetop platforms among old-growth cypresses. Get back to nature with an overnight stay in one of their custom-designed tree houses. In the Hill Country 30 minutes west of Austin.

✳ Outdoor Activities

Natural attractions in Wimberley include **Blue Hole** (512-660-9111; www .friendsofbluehole.org), a renowned natural swimming hole where folks come to splash and swing among the cypress trees, just a short walk from the center of town. Stunning scenery is visible from **Devil's Backbone**, a steep scenic ridge that offers stunning views; drive out RR 12 to RR 32 and turn west. **Jacob's Well** (512-214-4593; www .co.hays.tx.us/jwna.aspx) is what's called, in geological parlance, a "perennial karstic spring." The bubbling artesian spring, the headwaters of Cypress Creek, was discovered in the 1850s when curious settlers traced the creek to its source. The mouth of the spring is rather small, only 12 feet in diameter, and ringed with limestone cliffs and native vegetation. The depth of the cave system is truly amazing, with researchers reporting a 30-foot drop from the surface and 90 more vertical feet winding through several chambers and narrow passes. The water is deep, clear, inviting, and

HILL COUNTRY VISTA

a constantly cool 68 degrees. Swimming is permitted Memorial Day through Labor Day, but extreme caution is urged. The 80-plus acres surrounding the well have been consolidated and set aside as the **Jacob's Well Natural Area**, preserving this unique ecosystem, geologic wonder, and popular swimming hole for future generations. The park includes walking trails favored by birders and a nature center.

✳ Lodging

Blair House Inn (512-847-1111; www .blairhouseinn.com), 100 W Spoke Hill Dr. With deluxe cottages, a cooking school, an art gallery, and a restaurant, pool, and spa, once you arrive you'll have no reason to leave. The themed rooms revolve around Texas and the Southwest, with three archangel cottages thrown in. The Fort Worth Suite, for example, has a rich, leather sofa and chair, tan walls, a dark wood sleigh bed, crimson details, and a few requisite stars on the walls, just enough to capture the feel but not overly drawn out. Stunning views round out the luxurious offerings. $$$.

Creekhaven Inn (512-847-9344; www .creekhaveninn.com), 400 Mill Race Ln.

This inn may be relatively new, but it shares the banks of Cypress Creek with several towering cypress trees that are as old as anybody's guess. The 13 rooms are as unique and colorful as the wildflowers they're named for. $$$.

Cypress Creek Cottages (512-847-5950; www.cypresscreekcottages .com), 1 Woodcreek Circle. A dozen cottages range from cozy to spacious, each with a kitchen, deck, and private outdoor hot tub, and all pet and family friendly. There are studios, one-bedrooms, one-bedrooms plus loft, and two-bedroom color-coordinated cottages scattered about the peaceful property, with plenty of trees and tweeting birds, a dog park, a communal fire pit, and easy creek access. Guests appreciate the casual, relaxed atmosphere, removed

COUNTRY MUSIC ON A HOT AFTERNOON

from the bustle but just a minute's drive to town. $$.

Hotel Flora and Fauna (512-842-9110; www.hotelfloraandfauna.com), 400 River Rd. The sister property to Cypress Creek, this is a modern twist on the classic motor courts of the past. The boutique hotel complex, surrounding a courtyard and solar-powered pool, features 12 "king studios" equipped with a kitchenette, dining area, king-size beds with memory-foam mattresses, sleeper sofas, and even record players with a selection of vinyl. Unique touches include original artwork in each room and a breakfast voucher to the Sugar Shack, just a short stroll away. $$.

✳ Where to Eat

The **Leaning Pear** (512-847-7327; www .leaningpear.com), 111 River Rd., serves gourmet food in a bright, airy restaurant with soaring ceilings and a "tree house" out back. Perky salads, savory quiches, flavorful soups, a BLT with Brie, and roasted poblano pimento cheese sandwiches are just some of the many reasons diners line up for a seat in this popular—and delicious—lunch and dinner spot.

Stop by the **Sugar Shack Bakery** (512-847-0477; www.sugarshackbakery.net), 111 River Rd., for a treat; the macaroons are especially delicious. Or try a savory croissant for a light lunch on the shaded patio.

For atmospheric fine dining on the edge of town, head north to 16920 Ranch Rd 12 to **Jobell Café and Bistro** (512-847-5700; www.jobellcafe.com), where chicken and sweet potato dumplings, lamb-stuffed quail, and venison chili are all on the menu. Local ingredients abound, extending even to the luscious lavender pound cake dessert served with fresh berries. The bistro is set back from the road in a grove of trees and has a rustic farmhouse feel that pairs perfectly with its sophisticated cuisine.

NEARBY AND
IN BETWEEN

■

GEORGETOWN

NEW BRAUNFELS AND GRUENE

SAN MARCOS

NEARBY AND IN BETWEEN

nterstate 35, the highway connecting Austin and San Antonio, also passes **George-town**, **New Braunfels**, and **San Marcos**, which are great places to pull in for a meal, a day, or even a weekend. Thirty miles north of Austin, historic **Georgetown** (see below) is a remarkably well-preserved town with a restored courthouse at its center, antiques shops surrounding its square, and a lovely hike and bike trail. Thirty miles south of Austin, **San Marcos** (see page 192) has become known for its outlet malls, though nature enthusiasts will enjoy a trip to the educational Aquarena Center for a ride down the river on a glass-bottom boat. Another 20 miles south, **New Braunfels** has a reputation for some of the best river tubing in the area and is home to lovely historic **Gruene** (see page 186).

Georgetown

Straddling I-35, Georgetown is located at the spot where the fertile plains of East Texas start to give way to the jagged wooded ravines and sloping hills of the Hill Country. A pleasant side trip from Austin, Georgetown is home to Southwestern University. Chartered in 1875, Southwestern is often cited at the state's oldest university. Southwestern's relationship with Georgetown is one of quiet intermingling; the university's concerts, gallery shows, and theatrical productions are offered throughout the school year and are open to the public. Details at www.southwestern.edu.

Georgetown has won awards for its well-preserved, historic downtown, which comprises dozens of detail-rich buildings and homes dating to the 1880s gathered around a traditional Texas square with a courthouse in its center. The seat of Williamson County, Georgetown has become a popular commuter town for families and, with the construction of age-restricted developments, a home for retirees who come for the area's livability, climate, and access to Austin. Rapid growth has Georgetown focused on maintaining the small-town atmosphere that makes it such an enjoyable destination.

Stop in and say howdy at the friendly **Visitor Center** (800-436-8696; www .visit.georgetown.org), poke around the square's antiques and gift shops, and stay for a bite to eat.

✳ Things to See and Do

Theater buffs throughout the region frequent the **Georgetown Palace Theatre** (512-869-7469; www. georgetownpalace.com). Built in 1925, the Palace was originally a silent movie house. "Talkies" arrived in 1929, and the building was given its present art deco facade in 1936. A respite from the hard times during the Great Depression, World War II, and droughts in the 1950s, the Palace was the town's cultural and creative center. In 1989, the building was put up for sale; 300 concerned citizens bonded together to purchase, improve, and convert the Palace from a cinema to a theater. A true community endeavor, the now-thriving Palace stages spirited shows all year long, offering up both enjoyable theater and a slice of small-town Texas.

Georgetown's historic small-town ambience makes a scenic backdrop for a variety of festivals and special events. In April, Georgetown, the "Red Poppy Capital of Texas," hosts the weekend-long **Red Poppy Festival** (www.redpoppyfestival.com). **Market Days** (www.visit.georgetown.org) are held from 10 until 5 on the second Saturday of each month between March and December.

Stop by **Inner Space Cavern** (512-931-2283; www.myinnerspacecavern.com), located directly below busy I-35; it was discovered in 1963 during drilling to determine the stability of the ground prior to highway construction. As the holes were bored, the bit being used abruptly dropped dozens of feet, indicating the presence of a cavity beneath 40 feet of solid limestone. An adventurous highway worker rode a drill bit underground to take the first peek. Today, Inner Space Cavern is one of the more accessible caves in the region, with a unique cable car, paved trails, and a year-round temperature of 72 degrees.

✳ Lodging

The Sweet Lemon Inn (512-270-0812; www.sweetlemoninn.com), 812 S Church St. Located in a lovely restored 1918 bungalow, this bright green and yellow boutique B&B and café is just off the Georgetown Square. Rooms are bright and airy, with colorful furniture, bedding, and whimsical accents. $$$. When you wake, slip downstairs to the **Sweet Lemon Kitchen**. Try a cinnamon roll or a sweet or savory *kolache*, a Czech pastry popular in Central Texas. For lunch, the turkey and Brie sandwich is made special by their homemade spiced jam and locally baked poblano sourdough bread. Be sure to leave room to taste their buttery lemon cookies and lemon squares.

✳ Where to Eat

The **Monument Cafe** (512-930-9586; www.themonumentcafe.com), 500 S Austin Ave., opened in 1995, has become an institution; trying to get a seat in its '40s-style dining room or lunch counter at mealtime can take some patience. Fried whole catfish, Kobe steaks, and fried chicken with cream gravy are all served with generous side portions of comfort foods, many organic and/or locally sourced. Monument's signature chocolate pie is the real thing, from its thick, nutty crust made of toasted pecans, through its silky, rich, chocolate mousse filling, straight to the luscious, homemade whipped cream slathered on top.

THE SWEET LEMON INN, GEORGETOWN

'CUE

If you're coming to Texas, chances are you're expecting to sample some drip-down-your-chin juicy barbecue. Before you settle in with a dozen paper napkins and a pack of saltines, you might like to know the provenance of the tradition of which you are about to partake. Though the earliest details are somewhat murky, we know that folks around the world have been cooking outdoors since the dawn of time. At some point, these chefs began to dig pits to cook in, concentrating heat, smoke, and flavor and rendering even tough, stringy, and sinewy slabs of meat edible, moist, and tender. From clambakes to pig roasts, each culture has its version. The origins of the name—*barbecue*—are even more elusive, but theories abound. It may derive from *barbacoa*, the Spanish version of the name that the Taino Indians of the Caribbean gave to the process they had perfected of slow-cooking and smoking large pieces of meat over a pit fire.

In the US, the style and flavor of barbecue depend on the region. In the Southeast, folks love to drown their pork barbecue in a sweet tomato sauce with a vinegary twang, while the Southwest favors its meat dry-rubbed without any sauce at all. Chicago barbecue is heavy on both the sauce and the pepper. Generally speaking, the farther north you go, the greater the chance that if you order barbecue, you'll get chicken. In Texas, barbecue has always meant beef above all. Typically, the meat is dry-rubbed, smoked, and sauced with various signature concoctions that run the gamut from sweet and smoky to hot and spicy.

A PACKED DINING ROOM AT SMITTY'S IN LOCKHART

A few blocks downhill toward the river, you'll find **El Monumento** (512-591-7866; www.elmonumentogeorgetown .com), 205 2nd St., owned and operated by the same folks as the Monument, where the menu is centered on fresh, homestyle Mexican food, including rotisserie chicken, mesquite-grilled beef tenderloin, and *carne asada*. One of the best times to go is during the daily happy hour, when you can enjoy drinks, appetizers, and the real star of the show—the atmosphere and architecture. Built on a bluff overlooking Blue Hole and the San Gabriel River, the restaurant is both spacious and cozy with terrace seating, a charming interior courtyard, plenty of windows, and lush native landscaping.

BARBECUE WITH ALL THE FIXIN'S AT LULING CITY MARKET IN LULING

Some of the best barbecue anywhere is at **Franklin Barbecue** (see page 69) in Austin, **Cooper's** (see page 173) in Llano, and Louie Mueller Barbecue (512-352-6206; www.louiemuellerbarbecue.com) farther afield in Taylor. However, heading east of Austin and following the smell of the pits will take you on a self-guided tasting tour of some great, old-school 'cue. Starting in Lockhart at **Kreuz Market** (512-398-2361; www.kreuzmarket.com; pronounced "krites"), you will be served a huge hunk of hot-from-the-pit beef, pork, or sausage wrapped in butcher paper, a meal you will likely remember for years to come. No sauce and no utensils come with your order—the custom for over 100 years—you get just meat, some saltines, a huge pickle, and half an onion, and off you go to one of the communal tables to dig in. Many customers come for the brisket alone, but the prime rib and clod (shoulder) have garnered raves; and although it is very un-Texan, the pork chop is fabulous. When Kreuz moved from more modest digs down the street to this newer, larger space in 1999, it updated its menu by adding German potato salad, sauerkraut, and beans. Other than that, happily, the owners haven't changed a thing. **Black's BBQ** (512-398-2712; www.blacksbbq.com) and **Smitty's Market** (512-398-9344; www.smittysmarket.com) both rank high on locals' lists of regional favorites, and are open on Sunday, when Kreuz is closed. In Central Texas, barbecue is often served with a side of sausage—a smoky beef bratwurst—and the region's gold standard is Elgin sausage, made in Elgin, Texas. **Meyer's Elgin Smokehouse** (512-281-3331; www.meyerselginsausage .com) and **Southside Market** (512-281-4650; www.southsidemarket.com) are legendary.

Back on the square, **Wildfire** (512-869-3473; www.wildfiretexas.com), 812 S Austin Ave., is Georgetown's "date night" restaurant. The oak-fired grill serves as the inspiration for an inventive menu featuring southwestern fare. A casual yet sophisticated ambience pairs nicely with expertly prepared dishes such as ostrich medallions drizzled with a cilantro-citrus demiglaze and agave honey-glazed carrots, oak-grilled Jamaican jerk pork loin with habanero apple chutney, or *pepita*-encrusted American bison strip loin.

You'll find family-friendly fare at **Dos Salsas** (512-930-2343; www.dossalsas .com), 1104 1/2 S Main St., where tacos, enchiladas, tostadas, and tamales come stuffed with chicken, beef, brisket, pork, or *carne guisada* (slow-cooked beef tips with gravy) and are paired with rice, beans, or guacamole salad. This family-run restaurant on Main Street is a local favorite and, consequently, frequently packed.

When you're looking for something really special, **The Hollow** (512-868-3300; www.thehollowbrasserie.com), 708 S Austin Ave., is a destination restaurant for good reason. In the spirit of a French brasserie and with skill and creativity, Chef Jacob crafts the inventive seasonal menus around the freshest ingredients harvested by local partner farms. Each evening features a three-course prix fixe menu, a chef's tasting menu, and a bar menu. Past favorites have included such delicate dishes as carrots glazed in Meyer lemon and lavender with currants, feta, and sprouted lentils, or perfectly prepared hearty French classics like beef filet with sauce *au poivre* and pommes frites. From cuisine to presentation to atmosphere, The Hollow is a treat.

New Braunfels and Gruene

New Braunfels, located right off I-35 approximately 45 miles south of Austin and 30 miles north of San Antonio, was established under the auspices of the *Verein zum Schutze deutscher Einwanderer* in Texas, the "Society for the Protection of German Immigrants in Texas," or, simply, the Adelsverein.

As immigration to Texas picked up in the early 1800s, word of the region's potential reached a group of 21 enterprising noblemen near Mainz, Germany, who started

KICK UP YOUR HEELS ON THE CREAKY WOODEN DANCE FLOOR IN GRUENE HALL.

making plans for a mass immigration and sent two men to investigate the possibilities. In May 1842 Count Joseph Boos-Waldeck and Count Victor August of Leiningen-Westerburg-Alt-Leiningen arrived and approached Sam Houston, who offered them acreage in the hostile frontier west of Austin, which they politely declined.

In 1845, after much discussion and many failed attempts, the first wagon train of German immigrants staggered into Central Texas. The group founded New Braunfels, named for Prince Carl of Solms-Braunfels, and immediately began readying the parcel of land on the banks of the Comal River to receive more Germans, who would number between 300 and 400 by the following summer. Soon the operation was handed over to John I. Meusebach, who, confident he could deal diplomatically with the Native Americans in the Hill Country to the west, went on to phase two of Adelsverein and founded Fredericksburg in 1846.

New Braunfels quickly established itself as a commercial and manufacturing center in the region, feeding, clothing, and fixing the wagons of pioneers headed to the frontier. These days, visitors make the trip to New Braunfels for several reasons. One is Schlitterbahn (see below), the slippery, soaking wet, family magnet of a water park that draws visitors from near and far. Another is the Guadalupe and Comal Rivers, whose lazy courses are perfect for that beloved Central Texas pastime of tubing, floating slowly with the current on large inflatable inner tubes for hours and hours on end. And then there is Gruene.

In the 1850s, the tiny settlement of Gruene (pronounced "green") was founded by German farmers who built a thriving economy based on cotton growing and processing. By the 1870s a busy cotton gin was up and running, as were a mercantile store and dance hall. When the railroad passed through in the 1880s, commercial development grew and the town prospered. When the boll weevil blight of the 1920s decimated the cotton crops, however, and the Great Depression of the 1930s hit, many residents abandoned the town. In the 1970s interest in preserving the town grew, and it was placed on the National Register of Historic Places. These days, the restored town is a favorite of visitors who come for the restaurants and the music at the historic Gruene Hall (see below). Located just 3 miles north of downtown New Braunfels, Gruene is considered a historic district within that city's limits.

✻ Things to See and Do

HISTORY AND HERITAGE The Gruene Historic District (www.gruenetexas.com) is easily identifiable by its gray water tower, which is visible for miles. The town motto is "Gently resisting change," and the pace of life flows along as slowly as the nearby river.

Packed with shops and restaurants, Gruene is perhaps best known as home of **Gruene Hall** (830-606-1281; www.gruenehall.com), the oldest dance hall in Texas, with a reputation for fantastic music from the likes of Willie Nelson, Lyle Lovett, and George Strait. Folks come to kick up their heels and throw back a cool one, and the place is packed most weekends.

Stop in the **Museum of Texas Handmade Furniture** (830-629-6504; www .texashandmadefurniture.org) for a fascinating look at history through craft. The museum displays fine examples of Texas Biedermeier furniture from approximately 1845 to 1880. Located in New Braunfels Heritage Village, which is open by appointment only for area schoolchildren.

Families looking to meet some new friends or pass a rainy day will appreciate the **McKenna Children's Museum** (830-606-9525; www.mckennakids.org), a bright, cheerful, and educational museum in New Braunfels that appeals most to elementary school–aged children.

THE RIVERS

People come from far and wide to spend the afternoon just floating down the rivers in New Braunfels, an activity that can be wonderfully relaxing or invigorating. The gentle little Comal River, the shortest river in the world, begins at Comal Springs in Landa Park (see below) and travels 2.5 miles to meet the swifter and choppier Guadalupe River in downtown New Braunfels.

The Spanish discovered Comal Springs in 1691, stumbling upon the Native Americans who were living here. Early written references describe the springs and their almost unimaginable amounts of pure cool water surrounded by lovely groves; even today the springs gush 8 million gallons of water per hour, water that is both consistently clear and a refreshing 72 degrees.

The Comal is favored by families, while the Guadalupe has been known for its revelry, an image the city is working to shake. Local authorities are in no-nonsense mode after the public and politicians put pressure on them to keep the river clean and safe. While alcohol is legal on the rivers in certain areas, there are restrictions, and authorities issue stiff fines for infractions.

Smack in the middle of town, just north of the Main Plaza, **Landa Park** (830-221-4350; www .nbpard.org) is a terrific place for recreation. Fun for the whole family, the park has miniature golf and a miniature train, as well as the gentle 1.6-mile Panther Canyon Nature Trail (trail map available in the Parks and Recreation office). Adjacent **Prince Solms Park** (830-608-2165; www.nbpard.org) is home to the Chute, a section of the Comal River channeled by concrete that provides a smooth, swift ride for tubers. Admission, parking, and tube rental are $5 apiece. Fishing is another popular pastime in area parks; anglers enjoy the Guadalupe River for its rainbow and brown trout, though largemouth, smallmouth, striped, and Guadalupe bass, as well as sunfish, also swim the river.

TUBE RENTAL

There are dozens of tube rental places up and down the rivers, and all tend to follow the same general rules, routines, and pricing. Each outfit allows guests to park their cars at the rental location, to which a free shuttle service downstream will provide a lift back. Generally, rental fees run $18–$25, and life jackets are free. Consider paying a few dollars extra for the tube with a bottom in order to avoid scraping yours. The websites below post handy checklists of what to bring and expect, and many have coupons you can print and bring with you for dis-

✳ Lodging

In warm weather, water enthusiasts are drawn to New Braunfels like flies to honey. The city is an easy day trip from San Antonio or Austin, but if you plan to spend the night, it is necessary to book a room or campsite in advance.

There are several bed and breakfasts to choose from. **Gruene Mansion Inn B&B** (830-629-2641; www .gruenemansioninn.com), 1275 Gruene Rd. Within easy walking distance of anything in town, including the river, this historic inn is beside Gruene Hall. The converted stables, barns, corncrib, and carriage house are now home to 30 individually decorated rooms, each with its own porch for lounging. An authentic air of yesteryear is a big part of the charm. $$$$.

Gruene Homestead Inn (830-606-0216; www.gruenehomesteadinn.com), 832 Gruene Rd. This collection of historic homes, dating from the 1850s to 1900s, was moved to this location, renovated, and readied to receive guests on its 8-acre spread. Spend the night in a 1940s-era grain silo or a limestone root cellar underneath a 19th-century farmhouse featuring the exposed timber of traditional German *fachwerk*-style construction. $$$.

counts. Try **Texas Tubes** (830-626-9900; www.texastubes.com), **Gruene River Company** (830-625-2800; www.toobing.com), or **Rockin' R River Rides** (830-629-9999; www.rockinr.com).

NEARBY

For more water recreation, **Canyon Lake** (830-964-2223; www.canyonlakechamber.com), located 20 miles north of New Braunfels, has eight public parks around its 80 miles of shoreline. These seasonal parks, managed by the Army Corps of Engineers, offer plenty of opportunities for fishing, swimming, camping, boating, and picnicking. Thirty-seven miles west of New Braunfels, Guadalupe River State Park (see "Texas State Parks" on page 161) is a nice natural retreat with lots of swimming, tubing, and hiking trails.

CYPRESS TREES ALONG THE GUADALUPE RIVER

Kuebler Waldrip Haus and Danville Schoolhouse Bed and Breakfast (830-625-8300; www.kueblerwaldrip.com), 1620 Hueco Springs Loop Rd. West of New Braunfels, this is set on 43 rural acres teeming with deer. Three buildings, two dating from the mid-1800s, house the 11 rooms of this B&B, which is a particularly family-friendly place, and the size and configuration of the rooms are conducive to groups. $$$.

The region is also known for its camping, and opportunities are ample. Strap the bikes on the car, pack s'more fixings, slide on your flip-flops, and bring the family for that damp-swimsuit, dirty-feet, sticky-face,

stay-up-too-late-playing-cards kind of vacation that memories are made of. Campsites offer tube and raft rentals, and fishing advice is free. No pets, loud music, excessive drinking, or rowdy behavior allowed.

Camp Huaco Springs (830-625-5411; www.camphuacosprings.com) operates the first-come, first-served campsite and owns **Rockin' R River Rides** (830-629-9999; www.rockinr.com), which rents tubes at several locations in the area. **KL Ranch Camp** (830-625-1177; www.kl-river.com), on the Guadalupe River, has tent and RV camping, and **Mountain Breeze Camp** (830-964-2484; www.mountainbreezecamp.com) offers tent camping near the river, tiny cabins lined up in a row in a sunny field—each with air-conditioning and a bed—and some RV sites.

❋ Where to Eat

Huisache Grill and Wine Bar (830-620-9001; www.huisache.com), 303 W San Antonio St., started out in a rundown building in New Braunfels, but thanks to a renovation its wood floors and a soaring ceiling have grown to seem chic. The menu includes reworked southern staples like an Angus beef chicken-fried steak or pecan-encrusted pork chops served with a Jack Daniel's butter sauce. The Hot and Crunchy Rainbow Trout with a sesame almond breading and jalapeño tartar sauce is decidedly different, while the hot Cheezy Burger tastes familiar and homey.

Speaking of homey, **Naegelin's Bakery** (877-788-2895; www.naegelins.com), 129 S Seguin Ave., has been baking German strudels and cookies such as *springele, pfefernuesse* and *lebkuchen* since 1868, and stakes claim to being the oldest bakery in Texas. With apricot *kolaches,* bear claws, and 10 different kinds of bread pulled fresh from the oven, you really could follow your nose to Naegelin's.

After you've spent a day tubing, seafood sure hits the spot, and the **Clear Springs Restaurant** (830-629-3775; www.clearspringsrestaurant.com), 1692 TX-46, is a local favorite. The pan-seared tilapia, served with a Dijon peppercorn crawfish sauce, is popular, as are the blackened catfish fillets topped with crawfish étouffée; both are served with a scoop of garlic mashed potatoes and steamed vegetables. While this is the original eatery, located in a building that dates back to 1869, there are several Clear Springs locations in Texas, including Greune, where you'll find the **Gruene River Grill** (830-624-2300; www.gruenerivergrill.com), 1259 Gruene Rd.

NAEGELIN'S BAKERY IN NEW BRAUNFELS

The offerings here are similar to its sister restaurant—a few with a kick, such as the spicy southwestern meat loaf or the chipotle chicken Diablo in a spicy cream sauce. The patios and porches overlooking the river are a fantastic spot for a drink or dessert.

Located in the shell of an old cotton-gin mill, the **Gristmill River Restaurant & Bar** (830-625-0684; www.gristmillrestaurant.com), 1287 Gruene Rd., is situated behind Gruene Hall in historic Gruene. Seating is at well-worn wooden tables inside the rough-hewn mill, in the shady river grove, or on the decks overlooking the river. The atmosphere at the Gristmill is fantastic, as is the menu. There are chicken-fried steaks, Polish Wedding Sausage with barbecue sauce, meal-sized salads topped with grilled meats, and whatever fish is the catch of the day, served blackened or grilled. You can kick up the flavor of any sandwich or burger order with the addition of one of the Gristmill's homemade

TABLES IN GRUENE HALL, THE OLDEST DANCE HALL IN TEXAS

sauces: Spicy Queso, Garlicky Hot Sauce, Tomatillo Verde, or Gringo Pico de Gallo. The Gristmill can get crowded, so consider stopping in early.

Don't be fooled by **Dry Comal Creek Vineyards'** (830-885-4076; www .drycomalcreek.com), 1741 Herbelin Rd., whimsical labels, laid-back operation, and fanciful tasting room—they are serious about their wine. In a secluded valley west of New Braunfels, Dry Comal Creek Vineyards has coaxed native grapes into very dry, dark red wines, such as the 2004 Black Spanish, which has been declared the Texas Grand Star Winner at the Lone Star International Competition. For wine tasting in Gruene, stop in **The Grapevine** (830-606-0093; www.grapevineingruene.com), 1612 Hunter Rd.

✳ Special Events

FESTIVALS In May, the **New Braunfels Wein and Saengerfest** (830-221-4350; www.weinandsaengerfest.com) celebrates area music and wine making with dancing, food, and a "Grape Stomp." The tasty **Gruene Music and Wine Fest** (830-629-5077; www.gruenemusicandwine fest.org) ushers in October, and the cooler weather of November, brings the **Wurstfest** (830-625-9167; www.wurstfest

.com), New Braunfels's annual 10-day sausage festival. **Old Gruene Market Days** (830-832-1721; www .gruenemarketdays.com) occupy the third weekend of the month February through November, and a nightly lineup of talent makes **Gruene Hall** (830-606-1281; www.gruenehall.com) feel like a music festival that never ends.

THE GRISTMILL RIVER RESTAURANT & BAR IN GRUENE

San Marcos

San Marcos is located on I-35 at the eastern edge of the Hill Country, 30 miles south of Austin and 49 miles north of San Antonio, making it an easy day trip from either city. Home to a state university, two huge outlet shopping areas, and plenty of recreation, San Marcos makes an agreeable side trip.

Established in 1846, San Marcos has always been a crossroads. The site of several failed missions in the 1700s, it was an important stopping point for travelers on the Old San Antonio Road, the route from northern Mexico to Nacogdoches in East Texas, used

STATUE OF TEXAS RANGER JACK C. HAYS IN FRONT OF THE COURTHOUSE IN SAN MARCOS

Popular attractions in San Marcos are the Prime Outlets (512-396-2200; www.primeoutlets.com) and Tanger Outlets (512-396-7446; www.tangeroutlet.com), which straddle I-35 at Exit 200, approximately 30 minutes south of Austin and 45 minutes north of San Antonio. This is a mecca for discount shoppers, and things can get hectic here on the weekends.

by Native Americans and the Spanish crisscrossing Texas. It was on the Chisholm Trail, used for cattle drives between 1864 and 1884. Southwest Texas State Normal School, later Southwest Texas State University and now Texas State University–San Marcos, was chartered in 1899. The San Marcos Baptist Academy followed in 1907, establishing the city as an education center and diversifying its economy.

With lovely natural resources, San Marcos has long been a regional recreation destination. Aquarena Springs flows at a rate of 150 million gallons of crystal-clear water a day, feeding the San Marcos River, which runs through the city. By the 1960s a resort had grown up around Aquarena Springs, Wonder World was opened as an attraction, and the tourist industry became a reliable and growing source of income. At the same time, population growth, increasing water demands, and the constant threat of drought have been a cause for concern for the spring's future. Both the San Marcos River Foundation (www.sanmarcosriver.org) and Aquarena Center work to educate the public about the importance of their river, a fragile ecosystem that is home to several endangered species.

These days, San Marcos has the comfortable, lived-in feel of a college town, with an old-fashioned town square lined with casual eateries and shops, and is rapidly becoming a residence for commuters to Austin. Just minutes from Wimberley, San Marcos is also a good jumping-off point into the Hill Country.

✳ Things to See and Do

MUSEUMS It may be a little hard to locate, but the **Wittliff Gallery of Southwestern and Mexican Photography** (512-245-2313; www.thewittliffcollections.txstate.edu) curates provocative, insightful, and educational exhibits that appeal to both art aficionados and history buffs. Located on the seventh floor of the Albert B. Alkek Library on the Texas State University campus.

✳ Outdoor Activities

The spring-fed San Marcos River flows through town, joining the Blanco River and merging with the Guadalupe River farther along in South Texas before spilling into the Gulf of Mexico. The river guarantees water recreation in even the driest summer months; generally speaking, there is just enough current to keep tubing and boating interesting, but not enough to make it dangerous. The Rio Vista Dam in the **San Marcos City Park** (512-393-8400; www.toursanmarcos.com) is a good place to get your feet wet; when cracks were discovered recently in the hundred-year-old, low-water dam containing the San Marcos River, the city of San Marcos opted for a full-scale redesign of its urban park. Included in the project were provisions for saving wildlife, environmental enhancements to favor the endangered Texas wild rice, and the creation of three artificial rapids to provide for better water flow and more public recreation. The result is a great place for picnicking and swimming, with a family-friendly river chute for tubing at Rio Vista Dam. A charitable project of the local Lions Club, **Tube San Marcos** (512-396-5466; www.tubesanmarcos.com) rents tubes. The more adventurous can rent canoes and kayaks at **Austin Canoe and Kayak** (512-396-2386; www.austinkayak.com), located across from the Tanger Outlet Mall.

In 1994, Texas State University–San Marcos acquired the dilapidated Aquarena Springs Resort and re-created it as a nonprofit nature center whose focus is research and education to promote water and environmental stewardship. **The Meadows Center for Water and the Environment** (512-245-9200; www.meadowscenter.txstate.edu) runs a relaxing glass-bottom boat ride that offers underwater views of the Balcones Fault, the springs, and aquatic life. Additionally, you can stroll through the surrounding wetlands on the Floating Wetlands Boardwalk, or watch the 2 PM fish feeding at the modest aquarium, which is home to several San Marcos salamanders, fountain darters, and Texas blind salamanders, all federally protected species. Ecotourists, the naturally curious, and children will find the Meadows Center to be especially fascinating and informative.

Wonder World Park (www.wonderworldpark.com; 512-392-3760) gives visitors a rare view of the geological effects of earthquakes, one of which formed the Balcones Fault and the Balcones Fault Line Cave, the most-visited cave in Texas and Wonder World's main attraction. The cave is small, slippery, and wet, and since it was formed by an earthquake and not from the effects of millions of years of dripping water, it lacks the typical cave formations found in other area caves. The short tour concludes with a ride up the elevator to the top of the 110-foot Tejas Observation Tower for a view of the land aboveground. A train ride takes visitors through a petting zoo, where children can feed deer and other tame animals. The antigravity room is fun, and the gift shop is filled with rock candy and other amusements. Wonder World is well suited to families with elementary-age children.

❋ Where to Eat

San Marcos is a college town, with cuisine to match. Grab a cup of coffee and a quick bite to eat at **Tantra Coffeehouse** (512-558-2233; www.tantracoffeehouse .com), 217 W Hopkins St. Stop in for a fruit or sausage *kolache* at **Dos Gatos** (512-392-1444; www.dosgatoskolaches .com), 700 N LBJ Dr.; a breakfast taco at **Lolita's** (512-392-3441), 1501 Aquarena Springs Dr.; or a sandwich at **Alvin Ord's Sandwich Shop** (512-353-8042), 204 University Dr. Enjoy a slice of pizza at **Pie Society** (512-805-8900; www .piesmtx.com), 700 N LBJ Dr.; or duck into the **Root Cellar Café** (512-392-5158;

www.rootcellarcafe.com), 215 N LBJ Dr., where wood beams and exposed rock walls add ambiance to match the casual lunch menu and slightly more upscale dinner specials. Enjoy the lovely patio and extensive menu of steaks, pastas, poultry, and seafood at **Palmer's Restaurant Bar and Courtyard** (512-353-3500; www.palmerstexas.com), 218 Moore St.; or grab one of the remarkably popular macaroni and cheese burgers and a beer at the **Tap Room** (512-392-9824; www.taproomsanmarcos.com), 129 E Hopkins St.

✱ Special Events

FESTIVALS San Marcos festivals make a good day trip from either Austin or San Antonio. In April, the city of San Marcos celebrates the **Swing on the Square Festival** (www.smtxswingfest.com) with a weekend of Texas history, traditions, and music in Courthouse Square, featuring a farmers' market, craft beer tastings, and a cowboy gospel show. In May, the **Viva! Cinco de Mayo** & **State Menudo Cook-Off** (www.vivacincosmtx.com) are held together and add up to great fun. December brings the **Sights and Sounds of Christmas** (512-393-5900; www.sights-n-sounds.org), a festival of lights, food, and music along San Marcos Plaza and San Marcos City Park. Details of all city events can be found on the San Marcos Convention and Visitor Bureau website, www.toursanmarcos.com.

SUGGESTED BIBLIOGRAPHY

Whether you like to read up on your destination before you go or find that your curiosity is piqued by the trip, below are books recommended to enrich your experience, arranged here alphabetically by author.

Ajilvsgi, Geyata. *Wildflowers of Texas.* Fredericksburg, TX: Shearer Publishing, 2003.

Alsop, Fred J. III. *Birds of Texas.* New York: DK Publishing, 2002.

Awbrey, Betty Dooley. *Why Stop? Texas Roadside Markers: A Guide to Texas Historical Roadside Markers.* Lanham, MD: Taylor Trade Publishing, 2005.

Barkley, Roy, ed. *The Handbook of Texas Music.* Austin, TX: Texas State Historical Association, 2003.

Bryant, Helen. *Fixin' to Be Texan.* Plano, TX: Republic of Texas, 1998.

Bull, David. *The Driskill Hotel: Stories of Austin's Legendary Hotel/A Cookbook for Special Occasions.* Austin, TX: The Driskill Hotel. Packed with tidbits of juicy local lore and history.

Caro, Robert. *The Path to Power (The Years of Lyndon Johnson, Volume 1).* New York: Vintage Books, 1981.

———. *Means of Ascent (The Years of Lyndon Johnson, Volume 2).* New York: Vintage Books, 1990.

———. *Master of the Senate: The Years of Lyndon Johnson.* New York: Knopf, 2002.

Cerf, Bennett and **Van H. Cartmell,** eds. *The Best Short Stories of O. Henry.* New York: Modern Library, 1994. Though O. Henry's muse was New York City, he spent part of his formative years in Austin.

Cornell, Kari A. *Our Texas.* Osceola, WI: Voyageur Press, 2004. Coffee-table book.

Dallek, Robert. *Lyndon B. Johnson: Portrait of a President.* New York: Oxford University Press, 2004.

Fisher, Lewis F. *Saving San Antonio: The Precarious Preservation of a Heritage.* Lubbock, TX: Texas Tech University Press, 1996.

———. *The Spanish Missions of San Antonio.* San Antonio, TX: Maverick Publishing, 1998.

Ford, Norman D. *25 Bicycle Tours in the Texas Hill Country and West Texas.* Woodstock, VT: Countryman Press, 1995.

Friedman, Kinky. *Kinky Friedman's Guide to Texas Etiquette: Or How to Get to Heaven or Hell without Going Through Dallas–Fort Worth.* New York: HaperCollins, 2001. Kinky is a Texas original whose personality, politics, and antics are threaded through the contemporary social history of Central Texas.

Gilliland, Tom, Miguel Ravago, and **Virginia B. Wood,** *Fonda San Miguel: Thirty Years of Food and Art.* Frederickburg, TX: Shearer Publishing, 2005. A feast for the eyes as well as the palate.

Goodwin, Doris Kearns. *Lyndon Johnson and the American Dream.* New York: St. Martin's, 1991.

Ivins, Molly. *Molly Ivins Can't Say That, Can She?* New York: Vintage, 1992. Witty commentary on Texas politics.

Loughmiller, Campbell, Lynn Loughmiller, and **Damon Waitt.** *Texas Wildflowers: A Field Guide,* revised edition. Austin, TX: University of Texas Press, 2006. Updated version of a 1984 classic.

Meinzer, Wyman, and **John Graves** (introduction). *Texas Sky.* Austin, TX: University of Texas Press, 1998. Photographs of the awesome Texas sky.

Michener, James A. *Texas.* New York; Fawcett, 1987. Packed with drama and stereotypes, Michener's book paints a bold picture of the state.

Moran, Mark, Mike Sceurman, Wesley Treat, and **Heather Shades.** *Weird Texas.* New York: Sterling, 2005.

Peterson, Roger Tory. *Field Guide to the Birds of Texas.* Boston: Houghton Mifflin, 1998. Written by an expert.

Rather, Rebecca, and **Alison Oresman.** *The Pastry Queen: Royally Good Recipes from the Texas Hill Country's Rather Sweet Bakery & Café.* Berkeley, CA: Ten Speed Press, 2004.

Reid, Jan, and **Scott Newton.** *The Improbable Rise of Redneck Rock: New Edition* (Jack and Doris Smothers Series in Texas History, Life, and Culture). Austin, TX: University of Texas Press, 2004.

Richards, David. *Once Upon a Time in Texas: A Liberal in the Lone Star State.* Austin, TX: University of Texas Press, 2002.

Rucker, Sid, Clifford E. Shackelford, Madge M. Lindsay, C. Mark Klym, Shirly Rucker, and **Clemente Guzman III.** *Hummingbirds of Texas.* College Station, TX: Texas A&M Press, 2006.

Rybczyk, Mark Louis. *San Antonio Uncovered.* Plano, TX: Republic of Texas, 2000. A good look at the history of San Antonio.

Taylor, Tom, and **Johnny Molloy.** *60 Hikes Within 60 Miles: San Antonio and Austin.* Birmingham, AL: Menasha Ridge Press, 2004.

Tekiela, Stan. *Birds of Texas Field Guide.* Cambridge, MN: Adventure Publications, 2004.

Thompson, Karen R., and **Kathy R. Howell.** *Austin (Scenes of America).* Mount Pleasant, SC: Arcadia Publishing, 2006.

Tveten, John L. *The Birds of Texas.* Fredericksburg, TX: Shearer Publishing, 1993. Miraculous photos.

Walsh, Robb. *Legends of Texas Barbecue Cookbook: Recipes and Recollections from the Pit Bosses.* San Francisco: Chronicle Books, 2002.

Woods, Randall. *LBJ: Architect of American Ambition.* New York: Free Press, 2006.

INDEX

ABC Zilker Kite Festival, The (Austin), 83
accessible services, 23
Adams House Inn, The (Hyde Park), 60
Advantage car rental, 20
airport shuttle, 20, 21
air travel, 20–21
Alamo, The, 15, 88, 89, 96, 98, 99, 134
Alamo Bowl (San Antonio), 136
Alamo car rental, 20
Alamodome, The (San Antonio), 112
Alamo Drafthouse (San Antonio), 110
Alamo Drafthouse Cinema (Austin), 46
Alamo Heights, 95; restaurants, 130
Alamo IMAX Theater (San Antonio), 110
Alamo Quarry Market (San Antonio), 134
Alamo Springs Café (Hill Country), 159
Allens' Boots (South Austin), 82–83
Alvin Ord's Sandwich Shop (San Marcos), 194
American Yellow Checker Cab, 20, 21
AMOA-Arthouse. See Austin Museum of Art
    and the Arthouse
Amtrak, 21
Anglos, 17–19
Annual Kerrville EasterFest and Cook-Off
    (Kerrville), 169
Antone's (Austin), 74–75
Antone's Record Store (Downtown Austin), 82
Aquarena Springs (San Marcos), 12, 193, 194
area codes, 22
Arkey Blue's Silver Dollar (Bandera), 141
Armadillo Christmas Bazaar (Austin), 85
Arneson Theatre (San Antonio), 108
Art City Austin, 84
ARTS San Antonio, 108
AT&T Center, The (San Antonio), 112
AT&T Championship (San Antonio), 136
Austin: area code, 22; bars, 79–82; culture, 11;
    festivals, 83–85; fishing, 48; grocery stores,
    23; historic places in, 36–42; history, 31–34;
    hospitals, 23; lodging, 56–61; map, 30, 35;
    museums, 38–44; music, 74–79, 83–85;
    neighborhoods, 34–36; newspapers, 24–25;
    nightlife, 34, 74; outdoor activities, 50–54;
    performing arts in, 44–46; radio stations,
    25; restaurants, 24, 61–74; shopping, 82–83;
    swimming, 48, 51; tourist information, 26;
    transportation, 19–21, 34; tubing, 50. See
    also specific neighborhoods
Austin, Stephen F., 17, 37, 96
Austin-Bergstrom International Airport, 20

Austin Canoe and Kayak (San Marcos), 194
Austin Celtic Festival, 85
Austin Chamber Music Festival, 84
Austin Chronicle Hot Sauce Contest, 84
Austin City Limits, 76
Austin City Limits Music Festival, 83, 85
Austin City Limits Tour, The, 48
Austin Duck Adventures, 50
Austin Eats Tours, 48
Austin Film Festival, 85
Austin Film Society, 46
Austin Food and Wine Alliance, 83
Austin Gay and Lesbian International Film
    Festival, 85
Austin History Center, 38
Austin Ice Cream Festival, 84
Austin International Poetry Festival, 85
Austin Java Company, 68
Austin Land and Cattle (Clarksville), 72–73
Austin Motel (South Austin), 58
Austin Museum of Art and the Arthouse
    (AMOA-Arthouse), 41
Austin Nature and Science Center, 52
Austin Opera, 44–45
Austin Overtures, 48
Austin Powwow and American Indian Heritage
    Festival, 85
Austin Ridge Riders, 47
Austin Shakespeare Festival, 83
Austin Steam Train (Burnet), 50, 172
Austin Steam Train, The (Wimberley), 176
Austin String Band Festival, 85
Austin Symphony Orchestra, 45
Austin Zoo (South Austin), 54
Avery Ranch Golf, 48
Avis car rental, 20
Azúca Nuevo Latino (King William District),
    127

Backyard, The (Hill Country), 76
Bakery Lorraine (Museum Reach), 128
Balcones Escarpment, 12
Ballet Austin, 45
Bandera, 138, 162; festivals, 143; outdoor
    activities, 142; restaurants, 143; rodeos,
    141; sight-seeing, 139–42; tourist
    information, 26
Banger's Sausage House and Beer Garden
    (Downtown Austin), 63, 80
banks, 22

barbecue, 63–65, 69, 70, 133, 143, 184–85. *See also specific eateries*

Barley Swine (Hyde Park), 73–74, 81

bars, 21, 141; Austin, 79–82; Downtown Austin, 62, 63, 79–80; East Austin, 81–82; Gristmill River Restaurant & Bar (Gruene), 190–91; Huisache Grill and Wine Bar (New Braunfels), 190; Hyde Park, 81; Hyde Park Bar and Grill, 71–72; Palmer's Restaurant Bar and Courtyard (San Marcos), 195; San Antonio, 123, 133; South Austin, 80–81

Barton Creek Greenbelt, 56

Barton Springs (Austin), 12, 48, 51, 52, 65, 67

baseball, 46

Bastille Day (Austin), 84

Bat Boat, 54

Bat Fest (Austin), 84

B-cycle (San Antonio), 111, 113

Becker Vineyards (Hill Country), 142, 154

Bella on the River (Downtown San Antonio), 124, 131

Berges Fest (Boerne), 145

bicycling: Austin, 46–47, 56; San Antonio, 111; Wimberley, 176

Biga on the Banks (Downtown San Antonio), 123

Big Bib BBQ, The (San Antonio), 131

Bike Texas (Austin), 47

bird-watching: Austin, 47; San Antonio, 111; Wimberley, 176

Black's BBQ, 185

Blair House Inn (Wimberley), 179

Blanco: lodging, 144; outdoor activities, 142, 143, 160, 164; restaurants, 144–45; tourist information, 26

Blanco Bowling Club, 143, 144

Blanco County Fair and Rodeo (Johnson City), 164

Blanco County Inn, 144

Blanco Lavender Festival (Hill Country), 142, 143

Blanco State Park, 143, 160

Blue Bonnet Cafe (Marble Falls), 171

Bluebonnet Festival (Burnet), 172

bluebonnets, 149, 160

Bluebonnet Trail, The (Wimberley), 176

Blue Dahlia Bistro (East Austin), 69

Blue Hole (Wimberley), 177

Blue Star Arts Complex, The (San Antonio), 106, 108

boat cruises, 47, 50, 114, 172, 174, 176

boating, 47, 48, 50, 91, 176, 182; Bat Boat, 54; Canyon Lake, 189; Highland Lakes, 172; Inks Lake State Park, 173; Kerrville-Schreiner State Park, 167; Lake Austin, 174; Lake LBJ, 173; Lake Travis, 174; San Marcos River, 193; Wimberley, 176. *See also* canoeing; kayaking; Riverfest; tubing

Bob Bullock Museum, 37

Boerne: lodging, 146–47; outdoor activities, 145–46; restaurants, 147–48; sight-seeing, 145; tourist information, 27

Bonahan's Prime Steaks and Seafood (Downtown San Antonio), 124–25

Bonham Exchange (San Antonio), 132

Book People (Downtown Austin), 82

Boudro's on the Riverwalk (Downtown San Antonio), 123

Bouldin Creek Café (Austin), 68

Bowie, Jim, 96

Brackenridge Golf Course (San Antonio), 111

Brackenridge House, The (King William District), 120–21

Brackenridge Park (San Antonio), 95, 114–15; restaurants, 130

Brava House (Clarksville), 60

Brick's River Café (Bandera), 143

Bright Leaf Park, 56

Briscoe Center for American History, 14

Broken Spoke (South Austin), 76, 80

Bryan's on 290 (Johnson City), 164

Buckhorn Saloon and Museum and Texas Ranger Museum (San Antonio), 104

Budget car rental, 20

Bullock Texas State History Museum, 38, 40

Burger Tex II (Hyde Park), 71

Burnet, 172; hospital, 23; tourist information, 27

Burnet Road, restaurants, 73–74

Busbee's BBQ (Bandera), 143

By George (Downtown Austin), 82

Cactus Café (Austin), 76

Cactus Pear Music Festival (San Antonio), 135

Camp Ben McCulloch, 48

Camp Comfort, 150

Camp Huaco Springs (New Braunfels), 189

camping: Austin, 47–48; New Braunfels, 189–90; San Antonio, 111; Wimberley, 176

canoeing, 135–36, 194; Austin, 47; Wimberley, 176

Canyon Lake, 189

Canyon of the Eagles Resort and Nature Park (Burnet), 172

Canyon Springs Golf Club (San Antonio), 111–12

Capital Cruises (Austin), 47, 50

Capital Metro Bus, 20

Capitol. *See* Texas State Capitol

Capitol Visitors Center, 37–38

Cappy's (Alamo Heights), 130

car rentals, 20

Carver Community Cultural Center (San Antonio), 108

Casa Navarro State Historic Site (San Antonio), 101

Cascade Caverns (Boerne), 145

Casino el Camino (Austin), 76–77

Cave Without a Name (Boerne), 145–46

Cedar Street Courtyard (Austin), 77

Celebrate San Antonio, 136

Central Market (San Antonio), 63
Chart House Restaurant (San Antonio), 97
Chris Madrid's (Olmos Park), 130
Chuy's (Austin), 67
Cibolo Nature Center (Boerne), 146
Cinco de Mayo (Austin), 84
Cinco de Mayo (San Antonio), 135
CineFestival (San Antonio), 134
cinema (San Antonio), 110
Clarksville, 35; lodging, 60; restaurants, 72–73
Classics Burgers and More (Kerrville), 168–69
Clear River Ice Cream, Bakery, & Deli
    (Fredericksburg), 158
Clear Springs Restaurant (New Braunfels), 190
climbing, 48, 176
Comal Springs (New Braunfels), 12, 188
Comfort, 148; lodging, 150; restaurants, 150–51;
    tourist information, 27
Comfort Pizza, 151
Conchita's on Main (Kerrville), 169
conjunto music, 109
Contemporary Art Month (San Antonio), 135
Contemporary Austin, The, 41
Continental (South Austin), 77, 80
Cooper's Old Time Pit Bar-B-Que (Llano), 173,
    185
Corral Theatre (Wimberley), 175
Counter Café (Downtown Austin), 65
County Line, The (Lake Austin), 174
Cove, The (Olmos Park), 130
Cowboy Capital PRCA Rodeo (Bandera), 141
Cowboy Christmas (Boerne), 145
Cowboys Dancehall (San Antonio), 132
Cowboy Steak House (Kerrville), 169
Creekhaven Inn (Wimberley), 179
Creek Restaurant, The (Boerne), 147
Crockett, Davy, 37, 96, 99
Crossroads of San Antonio, 134
Crown & Anchor Pub (Hyde Park), 81
cruises. See boat cruises
Culinaria Wine & Food Festival (San Antonio),
    136
Cured (Museum Reach), 129
Cycle Texas, 47, 176
Cypress Creek Cottages (Wimberley), 179–80
Cypress Grille (Boerne), 147
Cypress Valley Canopy Tours (Wimberley),
    50, 177

dance (San Antonio), 110, 132–33
Das Garten Haus (Fredericksburg), 155
Dawn at the Alamo (San Antonio), 134
Daybreak Boat Rentals (Lake Travis), 174
Deep Eddy Pool (West Austin), 54
Devil's Backbone (Wimberley), 177
Día de los Muertos (San Antonio), 136
Día de los Muertos/Community Altars: A
    Celebration of Life (Austin), 85
Diez y Seis Celebration (Austin), 85
Diez y Seis Events (San Antonio), 136

dining. See restaurants
Dirty Martin's Place (Hyde Park), 71
disc golf, 48
Dixie Dude Ranch (Hill Country), 140
Dogleg Coffee (Bandera), 143
Dollar car rental, 20
DoSeum (San Antonio), 107
Dos Gatos (San Marcos), 194
Dos Salsas (Georgetown), 185–86
Double Horn Brewery (Marble Falls), 171
Dough Pizzeria (Olmos Park), 131
Downtown Austin, 34, 35; bars, 62, 63, 79–80;
    nightlife, 34, 57, 64; restaurants, 62–65;
    shopping, 82
Downtown San Antonio, 94; lodging, 118–20;
    restaurants, 24, 122–26, 133
Draught House (Hyde Park), 81
drinks. See bars
Driskill Grill (Downtown Austin), 62
Driskill Hotel, The (Austin), 57
drugstores, 23
Drury Plaza Hotel San Antonio Riverwalk, 119
Dry Comal Creek Vineyard (Hill Country), 154,
    191
dude ranches, 140

Eagle Eye Observatory (Burnet), 172
East Austin, 36; bars, 81–82; lodging, 60;
    nightlife, 81; restaurants, 68–70; shopping,
    83
Easter Fires Pageant (Fredericksburg), 159
East Main Grill (Johnson City), 164
Eastside Café (East Austin), 69–70
East Side Showroom (East Austin), 82
Easy Tiger (Downtown Austin), 80
Edwards Aquifer, 12
Edwards Plateau, 12, 31
Eeyore's Birthday (Austin), 84
814 A Texas Bistro (Comfort), 151
1886 Café and Bakery (Downtown Austin), 62
El Alma (South Austin), 81
El Dia de los Muertos. See Día de los Muertos
Elephant Room (Austin), 77
11th Street Cowboy Bar (Bandera), 141
Elisabet Ney Museum (Austin), 42
El Jarro de Arturo (San Antonio), 124
El Monumento (Georgetown), 184
Elysium (Austin), 78
emergency numbers, 21–22
EmilyAnn Theatre (Wimberley), 175
Emily Morgan, The (Downtown San Antonio),
    119
Emma Barrientos Mexican American Cultural
    Center (Austin), 42
Emma Long Metropolitan Park (Lake Austin),
    47, 174
Emo's (Austin), 78
Empire Theatre (San Antonio), 108–9
Enchanted Rock State Natural Area (Hill
    Country), 155, 161

Enoteca (Austin), 66, 67
Enterprise car rental, 20
Ernst, Johann Friedrich, 19
Esquire Tavern (San Antonio), 133
Esther's Follies (Austin), 45
Eva's Escape at the Gardenia Inn (King William
    District), 121

Fall Creek Vineyards (Hill Country), 154, 173
Ferguson, Miriam "Ma," 37
festivals, 142, 172, 183; Austin, 83–85; Bandera,
    143; Fredericksburg, 158–59; Gruene, 191;
    Hill Country, 158–59, 169; Kerrville, 169;
    New Braunfels, 191; San Antonio, 134–36;
    San Marcos, 195
Fiesta Noche del Rio (San Antonio), 108
Fiesta San Antonio!, 135
Fig Tree Restaurant (Downtown San Antonio),
    123–24
fire ants, 25–26
fishing: Austin, 48; licenses, 24; San Antonio,
    111; Wimberley, 176
flags of Texas, 16
Flags Over Texas (San Antonio), 97
Flatbed Press, The (East Austin), 83
Flat Creek Estate (Hill Country), 154
Flying L Guest Ranch (Hill Country), 140
Fonda San Miguel (Burnet Road), 74
food. See grocery stores; restaurants
Foodheads (Hyde Park), 71
Food Trailers Austin, 64
food trucks, 64
football, 48
Ford Canoe Challenge (San Antonio), 135–36
Fort Martin Scott (Fredericksburg), 153
FotoSeptiembre USA (San Antonio), 136
Four Seasons (Austin), 58
Fourth of July (San Antonio), 135
Fourth of July Fireworks & Symphony (Austin),
    84
Francisco's (Kerrville), 168
Frank (Downtown Austin), 62–63, 79
Franklin Barbecue (East Austin), 69, 70, 185
Freddie's (South Austin), 80
Fredericksburg, 152; festivals, 158–59; hospital,
    23; lodging, 155–56; outdoor activities, 155;
    restaurants, 156–58; sight-seeing, 153–54;
    Sunday houses, 153; tourist information,
    27
Fredericksburg Food and Wine Festival, 159
Fredericksburg Pie Company, 158
Fredericksburg Wine Road 290, 154
Fredericksburg Winery (Hill Country), 154
Freedmen's (Hyde Park), 71
French Legation Museum (East Austin), 39
Fricano's (Hyde Park), 71
Friedrich Wilderness Park (San Antonio), 116
Friendly Spot, The (King William District),
    126–27, 133
Frontier Times Museum (Bandera), 139–41

Full Moon Inn (Luckenbach), 170
Fun, Fun, Fun Fest (Austin), 85

Garcia Art Glass (San Antonio), 106
Gästehaus Schmidt (Fredericksburg), 155, 167
General Store (Luckenbach), 170
Georgetown: hospital, 24; lodging, 183;
    restaurants, 183–86; sight-seeing, 182–83;
    tourist information, 28; visitor center, 182
Georgetown Palace Theatre, 182–83
George Washington Carver Museum and
    Cultural Center (East Austin), 36, 39
Ginger Man (Downtown Austin), 80
Gliding Revolution's, 50
golf: Austin, 48; San Antonio, 111–12;
    Wimberley, 176
Go Texan marketing campaign, 176
Gourdough's (Austin), 68
Gourdough's Public House (Downtown Austin),
    80
Government Canyon State Natural Area, 116
Governor's Mansion, 38
Grape Creek Vineyards (Hill Country), 154
Grape Juice (Kerrville), 168
Grapevine, The (Gruene), 190–91
Green Vegetarian Cuisine (Museum Reach), 129
Greyhound, 21
Gristmill River Restaurant & Bar (Gruene),
    190–91
grocery stores, 23, 24
Gruene, 186–87; festivals, 191; lodging, 188–90;
    restaurants, 190–91; sight-seeing, 187–88
Gruene Hall, 187, 191
Gruene Homestead Inn, 188
Gruene Mansion Inn B&B, 188
Gruene Music and Wine Fest, 191
Gruene River Company, 189
Guadalupe Cultural Arts Center (San Antonio),
    109
Guadalupe River State Park, 161
Guajillo's (San Antonio), 124
Guenther House (King William District), 127–28
Güero's Taco Bar (South Austin), 65, 80

Halcyon (Downtown Austin), 80
Hamilton Pool, 48, 51
Hangar Hotel (Fredericksburg), 156
Haunted Texas Tours, 50
HEB, 23
Hecho a Mano/Made by Hand (San Antonio),
    136
HemisFair Park, 97
Henry Madison Log Cabin (East Austin), 39
Hertz car rental, 20
Heywood Hotel, The (East Austin), 60, 61
Hey!... You Gonna Eat or What? (Austin), 64,
    67–68
Hideout Coffee House and Theatre (Austin), 45
Highland Lakes, 172
High's (Comfort), 150–51

Hike and Bike Trail at Lady Bird Lake, 56
hiking, 56
Hill Country, 138–95, 152; area codes, 22;
     culture, 11; dude ranches, 140; festivals,
     158–59, 169; highways, 20; lavender
     farms, 142; lodging, 144, 146–47, 150,
     155–56, 164, 167–68, 170, 179–80; map,
     139; music, 76; newspapers, 24–25;
     outdoor activities, 142, 143, 145–46,
     155, 167, 177–79; radio stations, 25;
     restaurants, 143–45, 147–48, 150–51,
     156–58, 164–65, 168–69, 171, 180; rodeos,
     141; sight-seeing, 139–42, 145, 153–54,
     164, 166–67, 175; sinkholes of, 12; Texas'
     state parks, 160–63; tourist information,
     26–28; vineyards, 154. See also specific
     neighborhoods
Hill Country Bicycle Touring Club, 176
Hill Country Café (Kerrville), 169
Hill Country Cupboard (Johnson City), 164
Hill Country Equestrian Lodge, 140
Hill Country Lavender, 142
Hill Country State Natural Area, 142, 162
Hill Top Cafe (Fredericksburg), 158
Hippie Hollow (Lake Travis), 174
historic places: Austin, 36–42; San Antonio,
     96–104
history, 38, 40, 110, 169; Austin, 31–34; online
     information, 14; peoples of Texas in, 14–19;
     San Antonio, 11, 88–92
Hoffman Haus (Fredericksburg), 156
Holiday River Parade and Lighting Ceremony
     (San Antonio), 136
Hollow, The (Georgetown), 185–86
Holy Cacao (South Austin), 64
Home Slice Pizza (Austin), 66
Hondo's (Fredericksburg), 157
Hoover's Cooking (East Austin), 70
Hopdoddy Burger Bar (South Austin), 65, 80
hospitals, 23–24
Hotel Contessa, The (Downtown San Antonio),
     118–19
Hotel Ella, The (Austin), 58
Hotel Emma (Downtown San Antonio), 120
Hotel Faust (Comfort), 150
Hotel Flora and Fauna (Wimberley), 180
Hotel Havana (Downtown San Antonio), 120
hotels, 56–61. See also lodging
Hotel San José (South Austin), 58–59, 80
Hotel St. Cecilia (South Austin), 59
Hotel Valencia (Downtown San Antonio), 118
Hotel Van Zandt (Austin), 58
Hot Luck Food Festival (Austin), 84
Houston, Sam, 16, 31, 37, 38
Huisache Grill and Wine Bar (New Braunfels),
     190
Hula Hut (Lake Austin), 174
Hummingbird Farms (Hill Country), 142
hunting licenses, 24
Hut's Hamburgers (Downtown Austin), 65

Hyatt Hill Country Resort and Spa, The (Outer
     San Antonio), 121
Hyde Park, 35–36; bars, 81; lodging, 60;
     restaurants, 70–72
Hyde Park Bar and Grill, 71–72

Icenhauer's (Downtown Austin), 80
Il Sogno Osteria (Museum Reach), 129
Ingram Park Mall (San Antonio), 134
Inks Lake (Hill Country), 173
Inks Lake State Park (Hill Country), 173
Inner Space Cavern (Georgetown), 183
Inn of the Hills Resort and Conference Center
     (Kerrville), 168
Institute of Texan Cultures (ITC), 104
Instituto Cultural Mexicano, The (San Antonio),
     97
InterContinental Stephen F. Austin (Austin), 57
interstate highways, 20
ITC. See Institute of Texan Cultures

Jacala Mexican Restaurant (San Antonio), 124
Jack S. Blanton Museum (Austin), 39
Jacob's Well (Wimberley), 177
Jacob's Well Natural Area (Wimberley), 179
Japanese Tea Garden (San Antonio), 115–16
Jazz'SAlive (San Antonio), 136
Jobell Café and Bistro (Wimberley), 180
Joe's Bakery & Mexican Food (East Austin), 69
Johnson, Lyndon B., 33; boyhood home, 165;
     LBJ National Historical Park (Johnson
     City), 164; Lyndon Baines Johnson
     Museum and Library (Austin), 41; Lyndon
     B. Johnson State Park and Historic Site,
     162, 164, 165; National Park Service Visitor
     Center, 165
Johnson City: lodging, 164; restaurants, 164–65;
     sight-seeing, 164; tourist information, 27
John T. Floores Country Store (San Antonio), 133
Josephine Theatre (San Antonio), 110
Juan in a Million (East Austin), 69
Jump-Start Performance Company (San
     Antonio), 110
Juneteenth (Austin), 84
Juneteenth (San Antonio), 135
Just for Fun (Lake Travis), 174

kayaking, 47; Wimberley, 176
Keep Austin Weird Fest & 5K, 84
Kerbey Lane Cafe (Austin), 24, 70–71
Kerr Arts and Cultural Center (Kerrville), 167
Kerr County Fair, The (Kerrville), 169
Kerr County Market Days (Kerrville), 169
Kerrville: festivals, 169; hospital, 24;
     lodging, 167–68; outdoor activities, 167;
     restaurants, 168–69; sight-seeing, 166–67;
     tourist information, 28
Kerrville Folk Festival, 169
Kerrville-Schreiner State Park, 167
Kimber Modern Hotel (South Austin), 59

King William District, 92, 94, 132, 133; lodging, 120–21; restaurants, 126–28
King William Fair (San Antonio), 135
King William Manor (King William District), 121
KL Ranch Camp (New Braunfels), 189
Krause Springs, 48, 51
Kreuz Market (Lockhart), 185
Kuebler Waldrip Haus and Danville Schoolhouse Bed and Breakfast (New Braunfels), 189

La Barbecue (East Austin), 69
La Cantera Hill Country Resort and Spa (San Antonio), 112
La Condesa (Downtown Austin), 63
Lady Bird Johnson Municipal Golf Course (Wimberley), 176
Lady Bird Johnson Wildflower Center (South Austin), 54, 55
La Fogata (San Antonio), 124
La Fonda on Main (San Antonio), 124
La Frite Belgian Bistro (King William District), 127
Laguna Gloria (Austin), 41–42
La Hacienda de los Barrios (San Antonio), 124
Lake Austin (Hill Country), 49, 174
Lake Austin Riverboats, 50, 174
Lake Austin Spa and Resort, The (Outer Austin), 60–61
Lake Buchanan, 172
Lakehouse, The (Kerrville), 169
Lake LBJ (Hill Country), 173
Lake LBJ Resort, Marina, and Country Club (Hill Country), 173
Lake Marble Falls (Hill Country), 173
Lake Travis (Hill Country), 174
La Mansión Del Rio (Downtown San Antonio), 118, 119
Lamberts Downtown Barbecue (Downtown Austin), 63–65
lavender farms (Hill Country), 142
La Villita (San Antonio), 103
LBJ. See Johnson, Lyndon B.
LBJ National Historical Park (Johnson City), 164
Leaning Pear (Wimberley), 180
Liberty, The (East Austin), 81–82
Liberty Bar (King William District), 127, 133
licenses, 24
live music. See music
Llano, 173
lodging: Austin, 56–61; Blanco, 144; Boerne, 146–47; Clarksville, 60; Comfort, 150; Downtown San Antonio, 118–20; East Austin, 60; Fredericksburg, 155–56; Georgetown, 183; Gruene, 188–90; Hill Country, 144, 146–47, 150, 155–56, 164, 167–68, 170, 179–80; Hyde Park, 60; Johnson City, 164; Kerrville, 167–68; King

William District, 120–21; Luckenbach, 170; New Braunfels, 188–90; North Austin, 56–60; Outer San Antonio, 121–22; price codes, 10; Riverwalk, 118–20; San Antonio, 118–22; Southtown, 120–21; Wimberley, 179–80
Lolita's (San Marcos), 194
Lone Star Court (North Austin), 60
Lone Star Riverboat, 50
Long Center for the Performing Arts (Austin), 45
Longhorn Cavern State Park (Hill Country), 162, 173
Los Barrios (San Antonio), 124
Lost Creek Vineyard (Hill Country), 173
Lost Maples State Natural Area (Bandera), 142, 162
Louie Mueller Barbecue (Taylor), 185
Love Creek Orchards (Hill Country), 142, 167
Luckenbach, 155; lodging, 170
Lulu's (San Antonio), 24
Luna Fine Music Club (San Antonio), 132
Luxury, The (Museum Reach), 129
Lyndon Baines Johnson Museum and Library (Austin), 41
Lyndon B. Johnson State Park and Historic Site, 162

MadHatters Tea House and Café (King William District), 127
magazines, 24–25
Maggie Mae's (Austin), 78
Magik Children's Theatre (San Antonio), 110
Magnolia Café (Austin), 24, 66
Magnolia House (Fredericksburg), 155–56
Magnolia Pancake Haus (Olmos Park), 130–31
Main Street Bed and Breakfast Reservations Service (Fredericksburg), 155
Main Street Bed and Breakfast Reservations Service (Kerrville), 167
Majestic Theatre (San Antonio), 110
Marble Falls: hospitals, 24; restaurants, 171; tourist information, 28
Marble Falls LakeFest (Hill Country), 173
Mardi Gras (San Antonio), 134
Market Days (Georgetown), 183
Market Square/El Mercado (San Antonio), 133–34
Martin Luther King Jr. March (San Antonio), 134
Mayan Ranch (Hill Country), 140
Mayfield Park, 56
McCall Creek Farms (Blanco), 145
McKenna Children's Museum (New Braunfels), 187
McKinney Falls State Park, 47–48, 56
McNay Art Museum (San Antonio), 107
Meadows Center for Water and the Environment, The (San Marcos), 194
Medina, 167
Medina Highpoint Resort, 167

Medina Lake (Bandera), 142
Medina River Company (Bandera), 142
Menger Bar (Downtown San Antonio), 133
Menger Hotel (Downtown San Antonio), 119–20
Mexican free-tailed bat, 52
Mexic-Arte Museum (Austin), 42
Meyer Bed and Breakfast (Comfort), 150
Meyer's Elgin Smokehouse, 185
Mi Casa Gallery (South Austin), 83
Mid-Winter Music Festival, The (Austin), 83
Mission Concepción (San Antonio), 12, 100
Mission Kayak (San Antonio), 113
Mission Reach Ecosystem Restoration and
    Recreation Project (San Antonio), 113
missions (San Antonio), 12, 99–104
Mission San Antonio de Valero. See Alamo, The
Mission San Francisco de la Espada (San
    Antonio), 101, 102
Mission San José (San Antonio), 100, 101
Mission San Juan Capistrano (San Antonio), 101
Mitchell Lake (San Antonio), 116
Mi Tierra (Downtown San Antonio), 24, 125
Mokara Hotel and Spa (Downtown San
    Antonio), 118
Monte Vista, 95; restaurants, 130–31
Monument Cafe (Georgetown), 183
Moonshine Patio Bar & Grill (Downtown
    Austin), 63
MoPac, 20, 34
Mo Ranch Conference Center (Kerrville), 168
Mountain Breeze Camp (New Braunfels), 189
Mount Bonnell, 56
Mozart's Coffee Roasters (Lake Austin), 174
Museum of Texas Handmade Furniture (New
    Braunfels), 187
Museum of Western Art (Kerrville), 167
Museum Reach, 95; restaurants, 128–29
museums, 38–44
music: Austin, 74–79, 83–85; conjunto, 109; Hill
    Country, 76; San Antonio, 110, 131–32,
    135; South Lamar, 76. See also South by
    Southwest

Naegelin's Bakery (New Braunfels), 190
National car rental, 20
National Museum of the Pacific War
    (Fredericksburg), 153
National Park Service Visitor Center (Johnson
    City), 165
Native Americans, 16–17
Natural Bridge Caverns (San Antonio), 116
natural wonders, 12
Nau's Enfield Drug (Clarksville), 72
Neill-Cochran House Museum (Austin), 41
Nelson, Willie, 75
Nest, The (Fredericksburg), 157–58
New Braunfels, 12, 186–87; camping, 189–90;
    festivals, 191; hospital, 24; lodging, 188–90;
    restaurants, 190–91; sight-seeing, 187–88;
    tourist information, 28

New Braunfels Wein and Saengerfest, 191
newspapers, 24–25
Ney, Elisabet, 37
nightlife: Austin, 34, 74; Downtown Austin, 34,
    57, 64; East Austin, 81; San Antonio, 131.
    See also bars; dance; music
Noble Sandwiches (Burnet Road), 73
Noon Spoon Cafe (Marble Falls), 171
North Austin: lodging, 56–60; outdoor
    activities, 54–56
North Star Mall (San Antonio), 134

Oasis, The (Lake Travis), 174
Ocho Lounge (Museum Reach), 128, 133
Odd Duck (Austin), 68
Ogé House (King William District), 120
O. Henry Museum (Austin), 42, 104
Oktoberfest (Fredericksburg), 159
Oktoberfest-Wurst Braten (Boerne), 145
Old Gruene Market Days, 191
Old Settler's Music Festival (Austin), 84
Old Spanish Trail (Bandera), 143
Old Tunnel State Park, 163
Old Tunnel Wildlife Area (Hill Country), 159
Olmos Park, 95; restaurants, 130–31
Otto's (Fredericksburg), 157
outdoor activities: Austin, 50–56; Bandera, 142;
    Blanco, 142, 143, 160, 164; Boerne, 145–46;
    Fredericksburg, 155; Hill Country, 142,
    143, 145–46, 155, 167, 177–79; Kerrville, 167;
    North Austin, 54–56; San Antonio, 114–16;
    San Marcos, 193–94; South Austin, 54;
    West Austin, 54; Wimberley, 177–79
Outer San Antonio, lodging, 121–22
Out of Bounds Comedy Festival (Austin), 85

Pachanga Music Fest (Austin), 84
Page, Harvey L., 90
Palmer's Restaurant Bar and Courtyard (San
    Marcos), 195
Paloma Blanca Mexican Cuisine (Alamo
    Heights), 130
Paramount Theatre (Austin), 45
peaches, 151
Peach Tree Restaurant (Fredericksburg), 157
Pearl Brewery, 95
Pearl Brewery Complex, 126; restaurants,
    128–29
Pearl Brewery Farmers' Market, 128
Pecan Street Brewing (Johnson City), 164
Pecan Street Festival (Austin), 85
Pedernales Falls State Park (Hill Country), 163,
    165
Peggy's on the Green (Boerne), 147
performing arts: Austin, 44–46; San Antonio,
    107–10
Perla's (Austin), 65
pests, 25–26
Picante Grill (San Antonio), 124
Picnic, The (Austin), 64

Pico de Gallo (San Antonio), 125
Pie Society (San Marcos), 194
Pioneer Farms (North Austin), 54, 56
Pioneer Museum (Fredericksburg), 153
Polly's Chapel (Bandera), 141
PO PO Restaurant (Boerne), 147
Porter, William Sidney. *See* O. Henry Museum
Pridefest (San Antonio), 135
Prime Outlets (San Marcos), 193

Quarry Golf Club, The (San Antonio), 112

radio stations, 25
Rails Café at The Depot (Kerrville), 168
Rancho Cortez (Hill Country), 140
Real Ale Brewing Co. (Blanco), 145
Redbud Café Market and Pub (Blanco), 144–45
Red Poppy Festival (Georgetown), 183
religious services, 26
Remember the Alamo Weekend (San Antonio), 134
Republic of Texas Biker Rally (Austin), 84
restaurants: Alamo Heights, 130; Austin, 21, 61–74; Bandera, 143; Blanco, 144–45; Boerne, 147–48; Brackenridge Park, 130; Burnet Road, 73–74; Clarksville, 72–73; Comfort, 150–51; Downtown Austin, 62–65; Downtown San Antonio, 24, 122–26, 133; East Austin, 68–70; food trucks, 64; Fredericksburg, 156–58; Georgetown, 183–86; Gruene, 190–91; Hill Country, 143–45, 147–48, 150–51, 156–58, 164–65, 168–69, 171, 180; Hyde Park, 70–72; Johnson City, 164–65; Kerrville, 168–69; King William District, 126–28; late-night, 24; Marble Falls, 171; Monte Vista, 130–31; Museum Reach, 128–29; New Braunfels, 190–91; Olmos Park, 130–31; Pearl Brewery Complex, 128–29; Riverwalk, 122–26; San Antonio, 24, 63, 122–31; San Marcos, 194–95; Southtown, 126–28; Tex-Mex food, 124–25; Wimberley, 180
Rio San Antonio, 93
Rio San Antonio Tours, 114
River Center Mall (San Antonio), 134
Riverfest (Bandera), 143
Riverside Nature Center (Kerrville), 167
Riverwalk (San Antonio), 23, 91, 94; lodging, 118–20; restaurants, 122–26
Rockin' R River Rides (New Braunfels), 189
Rodeo Austin, 83–84
rodeos, 83–84, 134, 141, 164
Root Cellar Café (San Marcos), 194–95
Rosario's (King William District), 126, 132, 133
Rose Hill Manor (Johnson City), 164
Rough Creek Lavender (Hill Country), 142
Round Rock Express, 46
Rowing Dock, The, 47
Rustlin' Rob's (Fredericksburg), 158

Salty Sow, The (East Austin), 70, 82
Salvage Vanguard Theater (East Austin), 45
SAMA. *See* San Antonio Museum of Art
Sam's Burger Joint (San Antonio), 132
San Angel Folk Art Gallery (San Antonio), 106
San Antonio: area codes, 22; bars, 123, 133; bicycling in, 111; bird-watching in, 111; camping in, 111; cinema in, 110; culture, 11, 89–92; dance, 110, 132–33; festivals, 134–36; fishing, 111; galleries of, 105–7; golf in, 111–12; grocery stores, 23; historic places in, 96–104; history, 11, 88–92; hospitals, 24; lodging, 118–22; map, 89, 93; missions of, 99–104; music, 110, 131–32, 135; neighborhoods, 93–95; newspapers, 24–25; nightlife, 131; outdoor activities, 114–16; performing arts in, 107–10; radio stations, 25; restaurants, 24, 63, 122–31; shopping, 133–34; sports in, 112; swimming in, 112; theme parks in, 112–14; tourist information, 26; tours in, 114; transportation, 19–21, 92–93; tubing, 114. *See also specific neighborhoods*
San Antonio Botanical Garden, 114
San Antonio Cocktail Conference, 134
San Antonio Conjunto Shootout (San Antonio), 135
San Antonio Dance Umbrella, 110
San Antonio de Valero Mission. *See* Alamo, The
San Antonio Film Festival, 135
San Antonio International Airport, 21
San Antonio Living History Association, 110
San Antonio Missions National Historical Park, 12, 99–104
San Antonio Museum of Art (SAMA), 106
San Antonio Rampage, 112
San Antonio Riverwalk. *See* Riverwalk
San Antonio Silver Stars, 112
San Antonio Spurs, 112
San Antonio Stock Show and Rodeo, 134
San Antonio Symphony, 110
San Antonio Taxis, 21
San Antonio Wheelmen, 111
San Antonio Zoo, 115, 116
San Fernando Cathedral (San Antonio), 101, 103
San Marcos, 12, 192; festivals, 195; hospital, 24; outdoor activities, 193–94; outlet malls, 193; restaurants, 194–95; shopping, 193; sight-seeing, 193; tourist information, 28
San Marcos City Park, 193
San Pedro Playhouse (San Antonio), 110
San Pedro Springs Park (San Antonio), 112
Saxon Pub, The (Austin), 78
Schilo's Delicatessen (Downtown San Antonio), 123
Schlitterbahn (San Antonio), 112
Scholz Garten (Austin), 78
Schreiner Mansion (Kerrville), 166
Scoot Inn (Austin), 78–79
Scott Schreiner Golf Course (Wimberley), 176

SeaWorld San Antonio, 113
Second Bar and Kitchen (Downtown Austin), 62
Second Saturday Art Trail (Kerrville), 166
SegCity (San Antonio), 50, 114
Settler's Crossing (Fredericksburg), 156
Shady Grove (South Austin), 67, 80
Shangri-La (East Austin), 82
Shoal Creek Greenbelt, 56
shopping: Austin, 82–83; Downtown Austin,
    82; East Austin, 83; San Antonio, 133–34;
    San Marcos, 193; South Austin, 82–83;
    Southtown, 134; West Austin, 82
Shops at La Cantera, The (San Antonio), 134
Sights and Sounds of Christmas (San Marcos),
    195
sight-seeing: Bandera, 139–42; Boerne, 145;
    Fredericksburg, 153–54; Georgetown,
    182–83; Gruene, 187–88; Hill Country,
    139–42, 145, 153–54, 164, 166–67, 175;
    Johnson City, 164; Kerrville, 166–67;
    New Braunfels, 187–88; San Marcos, 193;
    Wimberley, 175
Silo Elevated Cuisine (San Antonio), 131
Silver Sage Corral Benefit Chili Cook-Off
    (Bandera), 143
Silver Spur Guest Ranch (Hill Country), 140
sinkholes (Hill Country), 12
Sister Creek Vineyards (Hill Country), 154
Six Flags Fiesta Texas (San Antonio), 113
Skies Over Texas (San Antonio), 97
Smitty's Market, 185
snakes, 26
SoCo. See South of Congress
South Austin, 34–35, 58–59, 65; bars, 80–81;
    outdoor activities, 54; shopping, 82–83
South Austin Trailer Park, 64
South by Southwest (SXSW), 83, 84
South Congress Café (South Austin), 66, 80
South Congress Hotel (South Austin), 59–60
South Lamar, music, 76
South of Congress (SoCo), 34–35
Southside Market (Elgin), 185
South Texas Off-Road Mountain Bikers (San
    Antonio), 111
Southtown, 94, 95; lodging, 120–21; restaurants,
    126–28; shopping, 134
Southwest School of Art and Craft (San
    Antonio), 105
Spanish Governor's Palace (San Antonio), 103–4
Spanish people, 15–16
special events. See festivals
Spicewood Vineyards (Hill Country), 173
Spider House (Hyde Park), 81
spiders, 26
SPLASH! Into the Edwards Aquifer (Austin), 52
Splashtown (San Antonio), 114
sports (San Antonio), 112
Stevie Ray Vaughan Memorial, 79
StoneMetal Press (San Antonio), 106
Stonewall, tourist information, 28

St. Patrick's Day (San Antonio), 134–35
Stubb's Bar-B-Q's (Austin), 78
Sugar Shack Bakery (Wimberley), 180
Sunday houses (Fredericksburg), 153
Sun & Fun Watercraft Rentals (Lake Austin), 174
Sunken Garden Theater (San Antonio), 110
Sunset Grill (Fredericksburg), 157
Sunset Station (San Antonio), 131–32
Super Shuttle, 20, 21
Sustainable Food Center's Farmers' Market, The
    (Austin), 83
Sweet Lemon Inn, The (Georgetown), 183
Sweet Lemon Kitchen (Georgetown), 183
swimming: Austin, 48, 51; San Antonio, 112;
    Wimberley, 176
Swing on the Square Festival (San Marcos), 195
SXSW. See South by Southwest

Taco Haven (San Antonio), 125
Tanger Outlets (San Marcos), 193
Tantra Coffeehouse (San Marcos), 194
Tap Room (San Marcos), 195
Tejano Conjunto Festival en San Antonio, 135
Tejanos, 14–15
Teka Molino (San Antonio), 125
Tesoros Trading Company (Downtown Austin),
    82
Texas Almanac, 14
Texas Archeological Research Lab, 14
Texas Climbing Adventures, 48, 176
Texas Department of Agriculture, 154
Texas Folklife Festival (San Antonio), 135
Texas Heritage Living History Weekend
    (Kerrville), 169
Texas Hill Country. See Hill Country
Texas Hill Country Wineries (Hill Country), 154
Texas Hill Country Wine Trail (Hill Country),
    142
Texas Hills Vineyard (Hill Country), 165
Texas Historical Commission, 14
Texas Lavender Trail (Wimberley), 176
Texas Memorial Museum (Austin), 41
Texas Military Forces Museum (Austin), 42, 44
Texas Outside, 176
Texas Parks and Wildlife, 14
Texas peaches, 151
Texas Rangers Heritage Center
    (Fredericksburg), 153
Texas Rock Fest (Austin), 84
Texas State Capitol, 36–37, 50
Texas State Cemetery (East Austin), 36, 39
Texas State Historical Association, The, 14
Texas State Park System, 160–63, 176
Texas Talent Musicians Association (San
    Antonio), 110
Texas Trolley Hop (San Antonio), 114
Texas Tubes (New Braunfels), 189
Texas Wine Trail (Wimberley), 173, 176
Tex-Mex food, 124–25
theme parks (San Antonio), 112–14

Thinkery, The (Austin), 44
Threadgill's World Headquarters (Austin), 66
Thrifty car rental, 20
Tobin Center for the Performing Arts (San Antonio), 107–8
Tomatillo's (San Antonio), 125
Tommy's Mesquite Flamed Pizza (Llano), 173
Torch of Friendship (San Antonio), 117
Torchy's Taco (South Austin), 64, 68
Torre di Pietra (Hill Country), 154
tourist information, 26–28
tours: Austin, 48–50; San Antonio, 114; Wimberley, 175, 177
Tow, 173
Tower of the Americas (San Antonio), 97
Trail of Lights and Zilker Christmas Tree (Austin), 85
transportation, 19–21; air travel, 20–21; Austin, 34
Travaasa (Outer Austin), 61
Travis, William, 96
TRIO (Austin), 58
Tube San Marcos (San Marcos), 194
tubing: Austin, 50; rental, 188–89; San Antonio, 114; Wimberley, 177
24 Diner (Austin), 24, 65
Twin Elm Guest Ranch (Hill Country), 140
Two Wee Cottages (Fredericksburg), 156

Uchi (Austin), 67
Uchiko (Clarksville), 67, 73
Umlauf Sculpture Garden and Museum (Austin), 52
Umlauf Sculpture Garden and Museum, The (Austin), 42
University of Texas at Austin, 35–36, 43; bars, 81; football, 48; lodging, 60; restaurants, 70–72; tours, 50; tower, 50; travels to airport, 20
University of Texas Longhorns, 48
University of Texas Performing Arts Center (UTPAC), 45–46
University of Texas Tower Tours, 50
UTPAC. See University of Texas Performing Arts Center

Valero Texas Open at La Cantera (San Antonio), 136
Vanishing Texas River Cruise (Burnet), 172
Vaudeville (Fredericksburg), 157
Vaughan (Stevie Ray) Memorial, 79
Veloway, 56
Vespaio (Austin), 66
VIA Metropolitan Transit, 21, 92
vineyards (Hill Country), 154
Vino Vino (Hyde Park), 81
visitors centers, 26–28, 37–38, 165, 182
Viva! Cinco de Mayo & State Menudo Cook-Off (San Marcos), 195

Watercolor Month (San Antonio), 135
Waterloo Records (Downtown Austin), 82
weather, 22–23
Weihnachts (Christmas) Fest Parade Weekend (Boerne), 145
Welfare Café (Boerne), 147–48
West Austin: outdoor activities, 54; shopping, 82
West End, 35
Weston La Cantera Resort (Outer San Antonio), 122
Whisler's (East Austin), 82
Whole Foods (Austin), 63
Wildfire (Georgetown), 185
wildflowers, 113, 149, 155, 159, 162, 167. See also bluebonnets; lavender farms
Wildseed Farms (Fredericksburg), 155
Wilhelm I, King, 92
Willow City Loop (Hill Country), 155
Wimberley: bicycling, 176; bird-watching, 176; boating, 176; camping, 176; canoeing, 176; climbing, 176; fishing, 176; golf, 176; hospital, 24; kayaking, 176; lodging, 179–80; outdoor activities, 177–79; restaurants, 180; sight-seeing, 175; swimming, 176; tourist information, 28; tours, 175, 177; tubing, 177; zip lining, 177
Wimberley Glass Works, 175
wineries. See vineyards
Wine Trail (Hill Country), 155
Wink (Clarksville), 72, 73
Witte Museum (San Antonio), 106–7
Wittliff Gallery of Southwestern and Mexican Photography (San Marcos), 193
Women and Their Work (Downtown Austin), 82
Wonder World Park (San Marcos), 194
Woodrose Winery (Hill Country), 154
Wurstfest (New Braunfels), 191

Yard Dog (South Austin), 83
Ye Kendall Inn (Boerne), 146–47
Yellow Checker Cab, 20, 21
Yellow Rose Bed and Breakfast, A (King William District), 121
Y. O. Ranch Resort and Conference Center (Kerrville), 168

ZACH Theatre (Austin), 46
Zilker Botanical Garden (Austin), 51–53
Zilker Metropolitan Park and Preserve (Austin), 50–51
Zilker Nature Preserve (Austin), 51
Zilker Park Boat Rentals, 47
Zilker Summer Musical (Austin), 84
Zilker Theatre Productions (Austin), 46
Zilker Zephyr (Austin), 52
Zinc Bistro & Wine Bar (Downtown San Antonio), 123, 133
zip lining, 50, 177